Trends and Innovations In Master-Planned Communities

PRINCIPAL AUTHORS

Adrienne Schmitz
Lloyd W. Bookout

CONTRIBUTING AUTHORS

Toni Alexander
Brian C. Canin
William Clark
V.R. Halter
Wayne S. Hyatt
Ehud Mouchly
Laurence Netherton
H. Pike Oliver
Michael Pawlukiewicz
Brooke Warrick

**Urban Land
Institute**

About ULI–the Urban Land Institute

ULI–the Urban Land Institute is a nonprofit education and research institute that is supported and directed by its members. Its mission is to provide responsible leadership in the use of land in order to enhance the total environment.

ULI sponsors educational programs and forums to encourage an open international exchange of ideas and sharing of experience; initiates research that anticipates emerging land use trends and issues and proposes creative solutions based on this research; provides advisory services; and publishes a wide variety of materials to disseminate information on land use and development.

Established in 1936, the Institute today has more than 14,000 members and associates from more than 50 countries representing the entire spectrum of the land use and development disciplines. They include developers, builders, property owners, investors, architects, public officials, planners, real estate brokers, appraisers, attorneys, engineers, financiers, academics, students, and librarians. ULI members contribute to higher standards of land use by sharing their knowledge and experience. The Institute has long been recognized as one of America's most respected and widely quoted sources of objective information on urban planning, growth, and development.

Richard M. Rosan
President

Recommended bibliographic listing:

Schmitz, Adrienne, et al. *Trends and Innovations in Master-Planned Communities.*
Washington, D.C.: ULI–the Urban Land Institute, 1998.

ULI Catalog Number: T02
International Standard Book Number: 0-87420-800-9
Library of Congress Catalog Card Number: 98-87161

Copyright 1998 by ULI–the Urban Land Institute
1025 Thomas Jefferson Street, N.W.
Suite 500 West
Washington, D.C. 20007-5201

ULI Project Staff

Rachelle L. Levitt
Senior Vice President, Policy and Practice

Lloyd W. Bookout
Vice President, Programs
Project Director

Gayle Berens
Vice President, Real Estate Development Practice

Adrienne Schmitz
Project Manager

Karen Danielsen
Director, Residential Development

Nancy H. Stewart
Director, Book Program

Barbara M. Fishel/Editech
Ann Lenney
Manuscript Editors

Helene Y. Redmond/HYR Graphics
Book Design/Layout

Meg Batdorff
Cover Design

Diann Stanley-Austin
Associate Director of Publishing Operations

Maria-Rose Cain
Joanne Nanez
Word Processors

About the Authors

Adrienne Schmitz is a senior associate in housing and community development at ULI. Before joining ULI, she was a market research consultant to real estate developers and homebuilders. She holds a master's degree in urban planning from the University of Virginia.

Lloyd W. Bookout is vice president of programs at ULI. He is the author of numerous books, research papers, and articles about real estate development. Before joining ULI, he was a planning, environmental, and entitlements consultant based in southern California, where he participated in development programs for several large master-planned communities.

Toni Alexander is president of InterCommunications, Newport Beach, California, a marketing company specializing in the development of branding and integrated communications programs for large-scale real estate and resort developments in the United States, the Caribbean, Mexico, and the Pacific Rim. She is a ULI trustee and frequent lecturer at ULI meetings and conferences.

Brian C. Canin is president of Canin Associates, urban and environmental planners and landscape architects in Orlando, Florida. Founded in 1980, Canin Associates has designed some of Florida's most successful master-planned communities, mixed-use projects, and resorts. Canin received a bachelor of architecture from the University of the Witwatersrand in South Africa and a master of architecture and urban design from Harvard University. He is a member of ULI's Community Development Council and has participated in a number of ULI forums.

William Clark is head of Clark Development, a Boise, Idaho–based real estate development and consulting firm with projects in the northwest United States. The firm's focus is the planning, economics, and development of commercial, residential, and recreational projects, particularly those involving complex and sensitive community and environmental relationships. Clark is also an adjunct professor at the University of Oregon, where he teaches real estate development.

V.R. Halter is president of V.R. Halter & Associates, a national real estate advisory firm. Active in residential development since 1969, Halter specializes in advising clients in planning, positioning, and sales and marketing of primary and resort master-planned communities in the United States, Mexico, and Europe. Halter is a ULI trustee and current chair of ULI's Recreational Development Council (Blue Flight).

Wayne S. Hyatt is a principal in the Atlanta law firm Hyatt & Stubblefield. He has over 25 years of experience in community association law, representing developers of planned communities. Hyatt, an adjunct professor at Emory University School of Law and Vanderbilt University School of Law, has written extensively about community association law, including *Condominium and Home Owner Associations: A Guide to the Development Process* and the recently published *Community Association Law: Case Materials on Common Interest Communities.*

Ehud Mouchly is managing director of PricewaterhouseCoopers LLP, a real estate consulting group. He is an expert in financial planning, operating management, and debt and equity financing for projects and portfolios. His practice includes national and international assignments in large-scale mixed-use development and redevelopment projects, master-planned communities, new towns, public/private joint ventures, and mixed-product portfolios.

Laurence Netherton, principal of Netherton and Associates in Newport Beach, California, began his real estate career as a market research analyst, moving to various senior management positions in large development organizations. Since 1981, he has been involved in the acquisition, planning, entitlement, and development of large landholdings in California. He holds undergraduate and graduate degrees in urban planning as well as an MBA.

H. Pike Oliver is a principal of the Presidio Group, a land development and management company active in the San Francisco Bay Area, Sacramento, and southern California. He also serves as vice chair of INTERRA, a strategic planning, financial analysis, and project management firm involved in community development and the reuse of military bases throughout California and the Pacific Rim.

Michael Pawlukiewicz is director of environmental land use policy at ULI. He previously worked in local policy development, addressing issues of growth and development related to water and sewerage, stormwater and flood management, and forest and habitat protection. He received a master's degree in regional planning from the University of Pennsylvania and a master's degree in public policy from the University of Maryland School of Public Affairs.

Brooke Warrick is president of San Francisco–based American LIVES. Warrick has been a leader in value- and lifestyle-based market research for 15 years, specializing in understanding what consumers want, segmenting the market, and finding niches for community and housing developers.

In Memory of D. Scott Middleton

Preface

Master-planned communities are usually a product of long-term, multiphase development programs that combine a complementary mix of land uses. Often they are held together by a unifying character or design element. A master-planned community provides an opportunity for a large tract of land to be planned comprehensively and implemented in logical stages.

Development of master-planned communities typically occurs on "greenfields," that is, tracts of formerly undeveloped land often at or beyond urban fringes. Increasingly, the most desirable sites no longer are available, and developers must turn to infill and "brownfield," or redevelopment, sites. Such sites provide new opportunities and challenges for community builders. Remote rural sites offer other kinds of opportunities.

The goal of this book is to provide practitioners with the most current practices and ideas in the development of master-planned communities. To do so, ULI has assembled a group of experts in the various disciplines of community development: developers, designers, and consultants from all parts of the country. No prior consensus had been reached to address common themes, yet common threads are woven throughout the book.

All development professionals face a major issue in the development of master-planned communities: public protests against new development. NIMBYism has become the most pervasive obstacle of new projects—urban, suburban, or rural and no matter how well conceived. Developers must acknowledge and address this issue, for it will not go away.

Other common themes in this book involve understanding the changing market for master-planned communities. "Psychographics" is the buzz word that has replaced "demographics" in terms of identifying and satisfying the market niches that make up today's home-buying public. Markets are more than just age cohorts; they are segmented into household types, lifestyles, and backgrounds. Aging is a major demographic factor that will change the face of community development. Immigration patterns are also to be considered. In response to these and other trends, developers are looking to ways of mixing ages and incomes within a community to broaden their markets.

Government bodies are cutting back, increasingly leaving social problems to be addressed by communities. Crime, education, low-income housing, and other formerly governmental responsibilities are being shifted to communities. Homeowners associations are becoming nonmunicipal systems of governance, taking on ever-broadening roles.

The key issues involving the character of development center around how to improve a community's livability. More mixing of uses is gaining favor. Facilitating access for pedestrians is increasingly important. Greater numbers of workers are setting up offices at home, spending more time in their homes and communities. The quality of life provided within a community will have greater impact on these people and will affect their home purchase decisions more than ever.

Several chapters discuss neotraditional design as one way to foster greater livability, and several discuss the issue of gating residential communities. All indications are that these threads are more than passing fads. They will be woven together to form the bases for how new communities are developed to meet the needs of future residents.

This book explores several topics: new trends, such as psychographics and changing lifestyles; consumer research about what homebuyers really want; new technologies, particularly in telecommunications, that are changing the way people live and work; the evolution in community governance; land planning to ameliorate the effects of crime, one of the most serious problems facing communities and governments today; environmentally responsible development strategies for master-planned communities; trends in community design and where those trends are headed; and the financial risks and rewards of developing master-planned communities, as well as some business strategies to improve the odds for success. The book concludes with three case studies of successful master-planned communities: the Woodlands, near Houston; Summerlin, in Las Vegas; and Celebration, in Orlando.

The primary focus throughout this book is understanding how people will live in the 21st century. Today's technologies make it possible for people to live like the science fiction cartoons of the 1960s, but most people don't want to live that way. People still want to walk to the corner store, to sit on the front porch, to have safe places for their children to play with neighborhood friends. However, this book is not a 1950s vision of how people will live. That corner store might be a business center. Mom is probably sitting on the porch with her laptop, connected via modem to her office in another city. And the kids playing outside might have come from all corners of the globe.

Acknowledgments

This book is the work of many hands and minds. We would first like to thank the chapter authors—Toni Alexander, Brian Canin, Bill Clark, Pete Halter, Wayne Hyatt, Ehud Mouchly, Larry Netherton, Pike Oliver, Michael Pawlukiewicz, and Brooke Warrick—who generously shared their expertise and insights. Much gratitude goes to Scott Middleton for his work on the three case studies. We wish to thank the contributors of several feature boxes: Pamela Blais, Metropole Consultants of Toronto; Charles E. Fraser, president of Charles E. Fraser Company, Hilton Head Island, South Carolina; and Buzz Koelbel, president of Koelbel and Company.

Thanks are also due ULI's research staff, especially Karen Danielsen, Michael Baker, and Jeff Hinkle, who worked tirelessly to edit materials, check and recheck facts, and assemble photographs and captions. Jeff Hinkle wrote the feature box on Harbortown. Nancy Stewart guided editing and production, Helene Redmond designed the book's layout, Meg Batdorff designed the cover, and Ann Lenney and Barbara Fishel edited the text. And special thanks go to all the developers and designers who provided information and materials on their master-planned communities.

Adrienne Schmitz
Lloyd W. Bookout

Contents

1. **Rethinking Master-Planned Communities**   1
   V.R. Halter

2. **Changing Consumer Preferences**   11
   Brooke Warrick and Toni Alexander

3. **The Implications of New Technologies**   25
   William Clark

4. **The Evolution in Community Governance**   37
   Wayne S. Hyatt

5. **Mastering Crime in the Master-Planned Community**   53
   Brian C. Canin

6. **Environmentally Responsible Development**   67
   Michael Pawlukiewicz

7. **New Visions in Community Design**   83
   Adrienne Schmitz

8. **The Business of Master-Planned Communities**   99
   Ehud Mouchly, H. Pike Oliver, and Laurence Netherton

Case Studies   113

The Woodlands   114
The Woodlands, Texas

Summerlin   128
Las Vegas, Nevada

Celebration   142
Celebration, Florida

Chapter 1

Rethinking Master-Planned Communities

V.R. Halter

Are developers creating master-planned communities that will be obsolete and unmarketable before they are ever completed? Just as today's office building developers are accommodating new technologies and striving to meet the expectations of sophisticated new businesses, today's residential developers must understand and respond to rapidly evolving consumer demands. Consumers of housing expect the same up-to-the-minute lifestyle features and technological innovations that they are used to at the office.

The 1990s have become the decade of subtle, but substantive, changes in consumer demographics and, more important, in psychographics. Unless consumer attitudes are better understood and integrated into their planning and sales processes, the developers of master-planned communities may find themselves at a competitive disadvantage. These developers could also end up investing in communities that will be literally obsolete or rejected by the consumer, because they fail to mirror and match the consumer's personal, technological, and psychographic needs. Many of these changes already are being anticipated and addressed in other areas of real estate, such as office and retail. But the planning

The Presidio at Williams Centre in Tucson, Arizona, established an upscale character on a high-density infill site of ten units per acre. A large percentage of the market for this moveup community has been single women.

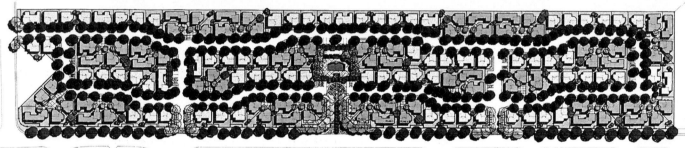

and development of *residential* real estate properties have lagged behind in focusing on the consumer. The rules are changing! How then will the master-planned community development business be different in the future?

First, the "typical" homeowner is very difficult to describe. Simply put, a mass market no longer exists. The buyer profile is now breaking apart into niche consumers, ranging from singles, retirees, married couples without children at home (at 54 percent, these households constitute the largest segment of the housing market), aging adults, college graduates who are once again living with their parents, and immigrants with diverse cultural mores, language, housing needs, and locational preferences. In essence, Ozzie and Harriet don't live here anymore. In spite of these identifiable changes, few developers or builders are designing their communities and products to address this reality.

Other important psychographic changes that affect homebuying demands and preferences

are occurring. Home-based offices have become an option, or even a necessity for many households. With the future growth of industry shifting from large corporations to small service-oriented businesses, there is concern for job security and the need to be flexible. Job locations are shifting from suburbia to penturbia, or rural areas beyond the outer suburbs. With the advent of corporate downsizing jeopardizing job and retirement security, Americans are changing how they think about work and retirement. The "fear of fear" is causing consumers to focus on personal safety, which, in turn, creates new realities for residential development and the strategies necessary for the positioning and marketing of master-planned communities. These psychographic and demographic factors are forcing a significant change in development strategies and partnerships. They are requiring new kinds of consumer research, housing products, and new types of infrastructure that focus on improved technology. This new infrastructure will have to provide for instant communication inside and outside the community. Builder programs must be designed to meet the needs of niche markets with adaptable housing products. These products must be able to meet the ever-increasing consumer demand for personalizing the homes and for satisfying their expectations for the level of quality and service that can now be found in almost every other consumer product. Fundamentally, success in the future will come from a new way of thinking by everybody associated with planning, development, construction, social community organization enhancement, and the sales, delivery, and service systems that interface with the consumer of the future.

What happened? Why is the customer different? During the last decade, major structural changes have taken place in America that are forcing community developers to take on new responsibilities. These new responsibilities are causing many developers to rethink their plans and positions in the community development and housing industry. The following sections discuss some of these changes affecting most developments today.

Entitlement or Extractions

Today, most municipalities will not or cannot fund the cost of added infrastructure and social value systems that they have bestowed upon their development concepts in the past. No longer will tax dollars be allocated for road construction, parks and amenities, or even educational facilities and social services, unless special bond districts that add taxes to the new development are voted upon and funded. The expected obligations of local governments, such as policy making, public education, and basic services such as trash collection, will be underwritten by the developer and the residents of the community. Beginning in 1998, for the next 15 years one baby boomer will turn 50 every eight seconds and will undoubtedly be the "900-pound gorilla" in terms of both its market size and its financial independence. This market no longer needs quality education. The children are grown. They no longer believe in higher taxes, because they no longer require many of the services funded by those taxes, and many have simply lost faith in the government's ability to manage fiscal responsibility. Many of these aging boomers hold their local public servants in low esteem. As one homeowner notes, "I can get pizza delivered to my

house faster than I can get a police officer here." The bottom line is that many of today's potential housing consumers are dealing with a crisis of confidence in their government and its elected officials. As a result, the psychographics of many of today's consumers have them searching for America "the way it used to be." This attempt to go home again is influencing the consumer to search for new developments that offer a way of life that truly is different from that of the 1970s and 1980s. The power of this subtle, but strong, psychographic trend cannot be underestimated in the planning, development, and implementation of any master-planned community of the future.

Radical Changes in the Homebuyer Profile

As noted above, a singular mass market no longer exists, even among the baby boomer market, if family size and psychographics are considered. In fact, the fastest-growing housing segment today is made up of couples with no children or no children at home. The stereotypical couple of the past with a core family unit (i.e., mom at home raising two or three children and dad off at the office providing for the family) no longer drives the housing market in America. In 1950, the average household was made up of 3.37 persons. Today's typical household comprises 2.6 persons. The aging of the boomers, the emergence of the X-generation market (perhaps one of the most challenging ever seen), and the dramatic increase in immigration and ethnic markets are creating demands for more flexible housing products. Who are today's consumers? What does he/she expect the home to be? What are the expectations and new definitions for *lifestyle?* All of these issues are becoming critical research and design elements that can affect the success of new communities and ongoing consumer acceptance of them in a way that they never have in the past. Selling to these buyers requires an extremely adaptable planning and delivery system, which includes the ability to create niche products, neighborhoods, way-of-life amenities, flexible floorplan designs, and even an understanding of the cultural requirements for design and sales as they relate to ethnic markets and cultural idiosyncracies. On any given day, any sales office in the country could welcome any of the following: the extremely bright, individualistic, affluent, and demanding X-generation customer, a single parent, a single female executive (a market few residential developers realize exists), an affluent African American, a baby boomer with no children at home, a "flex-exec" who can work anywhere, including at home, a retiree, or a recent Hispanic or Asian immigrant family, all looking for their own place—where they can feel connected and can find a personalized product to serve specific needs.

Regrettably, most community plans and sales delivery systems today are not prepared to deal with such diversity. Essentially, most planners, developers, and builders still target their programs, products, and amenities to a white, Anglo Saxon baby boomer market that has aged demographically and psychographically well beyond the word "baby." Planning for these emerging markets is critical for the survival of any new community. While the mix of demographics and niche markets may vary from region to region within the country, homebuilders should expect a far more diverse consumer base, irrespective of the geographic location.

The Changing Work Habits of the Housing Consumer

Today, work affects not only *where* people choose to live, but also *how* they live. As a result of the end of the industrial age (as it has been known) and the restructuring of corporate America that has occurred in the 1990s, the future of employment has shifted from production to service. The U.S. Census Bureau estimates that by 2000, 90 percent of the country's workforce will be in the service industry, 5 percent in production, and 3 percent in agriculture. The emergence of a service-oriented economy, thanks to advancements in technology, has changed forever the consumer's housing and community preferences. Today, more workers than ever are passing up a better location in order to get a better lifestyle. Work at home, outsourcing, and the flex-exec phenomenon give consumers far more freedom than ever in housing choices. Amazingly, only a few developers and builders have adapted the infrastructure in their developments to address changing lifestyles. Many are not even promoting technology features in their sales and marketing efforts. Ready or not, the trend will cause change to development infrastructure, housing

designs, technology applications and interface, and even to community governments in order for them to meet the demands of technology and the consumer of the future.

The Future Strength in Household Formation

Currently, one of the most overlooked and underestimated changes taking place is the increase in immigration and its effect on future household growth in America. In numbers not heretofore seen in America, the stage is being set for the emergence of minority household growth that will create diversity and niche markets, and will change dramatically the community development and housing industry. It is estimated that, within ten years, one-third of the housing market will be made up of a population now considered minorities. In fact, it is estimated that the real population growth during the next 20 years will result largely from both new immigrants and increases in the family size of existing immigrants. Family size among minorities will increase at a greater rate than in the family unit of their nonminority counterparts. Eighty percent of such growth will be driven by African Americans, Hispanics, Pacific Islanders, and Asians.

The vast majority of developers and builders are not prepared to deal with such consumers. The emergence of the minority consumer will raise planning issues as well as social challenges, such as language, education, cultural preferences, new housing types, and even new point-of-sale communication problems. For many markets (especially California, Texas, Arizona, Florida, and New York), minorities are already becoming a key element for both sales velocity and community development success.

Health in America

The American focus on health is no longer a fad, but a force that is driving many consumer decisions, including those relating to home purchases. The consumer is not just seeking health care, but is looking for wellness and is demanding the community amenities needed to maintain wellness. The aging baby boomer's pursuit of youth and longer life, the health consciousness of the X-generation, and the rising cost of health care are already becoming extremely relevant in planning communities of today and the future. Because of lifestyle changes resulting from the aging of baby boomers, by far the largest housing consumer group, health and wellness programs designed as a part of a community's way of life and delivery system will be essential. This is not just about more jogging trails. It is about interactive wellness programs offering individually prescribed exercise and diet regimens that are planned and managed in concert with neighborhood or community aerobic centers, personal physicians, and even employers' health maintenance organizations that may be located within a master-planned community's corporate campus. The use of technology to create such linkage and maintenance is clearly a trend of the future for a master-planned community of any size. In the past, such alliances were not considered a development discipline or even the responsibility of the developer. In the future, they will be planned and designed into the infrastructure of the community and considered an extremely relevant marketing amenity for attracting not only homeowners but also corporations, medical facilities, and retailers.

Time: The Amenity of the Future

The vast majority of today's housing consumers are in the lower end of the economic pyramid. Many of these households require dual incomes merely to survive, let alone to purchase and pay for a new home. Such economic requirements are causing change in the traditional family structure and in how the family members coexist. Middle American families are shrinking in size. Some families cannot cope with the stresses of modern life and become dysfunctional. The X-generation is deferring marriage and, in many cases, choosing not to begin families until later in their lives, if at all. Today, all people, including children, are facing more and more demands that pull them away from home. Yet many consumers, especially the aging boomers, clearly want life the way it used to be. They are searching for a place to come home to that offers not just shelter, but a true sense of belonging. For many, this desire to belong is not filled by the country club, the health club, or the neighborhood clubhouse. Instead, this is a broader desire to feel good about a place and, more important, to feel a part of it.

Clearly, many of these structural changes present unique challenges to developers, espe-

In an effort to tap immigrant and ethnic market niches, a few developers are devising ethnic housing. Mercado Apartments in San Diego, for example, was developed by the Metropolitan Area Advisory Committee, a nonprofit community development corporation.

cially to those planning larger communities that will have a marketing presence for five or more years. Planning for the future can no longer simply involve issues of land use and density. To avoid community obsolescence, developers will be pressed to accept even more financial and organizational responsibilities not only for the predevelopment process, but also for the social engineering process. For future communities to be truly competitive, they must provide quality of life for the community's residents. The consumer of the future will pass up a better location for a better lifestyle.

The New Community Developers

No doubt, many developers who review this book will wonder what has changed. In some form, these fundamentals have been factors in the development process for years. However, they have never been more relevant or more important than they are today. While developers have always been aware of factors such as crime, deteriorating education, minority markets, and even subtleties such as the search for a sense of belonging, these issues have never been essential to creating or protecting a community's long-term competitive edge and profit potential.

Accepting and dealing with the social relevance of building a community will likely tax the comfort zone of many developers. For this and other reasons, a structural change is occurring within the development fraternity. Some development companies are rethinking and retooling how their communities will be developed. Disney Development Company, DMB, John Wieland Homes, and Crescent Resources are some of those pioneering the change in community development. These progressive developers are asking the hard questions and are looking at master-planned communities in much the same way that General Motors looked at the auto industry before creating the Saturn. They are reinventing the process, changing the product, and creating new delivery systems that better meet the needs and values of the changing consumers. The result is a new kind of community, an expanded social planning role for the developer, and, most important, improved opportunities for those who invest in the community—the homeowners, educators, retailers, developers, and builders.

What are forward-thinking developers doing to benchmark new kinds of communities for the next century? Many are eschewing business as usual and are focusing on new kinds of consumer research. Market analysis typically has relied on two fundamental elements: 1) the collection and projection of historical hard data, and 2) developer intuition and desires. Future market research will be expanded to better understand the buyers and their desires for both the housing product and the lifestyle elements through the use of extensive consumer preference studies. Analysis will not be based on past choices, but rather on what consumers are saying about their current status and desires. Collecting this information will require surveying diverse interests, some of whom developers have never before considered relevant. Teachers, medical providers, telecommunication companies, shopkeepers, parents, realtors, builders, and even children of different age groups will all play roles in determining the shape of the new community. Surveys will include questions like "What educational systems can be planned to create opportunities for state-of-the-art training and educational alliances with local businesses?" "What kind of wellness and health care facilities are important and which ones should be designed to interact with any HMOs that may be part of a corporate client who is building in the community?" "What technological infrastructure is needed to deliver products and services to retailers, educators, and the community government?"

The second new research element will consist of innovative pilot programs (often initiated and financed by the developer) in partnership with government, business, educational institutions, and others to be integrated into the development plan for the community. These lifestyle innovations will prove critical in positioning the community to sustain a long-term competitive edge by offering a truly connected community lifestyle.

The third research element is a preprogrammed plan to gather continual, long-term consumer preference data. Such research will be used to fine-tune existing programs and to plan for future phases of the community. Simply opening the next phase by targeting the product price ranges will not carry the community over the long term. The product must be overlaid with the lifestyle preferences and needs of existing residents. Again, conducting such research and planning will be driven more by psychographics than by demographics. Talking *to* the customer and not *at* the customer will inevitably lead to differences that create and sustain a community's competitive edge and success.

Communities in the Future

Because of poor municipal planning, most new residential subdivisions today do not offer a true sense of community. They do not tie together the homes, businesses, schools, amenities, and health/wellness services in a way that creates synergy for the community and its residents or a stronger perceived value or sense of belonging. To accommodate consumer preferences, land use plans must provide opportunities for social inter-

At Spring Island, South Carolina, a 3,000-acre island community, the nonprofit Spring Island Trust maintains a 1,000-acre nature preserve and supports a staff of naturalists. Funding for the trust comes from a transfer fee on the sale of all lots. Developer: Chaffin/Light Associates.

action. Programs must be in place to establish civic and social organizations within the community and to rethink amenity packages as a means to draw residents together.

Creative developers will no longer view the location of a school site as an extraction or as the piece of land a developer has to give away in order to achieve planning approval. Instead, such sites will be seen as key amenities and may be placed in the heart of a community as opposed to its outer boundaries. Schools will be designed as community centers and will serve as a performing arts center, a center for adult education, and centers for cultural and social activities. This use of the schools will create a stronger sense of civic pride and place.

Integrating affordable housing into the site plan will become increasingly important and, in some areas, will be mandated by the municipality. Planning and positioning both rental and affordable for-sale housing will become a requirement for many master-planned communities of the future.

Many of today's new breed of developers are benefiting from working directly with environmental groups such as the Audubon Society during the planning and approval process. Such proactive cooperation is creating opportunities for developers to mediate affected areas during the site planning process and to use sensitive areas in ways that create an amenity and enhance the community's way of life. Alliances can be formed

with schools, homeowner associations, and environmental groups so that sensitive areas can become teaching and learning opportunities for community residents. As a result of such relationships, developers are creating land stewardship programs that become a part of their planning process, further enhancing the development's marketing image. Environmental alliances have been developed in the communities of Brookside in Stockton, California, Spring Island in South Carolina, and Celebration in Orlando, Florida. In all these communities, environmental alliances have led to significantly enhanced positioning and perceived values.

Broadening the Role of Community Associations

During the 1980s and 1990s, community associations evolved into service providers, offering residents more than just maintenance and accounting functions. In new communities, associations will provide and manage the community's technology services, cultural activities, and cross-alliances among businesses, schools, and residents. The community's Web site will allow residents to interact with one another, as well as with the community's businesses and schools. It will offer support staff for companies or residents who work at home. It will even serve as a clearinghouse for baby-sitters, tutors, and other service providers from the community.

Because of changes in consumers' work habits, developers are reconsidering what community governments will actually govern. They are redesigning the association documents not only to meet the demands of the new consumer, but also to protect development flexibility. Community associations must now manage issues such as satellite dishes, fiber-optics communications, security programming, community Web sites, and interaction between education and business.

Keeping Up with Technology

Developers are beginning to plan for private dedicated ISDN, broadband cable, and future fiber-optic cable that will allow high-speed interactive communication within the community and tie together home, office, school, and the world. Developers are planning for private community-dedicated fiber-optic television chan-

Fear, both real and perceived, motivates buyers and developers to rely on security gates.

nels that link the home to the school and allow students who are ill to attend classes from home. Such systems can also be used for adult education programs and personal services such as shopping with the community's retailers. New technologies will also offer visually interactive telephones that can communicate a resident's vital signs to the community's wellness/fitness provider. Developers are preplanning to provide multiple telephone lines to each home to meet the technological demands of residents who work at home. They know that before businesses locate in a new community, they will demand state-of-the-art communication facilities. Disney Development Company's community of Celebration in Orlando, Florida, has formed alliances with the school district and health care providers that integrate education and health/fitness into the community lifestyle, not only through site planning and programming of events and activities, but also through technology within the home. Developers today, and in the future, will need to face the ever-increasing demand for technology from both businesses and homeowners. Those communities with effectively preplanned technology options will make competing communities without such planning obsolete.

Capitalizing on Education

Developers recognize that the ultimate competitive edge of a new community will be superior educational opportunities offered to residents of all ages. Clearly, local governments will not be able to provide everything needed to ensure high-quality education. Therefore, state and local school districts, developers, builders, and businesses are forming strategic alliances to develop new kinds of facilities and curricula for their communities. These new curricula will require commitments of time and human resources from the developer, as well as from the community's business leaders, employees, and residents. High-quality education not only sells, but also is a key amenity for the future. Education has become so important to the housing consumer that it often is the deciding factor in purchasing a home.

Easing Fears

Developers also are initiating new approaches to ease consumers' fears about crime and about the trustworthiness of the developer and homebuilder. They are taking seriously what has been called the number one concern of consumers— crime, or simply "the fear of fear." In almost all consumer research conducted today, the fear of crime and the desire for safety are the most prominent concerns expressed by most housing consumers. Across the country, consumer surveys confirm that enhanced community security adds both perceived and real value to the community. To deal with these fears, developers are making public safety as much their responsibility as that of the local government. They are looking at innovations not only in crime control and prevention, but also in technology and better land planning. They are focusing on elements such as:

- Site plans that create smaller neighborhoods with homes featuring strong street orientation.
- A plan review process that broadens the focus on public safety from fire and accessibility requirements to crime prevention. To do this, developers are voluntarily involving police departments and other public safety consultants in the review of their land plans. Thus, the planning process has grown to include issues such as line of sight, site lighting, fencing, and even landscaping elements that help to reduce crime.
- Installation of association-controlled video monitoring of all cars entering and leaving the community.
- Association-managed security, including manned entries and roving security patrols in cars, on bicycles, and on foot. This increased patrol allows the security staff to come in

closer contact with residents and thus become a more relevant amenity for the community.

Creating a Different Kind of Builder Program

Consumers are more suspicious than ever of builders' and developers' ability to deliver on promises made. They take longer to make purchase decisions in order to be assured that the developer can deliver what he promises with regard to future development plans, amenities, and postsale service. In turn, developers are screening builders more carefully, focusing on independent owner satisfaction surveys, the quality of the builder's customer service programs, and the builder's willingness to offer extended warranties on the homes they build.

Reinventing the Sales and Marketing Delivery System

Because of the changes in development planning and consumer attitudes and expectations, developers are telling the story differently at the point of sale. They are developing new kinds of sales and information centers that humanize both the shopping and buying processes. Their sales programs are far more interactive, with sales managers and representatives trained to talk to and not at the customer. In the future, the goal will be to communicate to customers the community's unique selling qualities, thus adding a higher perceived value to living in the community.

Because of the emergence of numerous niche markets, developers want sales presentations to be designed in a way that will allow customers to better communicate their needs. The goal is to eliminate today's prescriptive and controlled sales presentation process, which essentially treats all visitors the same. Instead, sales representatives will focus on needs assessment. In

such an environment, prospects become guests and sales agents community representatives who interact with guests to understand their lifestyle needs in order to match them with housing.

Point-of-sale programs will become far more effective through the application of emerging visual technologies. Virtual reality will show existing and future phases of a community and how amenities and lifestyle enhancements will affect the community. Virtual reality can also be used instead of topographical table presentations, traditional wall-hung displays, and even model home demonstrations. In the information center of the future, guests will be invited to "experience" living in the community and to tour builder models from a comfortable seating area. With virtual reality, visitors will be able to drive the streets, see the architectural palette of the community, participate in previously held athletic and social activities, meet their potential neighbors, and tour a home, all without leaving their viewing chairs. Through this process, the potential buyer can actually "become" a part of the living environment and the housing product. Technology will never completely replace the need for personal communication between the customer and the sales associate or take the place of personal tours and product presentations, but it will change and enhance the communication process.

Getting Ready for the Future

For most in the industry, development concepts, consumer demands, buyer profiles, and developer responsibilities are changing. In the future, successful community developers will require expertise in the fields of planning, business development, education, health and wellness, and interactive social programs. The business is not getting easier. But for prepared developers, it will continue to be profitable and far more rewarding.

Chapter 2

Changing Consumer Preferences

Brooke Warrick and Toni Alexander

Development of planned communities has moved from a focus on mass-market standards to one on niche-market differentiation by both life stage and lifestyle. One of the problems of conventional builder and developer thinking, however, is that it has not always distinguished lifestyle from life stage. "Life stage" here refers to the stages of maturation in family life that call for different kinds of housing: from first-time buyers, to moveup buyers who want to display status, to empty-nester movedown buyers. Unfortunately, these phases are all too often referred to as "lifestyles."

In the building industry, income is seen as a standard counterbalance to life stage in determining the kind of house and community desired by a buyer. Income is perceived as the main predictor of the price people will pay for a house and community. But in reality, both house price and income serve simply as *constraints* on purchase, and the actual style that the homebuyer wants is still not specified. To specify what people actually want, one must know their "lifestyles."

By "lifestyle," most marketers, advertisers, market researchers, and social scientists mean the variety of consumers' ways of life and beliefs,

High-density housing can be a lifestyle preference as well as a cost consideration. At Kentlands in Gaithersburg, Maryland, high-quality townhouses meet the needs of buyers who prefer this type of housing.

Baby boomers are the single largest segment of the U.S. population. As they age, and as the bulge representing their generation moves through the age distribution curve, they are affecting everything that happens in community design. This has been especially true as they have entered their prime earning years, making enough disposable income to choose, and get, what they want in their homes and communities. But boomers are not all alike! And even if one can find out their income levels, upper-middle-class groups often live in different lifestyle "worlds" from one another. What one group wants is a scarcely noticeable factor to another. Becoming aware of this phenomenon is a central task for developers of master-planned communities.

At its best, the master-planned community should appeal to a collection of market niches by life stage, ranging from income-constrained first-time buyers, to moveup buyers who want to display their status, to movedown buyers who have markedly different needs. Awareness of this spectrum helps to maximize market differentiation and spreads the risk for developers and builders because they are then appealing to such a wide range of buyers. This does not mean, however, that a single developer should try to appeal to all conceivable market niches. A community can be sufficiently differentiated by offering a particular lifestyle, such as the neotraditional "new urbanism" community, the golf- and tennis-oriented recreational community, or the master-planned contemporary community.

Master Planning: Value and Infrastructure

From Unplanned Suburbs to Master-Planned Communities

In 1994, American LIVES and InterCommunications, Inc., did a nationwide study to obtain homebuyers' reactions to a wide variety of community amenities and features. As part of this study, people were asked to evaluate how much more it was worth to them to have the amenities and features they wanted in different kinds of communities. These four kinds of communities were:

1. The established suburban neighborhood;
2. The master-planned community;
3. The golf, tennis, or country club community;

including their preferred architectural styles, styles of furniture, kinds of cars, kinds of food, amounts and kinds of education, kinds of media use, and other behaviors that make up a way of life. American LIVES, Inc., has found that the best predictors of lifestyles as actually lived are the values and world views held by different market segments. It is not consumer psychology that determines values; it is the *values subcultures* to which households belong. Measurement of these differences can be made through surveys specially designed to discover the values of homebuyers. By knowing values and the meanings that people apply to the terms "home" and "community," one can segment the market.

Since the 1970s, there has been an evolution of community design from mass-market standards to the targeting of niche markets. During this time, master planning has become more common, tending to serve homebuyers who already own a home rather than first-time buyers. As American society has aged, the most active portion of the market has moved from a relatively undifferentiated, entry-level mass market to more mature buyers who are buying second or later homes. For these buyers, communities have become differentiated into many small niche markets, especially by lifestyle within life stage.

4. The master-planned community with extra community-participation capabilities.

What does the desire for master planning really mean? According to the American LIVES study, it is a preference for groups of items that people want, among them:

- *Natural Environment:* Lots of natural, open space; wilderness areas; a nature interpretive center for environmental awareness; preservation of historic sites.
- *Walks and Parks:* Interesting small parks; walking and biking paths; gardens with native plants and pedestrian pathways.
- *Cul-de-Sac Neighborhoods:* Cul-de-sac streets, circles, and courts instead of through streets; quiet, low-traffic areas.
- *Community Facilities and Shopping:* An amphitheater for public events and shows; a small cluster of convenience-oriented retail stores (dry cleaner, gourmet deli, corner grocer, and so on); a shopping center adjacent to the community; churches or other places of worship; a library where books circulate or can be read on site.
- *A Good Community Entrance:* A distinctive community gateway; an open yet clearly marked entrance.

The study showed that people were willing to pay a $13,500 premium for a master-planned community, compared with a $10,000 premium for the same house in an established suburban neighborhood; this $3,500 difference shows that master planning really does add value.

From Hard Infrastructure to Soft Programming

Designers and developers of master-planned communities have had to make tough choices about the hard infrastructure they put into their communities. Should they offer an Olympic-sized pool with diving boards or smaller, satellite swimming facilities that serve neighborhoods? Should there be tennis courts, and if so, how many? What about golf courses designed by expensive, big-name designers? How about pricey entry monuments that make the statement that "this community is about prestige and exclusivity"? How big should a community center be? Should any center be built at all? These are tough and expensive choices, because if a developer makes the wrong choice, it can be a costly mistake.

A prime example of the risks involved in these choices was the tennis craze of the 1980s. In 1982, tennis was taking off (with more than 21 million players nationwide), so many developers put in tennis courts to meet this market need. By 1995, however, there were barely more than 10 million tennis players nationwide. Hence, tennis complexes constructed in the mid-1980s often became a financial drag for communities still in the selling cycle a decade later.

Developers of master-planned communities who built golf courses in the early 1980s were on the right side of the demand curve for golf, and many are riding the wave of a sport that has taken off since the early to mid-1980s. Largely fueled by baby boomers whose knees have given out from playing tennis, the rise in golf has been steady year after year. But assuming that the fickle baby boomers will continue to support the game as they have in the past may be too risky.

Both homebuyer needs and the costs and risks of expensive "hard infrastructure" are part of a complex and changing landscape. Business decisions are difficult in such an environment. So it is important to ask what value is actually

Golf courses like this one at Brookside in Stockton, California, can increase prices of single-family lots for developers of master-planned communities. Developers must be aware, however, that the market for golf course communities is much narrower than many developers assume.

Figure 2.1. Summary of Features, by Percent of Respondents Saying Feature Is Very or Extremely Important

Feature	Percent
Quiet, low-traffic area	93.07
Designed with cul-de-sac streets, circles, and courts	77.72
Lots of natural, open space	77.72
Walking and biking paths	74.73
Established schools	69.84
Community controls over architectural styles and lot sizes	69.02
Sidewalk along one side of all streets	66.03
A security guard who patrols the community by car at night	65.22
Easy to meet people within the community	60.87
Easy access to freeway	60.60
Gardens with native plants and walking paths	56.39
A small cluster of convenience-oriented retail stores	55.30
Wilderness areas	52.99
An outdoor swimming pool	52.85
A community/recreation center	52.31
Easy to walk to parks, stores, etc.	52.17
A shopping center adjacent to the community	51.49
Interesting little parks	50.82
An exercise/fitness center	50.68
A town center with many small shops, coffee bars, meeting places	48.10
Joining in the community or neighborhood recreational activities	47.28
A library where you can check out books or sit and read	47.01
Churches or other places of worship	46.88
Preservation of historic sites	46.33
Opportunities for parents to interact around child-centered activities	46.06
Living in an area where I will meet lots of people	44.57
An open, yet clearly marked entrance	41.71
Organized programs for young children	41.71
Tennis courts	39.95
A golf course within the community	39.54
Organized sports programs (e.g., swimming, tennis)	37.64
A teen center with organized programs	36.68
Many opportunities to participate in community clubs, interest groups	36.55
A distinctive community entrance	35.73
A golf clubhouse with lockers, pro shop, and storage facilities	33.02
An amphitheater for public events and shows	26.36
A nature interpretive center	25.68
A community organizer to get clubs and community events started	23.91
A community "concierge"	18.48

Source: American LIVES, Inc., 1994.

produced by these amenities and features over the lifetime of a community's buildout. Many of these features may not pay their way.

Figure 2.1, compiled from the nationwide study conducted in 1994 by American LIVES, shows how a sample of home shoppers and homebuyers in master-planned communities rated a variety of community amenities and features.

Lifestyle elements are supported by hard amenities and soft ones alike. Soft programming features can increase the value to buyers but can at the same time easily be changed or eliminated. For example, a nature interpretive center can serve the needs of schoolchildren and/or turn into a community garden. To many families, these uses will outweigh golf or tennis.

Figure 2.1 identifies some of the soft programming elements that should be considered:

Opportunities for parents to interact around child-centered activities	46.06%
Organized programs for young children	41.71
A teen center with organized programs	36.68
Many opportunities to participate in community clubs, interest groups	36.55
A community organizer to get clubs and community events started	23.91

Collectively, these soft programming features can serve the needs of the community, but perhaps more important, they can "learn with the community" over time. That is, they can respond to the changing lifestyles of buyers over the life of the project because they are not fixed, hard infrastructure. Moreover, they are considerably less expensive and less risky in the face of a changing marketplace.

Some kinds of hard infrastructure are inherently more flexible and can respond to changing lifestyles. A good example is biking and walking paths. These inexpensive amenities are also popular, being favored by 75 percent of the shoppers and homebuyers who were surveyed to compile Figure 2.1. Biking and walking paths can serve the needs of mothers with strollers, kids biking to school, rollerbladers, runners, and other users. Regardless of which activity is in vogue, it seems that biking and walking paths are likely to respond to several needs.

Natural open space adds great value to master-planned communities for both developers and residents. Avenel, an upscale golf community in Potomac, Maryland, has maintained abundant green space by clustering homes into six distinct villages.

From Golf Courses to Open Space

The 1980s saw a proliferation of golf-oriented communities in which the golf course provided the focal point for the community's design and for its community image. Golf courses are indeed important visual amenities, and in most cases they create highly profitable lot premiums. Golf-oriented communities, however, appeal to a narrower segment of the homebuying population than most builders and developers realize.

While a substantial 39.5 percent of the sample in the 1994 study indicated that a golf course within a community was "very" or "extremely" important, 60.5 percent did not show this preference. Instead, they rated amenities and features like open space, wilderness areas, and gardens much higher than golf courses. Some of the items they did value highly were:

Lots of natural, open space	77.72%
Gardens with native plants and walking paths	56.39
Wilderness areas	52.99

These findings suggest that shoppers and buyers in the 1990s are looking for communities that use open space as an important feature in their master planning. What's more, they are willing to pay for it. The good news for the developer is that the cost of preserving open space is significantly less than the cost of fixing up a golf course. Yet the market of homebuyers who desire open space is double the size of that of buyers who want golf facilities.

From Single-Purpose Infrastructure To Multifunction Uses

Community features and amenities are supposed to add value to a community. What adds even more value, though, is features or amenities that serve more than one function simultaneously. The reason is that consumers are more diverse in what they want than most builders and developers think. When features and amenities can serve more than one purpose, they are likely to cover more facets of that diversity. The developer that offers multifunction uses has added to the likelihood that it has created value for more of its customers. This makes for a more competitive product.

Biking and walking trails, for example, are described as very or extremely important to 75 percent of the shoppers and homeowners surveyed by American LIVES, Inc., because respondents see more value to themselves in this multifunction amenity. Outdoor amphitheaters can be used for country music performances, meetings of the Grey Panthers (a senior group), chamber music concerts, and other events, thereby speaking to the needs of myriad community members. If community meeting rooms are designed with flexibility in mind, they can be used for weddings, homeowner meetings, private parties, community gatherings for holidays and special occasions, and so on and so on.

Parks are the amenity with the most varied uses: they serve as places to stroll, to play sports (from frisbee throwing to organized activities like soccer and volleyball), to picnic, to loaf, and more. These simple pleasures are coming back to resume a greater importance in the minds of homebuyers.

Interaction by Design

From Suburban Anonymity to a Sense of Community

Moving to the suburbs has for many homebuyers meant that they could get the houses they always dreamed of, with all the newest features and styles. In the previous generation, it didn't seem to matter that they didn't know any of their neighbors except for the people directly next door. But over time, disillusionment with the loss of community has set in. At this point, many buyers of new homes are fed up with suburbs and central cities alike and want a return to small-town life.

Status needs appear to be declining in importance, and other concerns have come to the fore. Merely being able to buy the "right" house in the "right" neighborhood is not enough for a majority in the 1990s—not if it means suburban anonymity. A desire, even a yearning, to feel rooted in the community they live in is growing among current homeowners and potential new-home buyers but is not being satisfied by the new housing and communities that builders and developers are providing. Better master planning is needed to meet a strong, already existing market demand for real community.

From Contemporary Styling to Neotraditional Forms

As lot sizes have diminished in most markets, a significant challenge to architects has been that of differentiating the elevation and styling of a house from those of similar available homes. Shrinking lot sizes seem to have forced the garage to the front of the house, making the big, blank garage door the focal point of the elevation and tending to emphasize the "cookie-cutter" effect, whereby the houses in any streetscape really don't differ that much from those in any other. Often, homebuyers today are looking for something else, anything else.

Over the last several years, a growing number of architects and planners have proposed designs for neotraditional styling in both houses and neighborhoods as a return to many of the architectural roots of small-town America. This movement goes well beyond just decorative features: Victorian detailing, gables, gingerbread trim, and picket fences. Communities offer town centers with cafés and walking spaces that encourage people to gather, and they are deliberately less automobile-oriented. There may be apartments over the stores, and neighborhoods near the center of town have narrow streets, small lots, and many larger trees. The traditionally styled houses have their garages hidden behind them, reached by driveways from the

front or off an alley, and the large front porches are supposed to encourage interaction among neighbors.

Results of a study done in 1995 by American LIVES, Inc., show the reactions of homebuyers and home shoppers to the eight key design elements of the neotraditional approach, or the *new urbanism,* compared with comparable designs in the standard suburbs (see Figure 2.2). The study results serve to segment the sample into the following three basic reactions to neotraditional styling:

- *Of the total respondents, 20.8 percent are in favor of the new urbanism.* They like the whole concept, including the higher densities, and are also unhappy with most suburbs as they are. These numbers are not huge, but they do represent a good niche market.
- *"Neutral" respondents (48.4 percent) like the image but want larger lots.* They like the town center idea in particular but would not really buy into the whole new urbanism concept. This segment did not like the higher density and the perceived lack of automobility, even though they do not like the suburbs as they are now. These consumers are not willing to sacrifice much for the new urbanism.
- *Finally, 30.8 percent like the suburbs the way they are now and reject the new urbanism.* They object to the higher densities and all conse-

quences that go with it, but some of these respondents are also attracted to neotraditional style.

From Sprawl to Compact Town Centers

Most buyers of new homes have come to loathe the kind of suburb that has miles of identical houses edged by strip commercial uses and malls. The suburban dream is imploding for these buyers. It is not that they want to go back to the central city; they don't. But they recognize the dysfunctionality of suburbs. The gridlock of traffic adds to their distaste for the suburban way of life. It does not suffice for developers to protest that "the market wants it this way"; this justification has come to be seen by new-home buyers as a self-serving falsehood. They want a product that is better designed.

In part, this change indicates that consumer standards have gone up. It also means, however, that the objections and complaints of architects and planners have finally trickled down to ordinary people, who find these pronouncements to be true. What they might once have rejected as elitist sentiment they now see as clear fact. Unplanned suburban sprawl is now viewed as thoughtless and foolish and not as evidence of the superior wisdom of the market. Standard

Figure 2.2. **Reactions to Eight Essential Design Elements**

For each of the numbered design elements, Item "A" describes the approach of the new urbanism, while Item "B" describes that of the standard contemporary suburb.

	% For	% Neutral	% Against
1. Town Center			
A. Town center has a village green surrounded by shops, civic buildings, churches, etc. The town center is the focal point for residential neighborhoods clustered around it.	86	8	6
B. No single community center exists: shopping and civic buildings are distributed along commercial strips and in malls.	23	20	57
2. Community Gathering Places			
A. Town center has lots of small parks, shops, cafés, and stores that have been explicitly planned to give places for people to gather and socialize (prices can be higher).	84	11	5
B. Commercial areas of the town are planned for ease of auto access and for convenient shopping to maximize store revenues (prices can be lower). Socializing is not planned for, so there are few community gathering places.	35	25	40
3. Street Pattern			
A. Narrow streets are centered on the town square and in a city-block grid to encourage walking and discourage in-town driving. Traffic flows through all residential and commercial streets.	55	17	28
B. Streets are wide to make it convenient to drive in town. Shopping areas are farther apart, so walking is not practical. Neighborhoods have culs-de-sac and courts that are linked by higher-speed, major streets.	46	20	34
4. Parking and Cars in Town			
A. Town is less automobile-oriented. Town center has parking structures instead of large lots. Higher-density development with walking and biking paths encourages people to get around town without cars.	69	16	15
B. Auto-oriented suburb has acres of parking around commercial and public areas. Things are far enough apart so that you need to drive to most places, especially shopping facilities.	25	21	54

suburban design does not work for many people, and the quality of life is often viewed as poor. Hence, master planning has ceased to be a luxury and has become one of the ordinary requirements to enter the market for a competent housing development.

Buyers of new homes are uniformly impressed by the idea of a town center and of towns that have boundaries to them. In the American LIVES study summed up in Figure 2.2, 86 percent of the sample wanted "a town center that has a village green surrounded by shops, civic buildings, churches, etc. The town center is the focal point for residential neighborhoods clustered around it." This consensus is too powerful to ignore. Homebuyers do not want an unbounded suburban cancer spreading across the landscape; they want urban growth to take the shape of nicely bounded small-town cells that have nuclei (town centers).

	% For	% Neutral	% Against
5. Density of Residential Areas			
A. Lots are smaller, with houses closer to the street and with smaller front yards in the style of small-town neighborhoods. Sidewalks are found on both sides of narrower streets. The focus is on shared community recreation areas instead of larger, private yards.	33	19	48
B. Larger lots and wider streets make for lower-density neighborhoods. Houses are set farther back from the streets, with larger yards. Less space is allotted to shared community recreation.	73	14	13
6. Look and Feel of the Neighborhood			
A. Styles of house and yard are often traditional, with garages hidden behind houses, front porches to encourage neighboring, and shade trees along the streets.	75	14	11
B. Styles of house and yard are contemporary, with houses set back from the street, garages facing the street, no porches, and shade trees, if any, only in yards.	32	23	45
7. Mix of Housing Types and Ages of Residents			
A. There is a wide range of housing types: single-family detached houses, rowhouses, duplexes, and apartments all exist in the neighborhoods. A town center also has apartments above the shops. The intention is to attract a wide range of ages, including seniors and young singles.	44	17	39
B. Strict zoning separates single-family areas from neighborhoods with higher-density housing. Narrow ranges of ages and family types prevail within the neighborhoods.	50	21	29
8. Architectural Styles			
A. All houses and stores are forced to follow a single, consistent architectural style that is either traditional or typical for the region.	48	17	35
B. With very few architectural controls, there is often one of two results: either a wide variety of styles that can be inconsistent, or cookie-cutter houses that lack a regional flavor.	17	28	55

Source: American LIVES, Inc., 1995.

From Status Display to Authenticity

Since the late 1980s, there has been less interest in the blatant display of status through the front elevations of homes, impressive streetscapes, and monumental entryways for master-planned communities. While there are still communities being designed using these styling standards, there is less pursuit of these norms than in the past.

Homebuyers are leaning away from status display in elevations (showy columns, bay windows, and massing of vertical spaces) in favor of greater differentiation of their own elevations from others. This styling allows for a more "authentic" feel. Homebuyers are also questioning the value of big, status-oriented entry monuments that serve no purpose other than to say, "We've made it." The movement over the last several years toward neotraditional community design is another response to homebuyers' desires to get back to community designs that are more genuine.

As the millennium approaches, there is an emerging dialogue among planners, designers, and developers about what really creates value for homebuyers. Many of the cherished notions that have driven community design for decades are being questioned. Golf courses are falling in favor of any or all of the following: biking and walking trails, open spaces that have been left untouched, eco-areas that are left as nature interpretive centers, large parks that serve multifunctional needs, and related features. This trend is likely to continue for the foreseeable future.

From Open Suburbs to Bounded Or Gated Communities

Along with a general rise in concerns about crime and security in recent years, there has been a parallel rise in homebuyers' security fears about their new homes and communities. In the American LIVES study of 1994, 65 percent of shoppers and homeowners indicated that a "security guard who patrols the community by car at night" is very or extremely important. In focus groups on community and house design, the issue of security always comes up, because it is one of the core concerns that all buyers can agree upon; it is not an issue that homeowners or developers of new communities can afford to neglect.

There are several techniques that developers and designers can employ to deal with safety and security fears. One obvious solution is to gate the community, but this does not address the real issue of people's safety and security fears. Feeling safe and secure is often more of a symbolic issue than one of simply putting more police on the streets. Feeling safe usually starts with the sense that the community has a clear boundary. When people who live in a community can spot outsiders and are doing some self-policing, a built-in sense of security results. Boundaries can be created with fences, but landscaping can be just as important in generating the image of a clear boundary.

Gated communities may not really solve the problem because most people realize the weak-

An open and distinctive entrance is important in establishing a new community's identity. The walkway and heavily landscaped colonnades at Addison Reserve in Delray Beach, Florida, welcome residents and visitors alike.

nesses of gated places: more than one car can enter if the gate is not manned; the time between the breakdown of carded gates and their repair can be long enough for many intruders to get through; and access codes to automatic gates can be learned easily by the wrong people.

American LIVES discovered that putting electronic security systems in all homes of a subdivision, rather than just offering them as an option, has a positive effect. Not only does this approach reduce crime in communities but also it gets the word out on the street that "this community is protected." An interesting byproduct of putting in security systems as standard features is the implied message to buyers that security in a community is not negotiable. Builders can make deals with installers of security systems to take advantage of economies of scale by installing a predetermined number of units per year. The cost to the builder will be significantly less than the perceived value of such a system to homebuyers.

Other kinds of protection that can be built into a community are more subtle but not costly. One of these techniques that can be used in large master-planned communities involves building at least some houses that are targeted at retired seniors. Retirees are at home most days and constitute an important early warning system about anything that looks suspicious. Developers can also start special programs to attract homebuyers who are policemen, detectives, and other security professionals who have trained eyes to spot activities that are questionable. Programs such as these have gone so far as to offer discounts on homes. It is surprising how fast the word gets out that there are police or detectives living within a community.

Speculations on the Future

As Yogi Berra once said, "Prediction is hard, especially about the future." Nevertheless, it is possible to make some forecasts about the future if one takes into account some trends that are already in motion. It is also important to bear in mind some current behaviors that cannot continue long into the future.

Developers may buy up inner-ring, older suburbs where the housing stock and infrastructure have long since decayed and depreciated, and may redevelop closer-in areas into highly bounded, attractive communities. Several factors favor this prediction. Demand from consumers favors closer-in

The growing desire for communities with a sense of place can be met by creating town centers with cafés and pedestrian-oriented spaces that encourage people to gather. The Reston Town Center in Virginia features retail and entertainment uses connected to an open-air civic plaza used for community events.

communities that are safe. If infill properties contain enough units to make the economics work, they offer the inducement that all infrastructure is already in place. The risk can be lower because the developer knows whether the location works. Hence, the critical task is to get the design right.

The cost of commuting—gas prices, time, and congestion—may get so high that America gets dense development along high-speed transit corridors or an expansion of denser, satellite cities around the urban cores. A growing amount of literature and public commentary has arisen over the last few years maintaining that the United States needs to take a close look at the real costs of cheap energy to its cities, that we need to do

Careful protection of natural amenities like this river at the Governor's Land at Two Rivers in Williamsburg, Virginia, can benefit both residents and the developer.

more of what the Europeans have been doing for decades: making it more expensive to drive, and restricting automobility. Americans' love affair with the automobile may have to give way to better public transit that meets the needs of more commuters. One consequence could be that development patterns would be oriented along high-speed transit corridors. Another interesting consequence might be that satellite cities could emerge in places served by these high-speed transit corridors.

What is now a niche market for neotraditional communities may gain in strength and become a major part of the landscape. Developers, builders, city planners, and many land planners are either currently involved in or planning neotraditional communities around the United States. Disney's neotraditional community, Celebration, in Orlando, Florida, has caught the media's attention and taken the idea of community design out of the design studios and brought it to the notice of the general public. An important new trend has been emerging as city planners encourage the development of neotraditional communities and discourage traditional suburban developments by making the approval process easier for the former and more difficult for the latter.

The American LIVES study on neotraditional styling has shown that home shoppers and home-buyers are strongly in favor of neotraditional *styling*, in part because it speaks to their yearning for community with gathering places, town centers, and a small-town character. They are more dubious about the higher-density features

of the currently proposed neotraditional town designs because high density implies noise problems, lack of visual privacy, and streets that are unsafe for children. While all of these issues can be overcome by clever design techniques, to date the design problems have not been solved.

A majority of Americans may set up home offices for home businesses and/or for telecommuting. The home office could become as universal as an extra room in the house. Out of a total of 99 million households in the United States in 1996, some 44 million had a place in the home they called an office. This office might be used simply as a room for writing checks, though for 12 million households it is a place to run a business, either part or full time. And these numbers are growing.

Builders and developers are now routinely including home offices as part of their development strategies. To some developers, this simply means putting in a dedicated power source and extra phone lines. But increasingly, it means that rooms devoted to the home office have a separate entry, are sound-buffered from the rest of the house or situated near the front door to receive clients, and do not allow views of the part of the house that is "lived in."

Providing for the home-office worker offers the developer other, unexpected benefits besides just another market niche to target. Home-office workers do not commute at high-traffic times, so they create less demand for large collector streets that can eat up much-needed infrastructure funds. But they may generate a demand for copying and other business services within the community.

Communities designed for the special needs of seniors will become more differentiated and will play a major part in the urban and social landscape. The single most important demographic trend in the United States is the aging of the population. It is impossible to overestimate the impact that this phenomenon will have on homes and communities over the next generation. Yet most builders and developers seem to assume that it is someone else's business. They are missing out on the direction in which a significant part of the market is headed.

It used to be that one could segment the all-important senior market according to its members' mobility: go-goes, slow-goes, and no-goes. However, the senior market is becoming more differentiated because elderly people now have more disposable income and thus more choice.

As the trend develops, the ways in which they want to live will become more diverse.

As demonstrated by the proliferation of active adult communities, especially in the Southwest and Southeast, many seniors want a lifestyle involving people like themselves and not including children. But this option does not suit all seniors. There is a much larger, age- and income-qualified group of seniors who reject active adult communities as "siren cities," places where the old go to die. These other seniors want to live in areas where there is as much diversity of age as there is of lifestyle. They want to move down to smaller homes because the kids are gone, but they still want all of the urban or suburban amenities and services they have become used to in the communities where they live now.

The market for continuing-care retirement communities (CCRCs) is differentiating even more. Going well beyond the old idea of nursing homes, CCRCs offer three levels of service: *independent living* for seniors who want to share meals, activities, and access to a clinic for checkups and routine health services; *assisted living* for seniors who have short-term needs for daily help with bathing, medication, and mobility while they are recovering from falls or temporary illnesses; and *skilled nursing* for residents who need 24-hour nursing attention, are probably not ambulatory, and need help with bathing and daily care. These communities are rapidly evolving and improving as they recognize the opportunity to go upscale (there are indeed seniors who are willing to pay lots of money to live in a CCRC). They are also discovering that they are not in the shelter business as much as in the business of providing safe and secure environments where people can get involved socially and form strong bonds of friendship with other community members.

Astute developers will become users of social research. Developers will need to look at community and design issues not just from a marketing standpoint but also from a social research viewpoint. Understanding changes in society that make people want to live differently—such as values, crime, aging, and women's issues—will result in the development of communities that meet the needs of a greater variety of homebuyers. Successful developers will be the ones to adopt a stance that anticipates the future, seeing trends coming and changing how their communities are built. Hiring social researchers as consultants could prove extremely helpful.

Environmental issues will gain in importance in development. Developers can lead the way in showing how a community can be designed for ecological sustainability and still be an enjoy-

Northwest Landing in Dupont, Washington, is a neotraditional development that offers residents charming streetscapes characterized by front porches and setbacks that are close to the street.

able place to live. A larger commitment to eco-designs can contribute more to a developer's bottom line than most community features. Because communities will last for generations, developers can guarantee their personal places in local history by leaving good legacies for future generations.

A developer's reputation adds to the credibility capital of a community, which will become ever more important in the future. Current research shows that a developer's reputation is already a major factor in the sales potential of a new community. There is every reason to believe that the importance of "credibility capital" will grow in the future. Credibility capital, as a term, is a better way of expressing what business often calls good will; it is a consumer's perception that he or she wants to do business with a particular company.

Homebuyers' current perception of most developers is relatively negative. Most developers are starting out with one foot in the hole by having to overcome the obstacle of poor community relations. Consumers want to buy from a developer and a builder who care. Any developer who undertakes good community relations as a strategy can be expected to prevail in the long run.

Developers and technology companies will form strategic partnerships. Technology will play an increasing role in community design, as seen in Disney's Celebration in Orlando, Florida, which combines the latest in fiber optics, interactivity, and consumer electronics in schools and homes to flexibly support innovative developments later on. As the world continues to shrink, we will see a continuing demand for technology that improves the ways in which we live.

Chapter 3

The Implications of New Technologies

William Clark

Throughout history, land development patterns have been determined by mobility. Forms of mobility have evolved rapidly over the past 100 years, bringing about changes in how and where people live. Most recently, the automobile and its associated infrastructure of roads and highways have opened the suburbs and defined a new lifestyle for Americans. Today, a new form of mobility is sweeping the world, brought by information and telecommunications technologies. Savvy developers are beginning to consider what these emerging technologies will mean to the business of building homes and communities in the years ahead.

Telecommunications progress has been linked closely to advances in information and computer technologies, as the use of fax machines, modems, networking, teleconferencing, and the Internet has expanded rapidly. These technological changes are occurring in tandem with economic and cultural shifts, such as those seen in corporate restructuring, "virtual organizations" (see "Technobuzz" on page 27), an increasingly international economy, and a greater emphasis on quality of life.

Employers are changing as well, offering greater flexibility in working hours and the option of working at home, at least part time, and establishing "virtual offices" staffed by a limited number of core employees. In today's fast-paced climate, businesses must be able to respond to immediate market opportunities and project needs. Increasingly, they rely on contract and temporary employees, decreasing security and stability for all workers.

Among the consequences of these advances in technology and shifts in employment is a rapidly growing population of home-based workers who are not constrained by commuting distances when selecting a new home and can choose to live in remote locations, even far from an urban or suburban area. Home-based workers also bring implications for the existing urban and suburban communities where they make up an increasing daytime population and require services, infrastructure, and zoning regulations to accommodate their needs.

Before continuing on the path of business-as-usual, residential developers and builders should consider some of the issues and oppor-tunities brought about by these emerging trends. Where are the new technologies headed, and what changes are likely in how people work and live? Is telecommuting a fad or the wave of the future? What kinds of technology-supporting features will consumers demand in their living environments? Are these broad-based demands, or do they apply only to certain niche markets? What are the potential effects on the location, type, and design of residential development?

Emerging Technology-Based Trends

Technological advances have been influencing employment trends for some time and are beginning to leave their mark on lifestyles and urban development patterns. Several technology-based trends that are receiving considerable attention have implications for residential developers.

The U.S. Census reports that home computer ownership grew from 8 percent of all households in 1984 to 23 percent in 1993.[1] According to estimates by *American Demographics* magazine, by

Broken Top, Inc.

Situated on the eastern slopes of the Cascade Mountains near Bend, Oregon, Broken Top is a master-planned community targeted squarely at "flexecutives." Since opening in 1992, 400 of a total of 1,100 approved lots have been sold at an average price of $150,000. The community, which is being developed by Broken Top, Inc., abuts the Deschutes National Forest and offers dramatic mountain views. Of the buyers to date, 70 percent have said that they intend to make Broken Top their primary home. Most of the buyers, whose ages average 47, come from a major metropolitan area, primarily Seattle, Portland, San Francisco, or southern California.

Technobuzz

Emerging technologies and changing cultural values are generating some new terms that are already being tossed around by real estate developers and builders:

- *Virtual organization.* One with a core workforce that might be situated in one location or in multiple locations. The organization depends on a network of geographically dispersed individuals and other businesses to perform its functions, typically on a project-by-project basis. The term also applies to large organizations with multiple locations that use technology and telecommunications to enhance the effectiveness of its personnel and to compete successfully in an international economy.
- *Virtual community.* A community of people drawn together by a common interest or purpose who communicate primarily via computer and telecommunications technologies.
- *Telecommuter.* A person who is in contact part or full time with his or her office and clients via telephone, computer modem, and/or other technologies.
- *Lone eagles.* Well-educated professionals able to live and work where they choose by using their brains and technology to cover distance.
- *Cappuccino cowboy/cowgirl.* One who lives and works (at least part time) in an upscale, recreation-based community somewhere in the West.
- *Neofrontier.* Rural area becoming popular for new planned communities.
- *Modem cowboy/cowgirl.* One who works from a computer terminal, usually portable, with at least one foot planted in a rural community.
- *Exurbia.* Communities beyond the urban fringes appealing to people looking for a rural quality of life and natural surroundings.
- *Telemedicine.* The practice of medicine by doctors and medical centers that evaluates and treats patients via video, voice, and computer communications from any distance.
- *Flexecutive.* An executive with the flexibility to work at home or in another place of choice, rather than being tied to a traditional office setting. ∎

1997 that statistic had grown to 37 percent of all households. As of 1996, nearly 50 percent of all computer equipment and software sold was for home use—the fastest-growing segment of the computer sales industry. The industry predicts that by 2000 more than 40 percent of all homes will have personal computers.

Home-Based Workers

Statistics vary, but according to the Bureau of Labor Statistics (BLS), in 1997 more than 23 million persons, or about 17 percent of the workforce, worked at home at least some of the time.[2] A widely quoted survey by the American Home Business Association of Salt Lake City reveals that the home-based workforce is increasing by 8,000 workers each day, or nearly 3 million people per year. According to the BLS, nearly 90 percent of home-based workers are in white-collar occupations, and about 60 percent use a computer for their work.

In addition to changing technologies, a major force behind the increase in home-based employment has been the restructuring and downsizing of business organizations. Downsizing has eliminated hordes of middle-level managers, causing many to seek self-employment or consulting arrangements with former employers.

The concept of the virtual organization has been another generator of home-based workers. This category comprises businesses with essentially no employees or physical location that depend on contract employees and other businesses to accomplish their objectives. The term also applies to businesses with a small core of employees working from remote locations, including other states and countries. The organization is tied together by telephone, computer, modem, fax, overnight express, and only occasional face-to-face meetings.

It is not only small and startup firms that are taking this path. For example, the Ford Motor Company has forged a worldwide link among its designers and engineers, who now can interact constantly through videoconferencing and instant graphic and data communication. Hewlett Packard now depends on a companywide Intranet system for communication within the organization, allowing about 10 percent of its employees to work at home at least part time.

Growth of Rural Communities

If technologies have enabled more home-based workers, the home-based workforce has spurred the growth of rural communities. Workers who once were tied to places because of their job sites are now free to choose where they live based on factors other than commuting times. Often, these workers choose to live in rural areas.

During the 1980s, a majority of nonmetropolitan counties lost population, but in the 1990s the trend was reversed. The U.S. Census Bureau estimates that between 1990 and 1994, 75 percent of nonmetropolitan counties grew in population, with an estimated 2 million people leaving their metropolitan homes for rural locales. The Census Bureau also estimates that employment growth in nonmetropolitan areas grew 5.8 percent, compared with 2.5 percent for metropolitan areas, between 1990 and 1994.

Employment growth in rural areas is even more impressive when one considers that the statistics include only wage- and salary-based employees and not self-employed workers, who have an even greater flexibility to live outside urban areas. The Census Bureau's estimates reflect the averages for all rural communities. Many small towns and recreation-based communities are experiencing growth rates of 5 percent or more, well above the average. These communities are often the favored locations for "flexecutives" (see "Technobuzz"), telecommuters, and others who do not necessarily have to live near an employment base.

In the West, these trends are evidenced in the phenomenal growth rate in the wine-country counties north of San Francisco and in the foothills of the Sierras. Growth in these areas is largely related to a rise in the number of part- and full-time residents who are able to work from their homes. More footloose telecommuters and independent businesspeople are contributing to the growth of recreational communities such as Sun Valley, Idaho, and Telluride, Colorado.

Perhaps in reaction to an increasingly machine-based world, some people are seeking a return to some of the more desirable aspects of earlier times. Many housing consumers are expressing a need for a greater sense of neighborhood and community, more control over their lives, closer contact with the natural environment, and more time to spend with family. These values are gaining in importance as factors in how and where people choose to live.

Real estate market surveys reveal a strong demand for communities that include the elements of traditional neighborhoods, promote interaction among residents, and offer strong links to the natural environment. Increasingly, master-planned communities are incorporating features that respond to these consumer preferences. Some developments focus on natural surroundings and recreation, others focus on neighborhood characteristics consistent with neotraditional planning concepts, and some of the best incorporate both environmental and neotraditional planning concepts. Examples of the new wave of market-driven communities include Prairie Crossing near Chicago, Kentlands near Washington, D.C., High Desert near Albuquerque, and Suisun City near San Francisco. Many of these concepts are being incorporated on a very large scale in the Valencia community north of Los Angeles.

Technology in Residential Design

The idea of "smart homes" has been around since the 1950s. The technology finally appears to be catching up with the notion. The concept of today's smart home goes beyond turning on the lights, sprinklers, and oven automatically. The smart home can be equipped to perform all of the following functions:

- Security, including alarms, door locks, and controls that allow the owner to open the door by remote control for a repairman to enter.
- Telecommunications functions such as telephone, TV, music, messaging, E-mail, the Internet, and faxing for the home, workplace, and individuals within the household.
- Monitoring and controlling electrical and HVAC functions, as programmed and in response to environmental conditions.
- A central computer with a number of stations, some for individuals and some for home functions, with the television usually among the stations linked to the computer.
- And, yes, turning on the lights, sprinklers, and oven.

All these conveniences are possible in today's homes. However, consumers will not necessarily use or pay for a technology just because it exists. A consortium of manufacturers of components for a system (without a computer) operating under the name Smart House has not had great success in marketing its product so far. And although videoconferencing apparently is on the

verge of widespread acceptance and use, similar technology has been available since the 1960s. A technology's broad acceptance results in large part from its ease of use and its time-saving capacity, as well as its affordability.

On the other hand, certain technological elements in homes have gained widespread market acceptance and even have become marketing necessities in some regions. Anecdotal reports indicate that apartments outfitted with high-speed Internet wiring are renting faster and at higher rents than comparable units without the wiring. One apartment developer reports that new construction typically includes as many as eight telephone lines per unit, up from the standard single line of only a few years ago.

Wiring in fact appears to be the most rapidly changing element of new home construction. Increasingly, buyers demand advanced wiring for integrated entertainment, security, and communications systems. Some builders offer systems that integrate telephones, cable TV, VCRs, computers, and HVAC controls with easy-to-use control panels. The cost of such systems can be relatively inexpensive.

There is unquestionably a trend toward including home offices in both single- and multi-family homes in new construction. According to a 1996 study commissioned by *Builder* magazine, 77 percent of builders have said that they are incorporating home offices into their products, and 65 percent foresaw an increase over this amount between then and 2000.

What's on the Horizon?

Where are these new technologies headed, and how might they further affect lifestyles and community preferences? The consensus is that technology will provide the tools to meet people's demands. But as George F. Colony of Forrester Research, Inc., stated in a *Wall Street Journal* interview, "If you ask consumers, 'What do you want?' they [don't] know." Colony believes it is essential to study people's values and needs in basic terms, then see how these preferences translate into products.

A sampling of some of the major technologies and their histories reveals how innovations have responded to consumers' basic values and needs and how they have in turn affected the ways in which people work and live. Telephones, automobiles, airplanes, photocopiers, fax machines, and personal computers have all changed how people work and live. Technology-based

29

Hidden Springs is a 915-unit planned community that opened in 1997 on a 1,700-acre parcel in the foothills near Boise, Idaho. The plan preserves about 75 percent of the site in a natural condition and provides for a community trail system that connects to a regional trail extending into the mountains above Boise. Hidden Springs, developed by Grossman Family Properties, includes a neotraditional village center with a general store, post office, fire station, small-scale commercial services, an independent school, playing fields, and a community center. A fiber-optic system is being installed throughout the community. All houses can be built with detached structures that can serve as home offices or accessory living units.

products of the future will likely respond to these needs and values, which are growing in importance:

- *Time.* This is the one commodity that everyone wants. Saving time, and having more of it available for personal use, will be an impetus for successful innovations of all kinds.
- *Personal security.* Despite statistics indicating that crime may be on a downturn, fear of crime in urban and suburban locations is influencing how people live. For many people, fear dictates the use of gates and fences, alarms, lighting, and interactive security systems.
- *Flexibility.* Adapting work and personal life to individual needs and rhythms is increasingly appealing and possible.
- *Contact with others.* The need to remain in contact with friends, family, and professional associates is a strong impetus for innovations in communications technologies.
- *Natural environment.* The view that the environment is in many ways threatened has made many people more aware and appreciative of their natural surroundings.

- *Community/neighborhood.* People are seeking living situations that promote interaction and familiarity with others, that enable a connection to a physical space in a way that technology cannot accommodate.
- *Predictability.* People want assurance that their surroundings will not be changed in a significantly negative way and that they have a reasonable chance to avoid becoming outmoded.

Not only the average person has trouble keeping up with the speed of change and envisioning what the future might hold. Technology experts as well have had difficulty in predicting the future with reliability. For example, in 1994 an interactive multimedia demonstration project undertaken by U.S. West and Time Warner was intended to pioneer a variety of video-related services. But the technologies being demonstrated were superseded by newer technologies even as they were introduced.

Despite the unpredictable fate of innovations, however, some leaders in telecommunications and information technology are projecting what will probably occur.

- *Competition.* An outgrowth of competing technologies and of the Telecommunications Reform Act of 1996 is that developers, builders, and individual customers will have choices as to who provides telephone and cable services. Developers will increasingly be able to take advantage of competition for improved quality of service, as well as reduced infrastructure costs and a potential additional source of revenue.
- *Wireless technology.* Wire, cable, and fiber-optic technologies will be superseded by global wireless technology. With wireless communication, small rural communities and even whole countries will be able to leapfrog cable and fiber-optic installation costs and achieve an equal footing with the most advanced metropolitan areas.
- *A major increase in telecommunications transmission capacity worldwide.* This rise will allow for the widespread and inexpensive availability of technologies that require large capacity, such as video transmission. This capacity will take both the wired and wireless forms.
- *Interactive video*, including teleconferencing, and video on demand. PCs with built-in video cameras for teleconferencing, combined with improvements in data transmission and increases in computer speed and memory, will allow for simultaneous video, audio, and data transmission and for interaction among parties in the normal course of business and personal communications. The quality, ease, and cost of teleconferencing are all improving dramatically, so that this technology will soon become commonplace.
- *Central home computer.* Home uses already account for nearly 50 percent of the total market for computer equipment and software. It is likely that a primary, powerful home computer will have PCs or terminal devices hooked into it, along with other functions such as telephones, lights, and security devices.
- *Television as computer.* Computers for homes now outsell televisions. With little difference between CD and VCR functions, televisions are expected to become routine parts of computer systems. CDs will replace videotapes and will be used for prerecorded programs and for recording.
- *Voice control of computers.* It was science fiction when Harrison Ford talked to his computer to examine and manipulate photographic files in the 1982 film *Blade Runner*. But IBM now produces voice-recognition software for PCs at reasonable prices. This is the first wave of technologies that will be able to detect the nuances of specific voices, to which they will respond. By voice instruction, users will be able to write and edit text, make audio/video calls, do research on information received, perform financial analyses, maneuver through the Internet (or Nextnet—see below), assemble and edit images, and provide personal reminders—basically, to do anything that computers are already capable of doing by keystroked command.
- *Speed and memory: no obstacles.* Speed and memory capabilities of PCs will exist at a level and cost that will no longer restrict other technologies or applications. Videoconferencing, extensive use of the Internet, and applications not yet conceived will be easily handled by the next generation of PCs.
- *Nextnet/Giganet.* The Internet as we know it will be superseded by new network systems with names like Nextnet and Giganet. Next-generation "nets" will be faster, will enhance the ability to maneuver through infinite sources of information and communication links, and will allow for improved communication through sophisticated video capacity and graphics.
- *Knowbots.* Personal information assistants will be available on verbal call through home- or office-based computers. These assistants, also referred to as intelligence agents, will be able to report back what they have learned, to communicate with other data sources through the Internet, to follow up on specifics, and in fact to do almost anything that is information related.

Undoubtedly, technology will continue to bring about enormous changes in how people live and work. Developers and builders are just beginning to consider how to respond to and incorporate advancing information and telecommunications technologies into their projects and how, by so doing, to gain a competitive edge in the market.

What Does Technology Mean for Residential Development?

Perhaps the most obvious implication of these technological developments is the fact they provide people with the flexibility to organize their

Montgomery Village, Canada's first telecommunity, is located in Orangeville, Ontario, a town of 20,000 people on the edge of the greater Toronto area. Planned for a total of 1,000 residential units, a regional high school, and a main street–style commercial component, this 250-acre master-planned community was brought to market in 1994 by the Toronto-based River Oaks Group.

The telecommunications component of the project involves both Bell Canada and the local cable company, Shaw Cable. Bell Canada is installing high-capacity fiber-optic cable and ISDN (integrated services digital network) connections as servicing and construction proceed. Shaw Cable now provides only basic cable service but is anticipating future telecommunications technology by installing a reserve conduit throughout the community. The cable service has been provided in a star configuration to allow for future services, including interactive television, videoconferencing, and telephone service, all provided by the cable company.

In addition, the River Oaks Group has formed an alliance with a local company to provide Internet services to Montgomery, as well as to the town of Orangeville and the surrounding country-side. The company has created a homepage for Montgomery and Orangeville area residents, focusing on local events, services, and businesses. Through an agreement with the River Oaks Group, Montgomery residents benefit from preferential hookup rates.

The phenomena of at-home work and of telecommuting were very much behind the concept for Montgomery from the outset. A small, early survey of residents showed that about half anticipated doing some paid work from their homes and that they planned to make use of the technology available at Montgomery. All homes in Montgomery are served by ISDN, a high-capacity linkup that allows simultaneous transmission of voice and video images, and data.

Flexible Home Plans

A wide variety of single-family houses, semidetached units, and townhouses are designed to be flexible and to accommodate a variety of work-at-home options and configurations, including optional third floors, basements, and accessory buildings. Basement levels are raised to provide daylight and are reached by a separate side door. Zoning permits a home office to be located at the back of the lot, either in a sepa-rate building beside a parking space or carport or as a second story over a garage. This office option will offer privacy and allow visitors to be received directly from the alley. Clients for a small business, for instance, need not go through the main residential unit.

Mixed Uses

Given that many more people will be working out of their homes, it is important to cater to their business needs within the community. One of the potential benefits of working at home is the reduced number of auto trips needed. This benefit will be realized, however, only if work-at-home support functions are provided within the community, ideally within walking distance. Montgomery's commercial component will address this need: Montgomery Boulevard, the community's mixed-use main street, is intended as the focal point of the community, and no home is more than a five-minute walk from Montgomery Boulevard.

Not yet under construction, Montgomery Boulevard is being planned for flexible live/work spaces in the form of townhouses whose ground floors can be converted (and deconverted) into offices or stores. Main-street buildings, like housing units, will be served by direct linkup to fiber-

work and living arrangements in ways more suited to their individual needs. So far, this flexibility has been evidenced mostly in how and where people have chosen to work. As described, technology has made possible increased numbers of home-based workers, telecommuters, and virtual offices, and greater flexibility in working hours and workdays.

The next issue is how increased flexibility in the workplace will translate into how and where people choose to *live*. For residential community developers, this prospect is at the heart of their business. A number of implications and opportunities brought about by these technological and economic trends bear consideration.

More Dispersion of Development

Since the invention of streetcars and then automobiles, America's cities have moved toward lower densities, especially in residential neighborhoods. Every survey continues to show that

optic cable. A wide range of uses is permitted in this commercial district, including office, service, institutional, and retail uses and the many activities that support home workers, such as copy centers, professional offices (accountants, lawyers, graphic designers), cafés, fitness clubs, and newsstands. The main street may also include multi- or single-user telecenters as alternatives to work-at-home arrangements.

High-Quality Environment And the Public Realm

With more people spending a greater portion of their time at home and in their communities, the quality of a community, its design and amenities, are of greater importance than in the past. Further, at-home workers need places for social interaction, and because there is a broader range of activities integrated into today's planned community, there is a greater emphasis on accessibility for pedestrians.

With these factors in mind, planners have paid careful attention to the quality of the streetscapes, parks, and other public areas in Montgomery. As in many neotraditional developments, all garages are placed out of sight, at the rear of the residence, and most are reached from alleys.

Porches line the fronts of homes, adding life to the street and making a more attractive and interesting place. Right-of-way widths are narrowed, and houses are brought close to the street to give a more intimate, human scale to the community. Streets are arranged in regular grid blocks to improve access and to keep walking distances to a minimum.

A new approach to parks has also been required, with the emphasis on smaller, easily accessible spaces for social contact. Corner parks provide for informal activities and casual meetings. Each quadrant of the community has its own small park, designed along the lines of formal English urban parks. An easily accessible, integrated trail system runs through the development and extends through Orangeville for longer walks, biking, and running.

Summary

With increases in the number of people working at home, communities must become more multipurpose and flexible, and must respond to a wider range of needs on site. But the quality of the environment and the public realm, together with the design of streets, homes, and parks, is much more essential than technology itself.

Technology supported Montgomery's initial success. When the project opened in 1994, Montgomery enjoyed being the first "wired community" in its market and indeed in Canada. But high-capacity telecommunications technology is rapidly becoming universally standard equipment, much like electricity, cable, or telephone service, and therefore will not continue to provide a competitive edge for new communities.

As advanced telecommunications technology becomes available in ever more remote places, competition will intensify and broaden as new locations are opened up for development. But technology will not provide an enduring competitive advantage as will the livability and quality of the community, and its building design and flexibility. While about half of Montgomery homebuyers surveyed expected to do some paid work at home, the ability to telecommute was only the fourth most important factor attracting homebuyers to Montgomery. The quality of the houses offered was the most important factor, followed by the quality of the neighborhood, and then the price of housing. ∎

Pamela Blais
President, Metropole Consultants
Toronto, Canada

the single-family house remains the strong preference of most consumers. During the past few decades, this preference has been modified somewhat by trends in spatial relationships between job and home, and in land and housing prices.

With the growing mobility spurred by technology and with the increased number of home-based workers, however, workers and their families will be less tied to employment centers. Conceivably, a sizable portion of the market will enjoy the flexibility to opt for exurban living, with a quality of life considered higher by some and with a cost of living lower than in urban areas. Thus, the trend toward a dispersal of urban development can be expected to continue.

Some residential developers already are seeing opportunities for planned residential communities —particularly recreation-based developments— in remote rural places. Just a few years ago, these communities might have appealed only to the market for second homes. Now, however, buyers are spending more (or all) of their time in these

Telecommuting makes resort living a possibility for more people. Las Campanas, in the rolling New Mexico countryside, provides golf, riding, and other resort activities for residents.

communities and are telecommuting to their places of employment. Some communities that have benefited from this trend include Las Campanas, New Mexico, Fairview Village, Oregon, Dewees Island, South Carolina, Farmview, Pennsylvania, Valencia, California, and Hidden Springs, Idaho. These and similar communities, and more that are on the drawing boards, are just beginning to affect residential development patterns, but the trend is evident.

If the dispersal continues, traffic congestion during peak hours could decrease because there would be fewer commuters, traveling at staggered times, distributed over longer periods. The burdens of long-distance commuting could diminish and could become an additional factor causing people to move farther from urban centers.

More Mixed-Use Residential Communities

Whether they realize it or not, most workers have come to rely on their offices as their primary places of social interaction. For the increased numbers of home-based workers, the social interaction that has been a daily part of working in an office will not exist. This will cause a need for such interaction in other parts of people's lives, like in the local community and neighborhood. Thus, the purely residential community will have more need for the corner store, the coffee shop, the pocket park, and other gathering spots.

There will also be a need for the kinds of support services typically available to workers in employment centers. Eating and meeting places, convenience stores, copy centers, business support centers, athletic facilities, and even the often-disdained gas station will have their places in the residential community. What all this means is that mixed uses will be the way of future development, while bedroom communities will become obsolete and will eventually have to be retrofitted to become more livable and competitive.

Many developers are responding to a growing market demand for *real* communities, not just bedroom suburbs. These developers are incorporating such features as neighborhood gathering places, civic spaces, commercial services accessible to pedestrians and bicyclists, natural open space, and a wider range of recreational opportunities. They are taking on a larger responsibility for coordinating social activities and working to establish a social infrastructure.

Neotraditional planning theory recognizes the need for residential communities to foster increased opportunities for interaction among residents. Many developers are adopting at least some neotraditional elements in their projects and are incorporating them as major features of their marketing plans.

Technology Infrastructure

Builders and developers will find a competitive advantage in offering fully wired homes and communities able to accommodate a broad range of work activities, as well as smart-home elements or options. Making such an offering will entail telecommunications infrastructure (with a capacity allowing for its rapid evolution), community Web sites, workstations in the home for all household members, and flexible floorplans that will accommodate one or more offices. Home offices have different requirements from bedrooms, affecting factors like location within the home, windows, and storage. For this reason, home offices should not be seen as interchangeable with a simple change of label on the floorplan. These features might be considered niche opportunities now but are likely to become market requirements in the near future.

Are These Patterns Mainstream Trends?

Advances in technology and telecommunications will not change the residential development business overnight. A key to the rate of change will be the number of households that actually have the kind of flexibility discussed here. Some observers argue that only those at the top end of the workforce will in fact be able to modify their living and working styles as a result of technology. However, given that almost 50 percent of computer equipment and software sold is for home use, that about 40 percent of all homes are now equipped with PCs, and that 20 percent of all companies already have telecommuting programs, clearly these changes are not just upper-income phenomena. These quickly rising percentages suggest that there will be a mainstream market for communities responsive to new technologies and to the resultant lifestyle changes and preferences.

What are some of the factors limiting the size or timing of this emerging market? Even with advancing telecommunications technology, many jobs in the foreseeable future will still require a physical presence. Flexibility also will be limited by the large percentage of two-worker households. Both workers might not have the same level of flexibility in their hours and workplaces. Moreover, there is still no clear indication that the mainstream market is unhappy with, or ready to give up, conventional living and working patterns. Finally, virtual organizations, telecommuting, and other forms of alternative work styles are still in their infancy, and it is not known

whether these work styles will permit the needed amount of efficiency and competitiveness over the long term.

The market for houses, apartments, and planned communities targeted at the technologically literate is still considered small, but the consumer response to developments that incorporate these elements has been highly positive. Although there are other lifestyle and consumer preference issues beyond technology that affect the decisions of developers and builders, technology-based trends will certainly be an increasingly important factor in home and community design and in buyers' choices. Over the longer term, the effects of technology on residential markets should become clearer. Developers should watch and be ready to react accordingly.

Dewees Island, South Carolina, is a private oceanfront island retreat accessible only by ferry. No cars are permitted on the island. Residents enjoy an environment protected by extensive covenants and design guidelines. Developer: Island Preservation Partnership.

Conclusion

Advancing information and telecommunications technologies, in combination with economic and cultural trends, are certainly bringing about changes in how people work and live. Impacts on residential real estate markets will be substantial. The forms that these changes will take will be diverse and will result from much trial and error.

The most notable effect of technology on residential market demand will be indirect, and accommodating technology will not require significant changes in the way homes are built. Currently, new types of infrastructure, other than high-capacity telecommunications wiring, are not needed in residential communities. Providing home offices that can double for other uses, such as dens or guest rooms, is an idea with widespread market appeal. Beyond this sort of accommodation, technologies are largely independent of floor plans and community designs.

Indirectly, technology can be expected to open up a larger range of locational choices for housing consumers. More households will be able to make choices based on quality-of-life considerations rather than on the duration of rush-hour commutes. For their part, local commercial services will become more important for supporting the growing populations of home-based workers in communities.

Where will the effects of technology be felt most, and who stands to gain? Exurban recreation-based communities are the obvious near-term beneficiaries—especially those in sought-after locations with attractive natural surroundings. Some existing suburban neighborhoods are adapting to the demands of larger daytime populations and will likely further retool to keep pace with residents' changing needs. Urban neighborhoods, especially newly revitalized ones, will continue to attract that segment of the population preferring an urban lifestyle. With a potentially shrinking demand for office space, there could be increased opportunities to recycle obsolete office buildings into multifamily housing units.

Residential developers will need to do what they always have done: look closely at what consumers want and then provide it. What will be different is that technology and the new form of mobility it brings will allow individuals a much broader range of choices in how and where they can live.

Notes

1. U.S. Census Bureau, October 1993.
2. "Work at Home in 1997," BLS news release, March 11, 1998.

Chapter 4

The Evolution in Community Governance

Wayne S. Hyatt

You *can dream, create, design, and build the most wonderful place in the world, but it requires people to make the dream a reality.*

—Walt Disney

This chapter identifies and explores the potential for change and growth in community association law. Included are discussions of three key aspects of the present and future development and operation of community associations:

1. The expanding roles of community associations;

2. Impediments to growth and change as these roles expand;

3. Innovative principles and practices in community association governance and operation.

Positive change will come neither smoothly nor successfully without a joint and concerted effort among developers, attorneys, and other involved parties. Much of the evolution in community association law in the latter part of the 20th century has come without a coordinated, mutual effort. It has come as one segment of the industry or another has asserted a position while other segments have resisted or opted out of the discussion. So much more can be accomplished with a common effort. There must be a synergy between the need and the capacity for governance. Planners, developers, and attorneys must therefore understand what those needs are and what they will be in the future.

Expanding Roles and Responsibilities: Beyond Property Management

How can a community association exercise properly the power of governance while maintaining a sense of community among residents? What principles and procedures must guide the administrators of a community association as they seek to discharge obligations, protecting the delicate balance between the rights of the community and the rights of the individual community resident?

A *community association* is a mandatory membership entity comprising all property owners in a real estate development. A successful community association is one with a workable internal society as well as working relationships with the larger, external society. It has an internal social structure that is, of course, at least in part a function of governance.

A discussion of governance systems must recognize the impact that governance has upon various facets of community association activity. First, there is an obvious concern: the balance between the rights of the community and the rights of the individual residing within that community. While simplicity and flexibility are desirable, individuals should expect a degree of certainty regarding what the rules are, and a reasonable assurance that the rules will not change so drastically as to make ownership no longer desirable.

Beyond those matters that are directly and naturally involved in the running of community associations, there are broader, societal concerns. If the public should become convinced that community association living means conformity, control, and constraint, buyers will avoid this form of community. Eventually, this perception will significantly reduce the available housing stock, because the relative unpopularity of such existing and ongoing projects will mean that their units are in effect no longer part of the "available" stock. This would have a negative impact on housing producers, owners, and local governments. And these effects would have no

compensating benefit because there is no technical or anecdotal evidence that the more highly regulated a community is, the better that community is. Indeed, evidence increasingly suggests that excessive regulation results in a diminution of the quality of life.

Quality of life and lifestyle present another area of concern. The highly individualistic person perhaps does not belong in a place where his interests run strongly counter to the degree of conformity required in any planned community. By the same token, community is not synonymous with conformity, and making this differentiation is a challenge for developers and operators of community associations. Highly regulated and formalized governance structures are perhaps inconsistent with the amount and type of flexibility necessary to make a community successful.

The goal, then, for anyone drafting governance documents should be to devise a system that balances multiple interests, preserves the functions of the community association, protects its flexibility, and provides the powers necessary to permit it to remain dynamic in periods of change while reasonably protecting the property owners' interests and expectations for an appropriate degree of certainty.

This chapter explores these issues and identifies trends in community association activity. These trends—which range from new ways to create and structure associations to the innovative and exciting new roles of community associations in the years to come—make bringing about changes in governance not only desirable but imperative.

Some Fundamental Shifts

Some of the trends affecting community associations include changes in technology, demographics, and lifestyles; the increasing privatization of services; and the challenges inherent in renewing the form of planned-community governance. Change comes from many directions. Technological changes and their results may constitute the most significant type of change because of their effects on so many, broader aspects of life. From the wiring of homes for multiple technological uses to voting and assessment collection by computer, the range of potential impacts is enormous.

Also of substantial importance are changes in the demographics, sophistication, and expectations of the real estate market. Community

At Weyerhaeuser's Northwest Landing, homeowners share a large common green. Common area maintenance has always been a major responsibility of community associations. Today, roles are expanding to address activities programming and many of the economic and social issues facing communities.

association law itself, as well as attitudes in the industry, are changing as more and more options rely upon some form of community association structure.

Changing Demographics, Attitudes, And Lifestyles

Consumers' desires for amenities and services are altering. The consumer pool is aging and is increasingly composed of working couples. This trend shows a need not only for more streamlined association governance but also for a greater range of association-provided services. More services may need to be offered as options so that people can pick and choose as their requirements change.

Child care is an example of a service needed by today's households. How, if at all, should the community association play a role in providing this service? What are the risk factors, and how can they be addressed?

Security is another example. Is it needed, or is it a marketing issue? And does the distinction matter? What does security mean in a community's particular context, what should it entail, and how can it be paid for?

An issue of considerable importance is the drastically different paradigms for large and small communities. Today, there is often little difference among the *basic* structures of community governance. In the future, however, there will have to be much greater variance because of the real differences in what large and small associations will do.

If elitism is a drawback of some community associations, as it is frequently alleged to be, then one way to defuse that charge is to address the need for greater inclusiveness and the incipient trend of finding ways to foster inclusiveness. The need is real. Community associations of the future will have to address multiple aspects of this issue. One challenge will be to ensure that there is affordable housing within a community. Will this housing be affordable only at the time of initial sale, or will covenants ensure that it remains so, sale after sale? The latter is being accomplished in some communities now, and such covenants will become more common and more creative in their execution as time goes on.

Another concern and challenge deals with aging. Governance structures will have to meet the needs of an aging population but without necessarily segregating older people in retirement communities. Communities for people over a certain age will have different needs, services, amenities, and activities than they do today—all of which will have to be reflected in the governance of these communities.

Related to changing demographics is the effect that an aging population will have on positions of authority within associations. On the one hand, working couples will have less time to serve on an association board and will want a more streamlined system. On the other, there will be people who have retired and are eager to serve. There will be some residents in a community who are accustomed to corporate governance and some who are not. Association governance will have to be tailored more effectively to the individual situation of each community.

Restructured boards, a greater reliance on professional management, more meaningful committees, and volunteer programs are all legitimate responses to these needs. Yet it must be noted that *service* remains vital to the success of any community. As University of Chicago ethics professor Jean Bethke Elshtain writes, "One cannot create community without asking how communities are to be sustained. By whom? To what ends? To have community, you must have people prepared to shoulder responsibility, to be accountable. Otherwise, you have lots of feelings about wanting to do good, but these evaporate like the early morning's dew at the first sign of difficulty."

A major chance to innovate in governance arises from the exciting evolution in community design. From the neotraditional movement comes a laudable emphasis on people and on people-friendly, activity-oriented spaces. Governance must be as innovative and as responsive as new design concepts. New community design techniques will require not only new approval and regulatory approaches but also new approaches to maintenance, ownership, use restrictions, and many other adjustments to fit new structures.

Innovation in building methods and materials, such as the use of steel studs and manufactured housing, will affect community governance. New techniques will make some covenants and design guidelines obsolete and irrational. Governance structures will have to be flexible enough to adapt and strong enough to permit reviewers to make judgments and decisions without spewing out pages of predigested design dogma. Provisions will have to be enforceable yet subjective. This balance will be possible, but it will require better documentation than is currently the norm.

Environmental management might fall under the expanded roles of community government. At Dewees Island, South Carolina, the community's environmental character is its primary amenity. Strict covenants control development to protect the island's vegetation and wildlife.

More Privatization of Services

Privatization is, of course, a major change factor in community association law and practice. As more responsibilities move from the public sector to the private, it becomes necessary to broaden the economic base available to accept these responsibilities and the demographic base necessary to discharge them. Community associations are increasingly becoming the entities ultimately responsible for many activities and services previously the province of local governments. For these new activities to be accepted and properly discharged, old forms, formulas, and attitudes must be altered, and new powers, procedures, personal involvement levels, and accountability standards adopted.

A significant portion of the U.S. population apparently desires less government. On the other hand, an equally vocal and sincere group expresses a sense that government does not go far enough to meet the needs of citizens; in many instances, there is no formal governing body empowered to meet these needs. Community associations must be structured to address both viewpoints. They must have the capacity and willingness to meet public needs without the traditional attributes of government.

The pressures upon public funding sources will place an even greater reliance upon community associations to meet needs previously met by the public sector. This role will require more flexibility in the way associations are financed and in the permitted expenditure of these finances. By the same token, it will be necessary to protect the minority interests within an association from unanticipated and perhaps undesired expenditures by the majority. Balance and process will become ever more important.

Education, for example, is becoming a responsibility of community associations. Education means many activities, all of which will affect governance in the future. One activity involves helping diverse populations to learn from each other. An association can place a great emphasis upon this goal and channel resources into ensuring that there are ways and means of meeting it. Another responsibility is the more formal one of implementing genuine cooperative efforts between the association and local school systems to foster, help finance, and participate in public schools.

Another educational activity for the larger community associations will be helping to provide adult education opportunities, both on their own and in a variety of partnerships. These opportunities might extend beyond the boundaries of the association into the greater community. Funding, the use of facilities, curriculum decisions, and the nature of the programs all are subjects and challenges that current governance structures rarely address or that they address inadequately.

Other Opportunities and Challenges for Renewal

Community associations must not become merely enclaves of private wealth and insular thinking. Certainly, some community associations do have these characteristics, but more significantly, associations can create a genuine feeling of cohesiveness and can discharge tasks that neither government nor business can assume. For example, community associations often undertake activities that bring people together, instill a sense of community, and enable people to make a difference in their own neighborhoods. Pressures to fill the voids left by public unwillingness or incapacity, balanced against the very real need to avoid creating "privatopias," are perhaps the greatest challenges—and opportunities—facing today's associations.

Obsolescence of existing association properties will accelerate as buildings from the 1970s age and as much older buildings that were condominium conversions require major repairs or reconstruction. The results will be governance structures faced with the challenge of resolving questions of whether or not to rebuild and, if not, what to do. If the answer is to rebuild, the issues of finance will be acute, as will questions of design and ownership. Current governance structures are largely unprepared to meet these needs. For example, few association documents meaningfully address the power to borrow and the ability to collateralize a loan.

In many communities, voluntarism is on the rise, and in many others, it can and should be. In their governance structures, forward-looking communities encourage and foster this trend. Yet too few have set forth realistic and sufficient procedures for doing so. Governance approaches must facilitate and encourage voluntarism.

Environmental responsibility in the founding and operation of a community association is now an issue and a challenge. Both individual and group interests are involved. The association of the future will become increasingly involved in the environmental approval and postapproval processes. This involvement may be direct or it may be relational, as the association supports and benefits from, for example, a tax-exempt organization maintaining sensitive areas. Involvement may be indirect, as the association's committees or volunteers play a role. The association may become an aspect of an educational program. All of these forms of involvement will require governance structures to facilitate them.

Finally, advances in telecommunications are a major trend. Though a discussion of all that is involved is well beyond this chapter's scope, the effects of the telecommunications revolution will substantially influence community governance. Some issues that will demand attention include the changing restrictions on commercial activity and on working at home, and the need to provide the opportunities for socialization that will soon be missing from the traditional workplace. Overall, greater creativity and flexibility will be required of community governance.

Most community association documentation reflects a limited view of what an association is and does. The emphasis has been on property management. The result is that many documents narrowly define *common expense,* thus limiting the use of the association's funds. Documents narrowly define the association's purposes, who may use its facilities, and its capacity for outreach.

Association documentation must be taken to a new level. Scholars, judges, developers, and attorneys all have a role in revising these documents, as do professional community managers. Certainly, consumers and the professionals who train, represent, and assist them all will fill major functions as well.

Impediments and Inertia: Overcoming Obstacles To Change

Nothing will ever be attempted if all possible objections must first be overcome.

—Samuel Johnson

Change is not easy, nor does it come in a smooth, linear way. Both practical and structural obstacles must be overcome. Some obstacles can be dealt with quickly, with the tools of determination and imagination. Jumping other

hurdles will require changes in the law, while still others will call for cultural changes.

No one can deny the impact of litigation upon every participant in the housing industry, including the builder/developer, the community manager, and the housing consumer. The effects include greatly increased risks, costs, time delays, overly defensive engineering, a reduced willingness to build, and increased costs. All of these consequences ultimately lead to lower housing stocks, higher prices, and lower returns. To affect the pace and direction of change, it will be critical to establish the concept of preventive law and practice.

Rather than awaiting changes in the very nature of lawyers or in the laws of liability as a panacea for excessive litigation, the development industry will need to become proactive in effecting change. Before meaningful changes can occur, however, there must be an alteration in attitudes and practices both for the consumer and for the producer of products in master-planned communities.

Besides basic business practices, which can alter the developer/association relationship, some practices and procedures can even directly prevent litigation. A prevention-oriented developer will have a designated manager whose primary responsibility is risk management. That developer will use risk-preventive documentary provisions and management practices. Marketing as well as construction will be supervised, and management will ensure that lines of communication remain open among departments, as well as between the development organization and the customer.

People often sue not because a defect is so bad but because they feel deceived, misled, or taken advantage of. A business must build and maintain the confidence of its customers, and focused, preventive marketing is part of this process. Education of both the consumer and the sales staff also plays a major part. The prevention-oriented development firm will train and test its staff on a continuing basis.

Sales documents are not usually thought of as opportunities to manage risk, but they are. These documents can also help to condition expectations with properly drafted disclosures and disclaimers. The documents should contain balanced yet defensible provisions.

Archaic laws and regulations in some states and localities greatly complicate the process of change. It is vital for courts to understand the

New kinds of communities are responding to changes in demographics and lifestyles. Accessory apartments, typically forbidden by covenants, are encouraged as a way to increase diversity at Kentlands in Gaithersburg, Maryland. Developer: Joseph Alfandre & Co.

dynamics of association operation and to permit associations the power and flexibility to meet their responsibilities. Certainly, there must be limits and the rights of minority interests must be protected; however, holding to outdated legal principles and strictly construing them rather than giving effect to the intent implied by the facts and circumstances are highly questionable practices.

Increasingly, local governments are resisting approvals of community associations. In many cases, they are balking because of the nature of the project planned or because the association is seen as the province of the elite. Addressing the issues of affordable housing, demographic shifts, and inclusiveness can and will improve this situation.

The industry continues to struggle with the effects of inadequate training for the people who will operate community associations. While there are programs and organizations that provide some training, they are not as widely used as they should be for the growth and evolution of association governance. The effects of this lack of training and understanding also touch the legal and other professionals involved in the industry. If community governance is to evolve, so must the persons managing it.

A companion problem to lack of training is the developer's fear of new approaches. Whether in design, governance, or other aspects of community development and management, the developer, as the key player, must be willing to abandon old methods and try new approaches. Parenthetically, the same can be said for the management and legal professionals. Developers, managers, and lawyers all must be willing to do new things and not assert, as one manager did, "I don't want the board to use judgment. It makes my job harder."

The Present Structure and Its Problems

The unfortunate thing about this world is that good habits are so much easier to give up than bad ones.
—W. Somerset Maugham

By provisions in their governing documents, community associations are automatic, mandatory membership entities. An association has a separate existence from its creator, the "declarant," usually the master developer. Perhaps most significantly, it has broad powers to assess, control, and administer—to *govern* the community—

Golf is a desirable but expensive amenity. Community associations must seek creative new ways to fund the operating costs of such amenities.

Timber Pines/U.S. Home Corporation

although it is certainly not the real government and is not intended to be.

The community association and the underlying body of community association law provide a legally recognized framework with considerable power and almost infinite flexibility upon which to build the governing process of a real estate development. In the fundamental principles of community associations can be found the first major reason for the existence of associations, namely, their functions: they can own, maintain, manage, serve, and enforce. A second reason is the recognized, growing body of law applicable to the concept. The law is empowering and guiding and is evolving within a modern setting, freeing the association and its creator from many restraints of the old interpretations of basic principles of real estate law.

The association gives the developer an exit strategy. As an entity that will accept ultimate ownership and responsibility, the association has a legitimate interest in ensuring that what are initially developmental responsibilities are properly discharged long after the developer has sold out of the project and transferred control. Many of these responsibilities derive from development agreements, zoning ordinances, and other governmental actions agreed to by the developer as part of the permitting process.

Community associations are infinitely flexible in their control and in their responses to change. They have the capacity to respond to negatives,

as well as to react within the governing structure to market change. There is the ability to innovate and to create inventory. And there is the capacity to provide integrated services within a context of legally enforceable relationships. The structure is in place and works if the community association is properly planned and operated. For the community of the future, however, this might not be enough.

What is wrong with the way things are? Why is there a need for structural change in the way community associations are organized? First, associations need to be made less restrictive and more user friendly. A perception exists that the restrictiveness of some associations adversely affects sales, quality of life, and public image.

Another reason for change is a shift in focus as community associations and community association law and practice mature and identify new ways of doing things and new responsibilities to take on. This shift reflects the results of the privatization of certain functions and the fact that in many cases an association will become the party ultimately responsible as tasks and obligations go from public to private.

This shift is a response both to technological advances and to changes in consumer preferences and needs. It also results from a movement from property management as the focus to management of people and services—with property management as a lesser, though still significant, duty. The transition also reflects the new urbanism. It responds to the fact that new design structures lend themselves to advanced governance structures with heightened levels of participation, service, and community inclusiveness.

Finally, the changes respond directly to alterations in the law. Governance systems must be based upon the power to govern rather than on a listing of rules. "Govern" must be broadly defined to allow associations to meet their increasing obligations and opportunities. This is the direction the law is taking. The industry should lead this trend through the structuring and use of community associations.

Meeting Tomorrow's Challenges

Following are some areas for change in the customary ways of conducting community association business. Many of the ideas expressed are already in use by some associations and are under discussion by others. These suggestions cover a broad spectrum but do not constitute an exhaustive list. Ideally, the reader will add to the list, modify it, and borrow from it.

Structure and Role of the Board

There is a need for evolution in board structure, powers, and responsibilities. Changes in these areas are the predicates for changes in many other areas and perhaps are in turn driven by the evolution in these areas.

Community association boards have broad express and implied authority. There are, however, limits. For example, a regulation may fail because it seeks to regulate a matter over which the association has no jurisdiction. A board may seek to exercise implied powers but find that only such implied powers as are necessary to the express powers will be upheld, not those that are merely convenient or desirable.

Courts have continued to shape an evolving board power while at the same time identifying a reasonably recognized procedure as the standard for board decision making. This standard is the *business judgment rule*, which requires that the board act within its authority, with good faith, and in a nondiscriminatory manner. The board's decision must further the legitimate interests of the association. So long as the board acts in accordance with the business judgment rule, courts will not question the soundness of its decisions.

If the basic underlying principles are reasonableness, business judgment, and acting *intra vires*—or within the authority given—then the board is assumed to be vested with discretion, power, and responsibility and to be an active part of the regulatory process, so long as it follows the rules set out in the association's governing instruments and in the general principles of community association law.

Acknowledging these principles does not diminish the need for a board to seek a more flexible approach to governance or for the governing documents to allow the rule-making process to be a dynamic one rather than a static recitation of "thou shalt nots," many of which will never apply to a given community. It is best, therefore, to look for a new approach.

What community governance needs is a legal framework within which the board and the association member may operate to implement and manage existing structural law. The covenants must permit the governance process to evolve with the changing needs of the community. Recognizing the difference between regulation and prohibition, the alternative approach involves creating a more legitimate governance structure and construction of the governing documents to contain only the limited number of prohibitions and/or restrictions that are vital to the overall development plan for the community. Accompanying these initial provisions should be a method of permitting the modification of restrictions and the adoption, modification, or abrogation of regulations to be made in the legislative process of the community as circumstances change.

The governance system needs checks and balances, disclosure of the potential consequences to purchasers, and specific protections for vested rights that might have arisen as part of a purchaser's initial acquisition. For these reasons, the alternative approach should contain not only empowering sections but also a "bill of rights" for homeowners and for the developer.

Both the business and governmental roles of the board will continue to grow, with divisions in function justifying changes in form. Future associations may have two governing boards, one taking on each role, though preferably one board would function through two committees. The powers and methods of operation of boards should be strengthened, and the hierarchical relationship among committees should be established. Taking this step would address a number of operational and legal questions now vexing association practitioners and would strengthen both boards to meet the new obligations.

The new framework should more clearly delineate the policy-making role, the law-giving role, and the judicial role of the association. The business role will increase to meet greater needs. Issues of contracting capacity, delegation, individualized services, and technological innovations and their effects on the association's powers all will be important. Associations may take on the style of the strong city-manager form of government as they adapt to meet new needs and constraints.

A key is to seek answers before establishing the association and its board. For example, should boards be structured to ensure that different age groups are represented? In second-home developments or communities of mixed retirement and nonretirement residents, this is a significant question. Should there be built-in procedures to reconcile the desires of retirees versus those of working families, and what should these procedures be? Should there be a mandatory balance of demographics, as there often is among product types? And, most important, how should one structure the governance?

A comparable issue is the need to ensure a balance in board members' understanding of and experience in corporate governance. The eventual possibility that there will be professional board members is a real one and not to be rejected out of hand. Yet the desire of homeowners to participate should not, of course, be overlooked. Homeowners may look to professional officers yet continue to serve in the policy-setting role. The important point is that professionalism and compensation are both possible in the future of board operation. Current management professionals must be willing to accept and indeed to lead change.

Corporate Governance Analogies

Courts have long applied the business judgment rule (defined under the previous subhead) to community association boards, but this is an inexact standard. For example, the rule has a kickout provision covering situations in which a conflict of interest is inherent in the board members' decision. On an association board, the members *always* have some degree of conflicting interest because they live in the community and have to pay for a decision's results. Association governance must therefore evolve to accommodate this anomaly.

The rule will continue to be applied by analogy, but increasingly it will be fashioned to fit the realities of community association governance. As a result, it will become a new and in-

Condo Commandos: An Abuse of Power?

Land use covenants in master-planned communities and condominium buildings are enforced by human beings serving on boards and committees. These committees, sometimes referred to as condo commandos, exercise major powers over the daily behavior of residents and over the nature and form of the building modifications that are inevitably required in order to adapt to the needs of successive owners. Such control by the arbitrary few (or, as often happens, control over the young by the old) has a long history in human affairs in prior eras of autocratic governments. Sadly, this unfortunate pattern in human affairs has been inflicted on most U.S. master-planned communities because attorneys have given too little thought to the need to restrain abuses of power.

The long history of battles against the arbitrary power exercised by kings, dukes, prison wardens, man-of-war captains, royal judges, bishops, religious courts, sheriffs, and prosecutors tells us that Lord Anton was right when

he wrote, "Power corrupts, and absolute power corrupts absolutely." While no one is cast into prison and physically tortured by self-perpetuating master-planned-community property owners or condominium association boards, there is often a virtually unchecked focus on the self-interests of the male resident aged 70 and older. This is the profile of the people who usually come to dominate such boards gradually, through the nominating committee process. All sociological studies of differences among age groups conducted over the past 50 years show sharp differences in the life interests of people 35 years old and those of people 70 to 80 years old, and most particularly between the interests of 35-year-old mothers and those of childless or empty-nester 70-year-old males.

These vast differences of attitude and approach can lead community association boards to neglect to budget association dollars for children and young families in the community, and to pass rules stifling community events

popular with the younger half of their constituencies. Who is principally to blame for this state of affairs? Community builders and their lawyers! And how can this situation be changed? By introducing proportional representation on condominium and community boards that would divide board membership into 50 percent women and 50 percent men, then divide each half among three age groups: over age 70, ages 55 to 70, and under age 55.

Besides the addition of new language to future legal documents covering board composition, there needs to be a "spirit-of-freedom clause" to allow for individual choice in areas not demonstrably influencing property values or peaceful coexistence by next-door neighbors. For example, while it may be reasonable to prohibit barking dogs, it is not reasonable to prohibit the use of 18-inch satellite dishes.

Charles E. Fraser
President, Charles E. Fraser Co.
Developer of Sea Pines Plantation

dependent rule. Areas of concern and change will include board roles and powers and the rules applicable to both.

Provision of Services

The association will be empowered to provide services for the community, groups, and individuals, as well as services beyond the community boundary, at common expense and for user or fixed fees. Services might include anything from supplying firewood and mowing lawns to providing social services. Many of these services will be implemented solely by the development team and the association. Others will be delivered through partnerships with local governments or other agencies. All of these functions can serve to raise levels of interaction, participation, and citizenship among residents.

New assessment techniques will allow for the financing of added services. The definition of *common expense* will be broadened as property management gives way to community building and community management. Learning centers, business centers that supplement home offices, and strategic services for working families will all become parts of the authorized activities of the association.

Interaction with Other Organizations

Organizations that are tax exempt under Internal Revenue Code Sections 501(c)(3) and (c)(4) will come into play for social, educational, environmental, wellness, transportation, and many other purposes. The association's documentation will authorize it to become involved in such activities, but the 501(c)(3) organization, for example, can in a proper case undertake these activities with tax-exempt, tax-deductible financing. Activities in these areas will range from direct involvement in management to education and funding incentives that encourage certain activities.

Developers will shift some activities away from the community association to the 501(c)(3) or (c)(4) organization. The association and the tax-exempt organization will work together to achieve the maximum return for the community. The results can be far greater, and can be accomplished for far less cost, at a higher level of public trust and acceptability.

As they take on expanded roles, many community associations are providing social programming of such events as this celebration at Summerlin in Las Vegas.

Finance Mechanisms and Systems

As communities age and thus need rebuilding and restoring, and as associations undertake new responsibilities, new funding systems will be needed. The power to borrow without artificial constraints will be enhanced, as will the capacity to pledge property or income streams as collateral.

Different assessment levels and types of fees will meet new needs. Caps, recaptures, percentage charges on resales, and transfer fees will in appropriate cases keep units affordable, fund 501(c)(3) activities, lower ongoing operating costs, and meet other needs. Assessments will be restructured to reflect individual as well as group services. And there will be new approaches to formulas for certain services.

For example, amenity preference surveys show that consumer interest in golf courses is waning, but the concept of the club is still a vital part of many development plans. Charging all homeowners a social membership fee for the club can shift some operating costs from the association assessment to the revenues generated by golf and other activities involving nonmembers of the association. New ways will arise to work with clubs, to destigmatize club membership by broadening the club's reach.

Individual versus Group Interests

The same orientation that leads to neighborhood entities and lowered restrictiveness will permit a greater capacity to individualize and an improved ease of dealing separately with different parts of the community. Services, rules, costs,

A Case in Point: Unique Goals Require Unique Governance

Some innovative developers are incorporating tomorrow's governance systems into today's developments. One developer, DMB Associates, has a vision for its mixed-use community, DC Ranch in Scottsdale, Arizona—preserving the distinctive character and stark beauty of an environmentally sensitive site while offering property owners a community rich in educational, cultural, and social opportunities.

The developer realized that the community needed a governance structure as special as the physical qualities the development would offer to community residents. The internal governance system that was created combines a sense of stewardship with enforcement techniques that truly work. The developer has put in place a system that will work not only while the community is under developer control but also after the developer passes the powers on to the property owners. The entire structure engenders a sense of the genuine value to be realized from its effective operations.

How Governance Will Work

This community combines standards of excellence both for the product and for the process. While the product is that which is built or developed, the process is the achievement of a sense of community through the governance structure and the way in which the values and qualities of that community are created and protected.

Governance within DC Ranch rests upon a foundation of covenants and restrictions that will be recorded in the land records and will bind all present and future owners. In addition to containing the standards and guidelines for the development, operation, use, and maintenance of the community, these covenants establish the community council and the residential community associations, which administer and enforce the process. The covenants also set up the covenant commission, which enforces and administers guidelines within the community. These entities are nonprofit corporations with broad powers and specific responsibilities. Each residential property owner is a member of a community association, and all property owners are subject to governance by the council and design review and administration by the commission.

These entities constitute a hierarchy designed to vest governance roles and responsibilities in ways and at levels most appropriate to accomplishing community objectives and purposes.

Community Council

The community council encompasses the entire community and is responsible for establishing and implementing communitywide standards for all residential and nonresidential properties, including standards for operation and maintenance. It coordinates and facilitates activities and regulation among all components of the community. For example, if a commercial use is located next to a residential neighborhood, the council works to protect the interests of both groups while considering the interests of the community as a whole.

The council functions much as a council of governments would but also with the very real power to require or prohibit actions on a communitywide basis. It has power over all community associations within the development. In addition to its broad corporate authority, the council possesses powers and responsibilities that arise from covenants recorded on all properties within the community.

The council appoints one or more members of each community association and one or more owners of nonresidential property to a liaison committee, which acts as a contact point for the exchange of ideas between the council and owners of property, subject to the covenants and easements. The committee meets with the council regularly.

In accordance with the developer's vision and the covenants and easements, the council's responsibilities may include the following:

- Owning, operating, controlling, and maintaining community facilities and property;
- Resolving community disputes;
- Administering flexible and evolving systems of rule making and enforcement;
- Managing transportation;
- Levying and collecting assessments to fund activities;
- Sponsoring cultural programs;
- Preserving and managing open space;
- Curing nuisances and abating conditions that violate covenants and rules;
- Establishing regulations, restrictions, and controls for habitat and wildlife;
- Carrying on cooperative activities with community associations and other entities;
- Supporting the arts;
- Operating historical and/or archeological sites;
- Establishing fire prevention measures;
- Enhancing community security;
- Operating communitywide video facilities and technology;

Half of DC Ranch's 8,300 acres is dedicated to open space. Designs of a retaining wall and golf course were sensitive to the spectacular beauty and environmental conditions of the site. Design guidelines are enforced by an internal governance structure for the development.

- Overseeing health and wellness programs;
- Administering lifelong education programs;
- Supervising community service programs;
- Coordinating community clubs and volunteer clearinghouses.

Residential Community Associations

Within the community, one or more residential associations implement and enforce any standards applicable to residential development, as well as maintain, manage, and operate the residential common properties. The association structure is divided into neighborhoods or districts to avoid the confusion and layering that can result from subassociations. This structure ensures a degree of autonomy, tailored service levels, and fair representation on boards.

The legal documentation for all associations is flexible yet rational, enforceable, and, most important, understandable; the documentation blends professional management and decision making with owner participation to effect both a sense of community and competent governance, and provides for the adequate funding of the associations.

The representative system of voting at the association level provides for ease of administration. Each neighborhood elects a voting member to exercise the vote of that neighborhood's members—except for the developer's votes—in director elections and on issues related to special assessments, community rules, amendment of the declaration, and expansion of the community.

Nonresidential Governance

Nonresidential property is governed not by a community association but primarily by the council and by one or more cost-sharing and joint-use agreements between the nonresidential properties and one or more associations. In addition to setting forth maintenance and use restrictions applicable to the nonresidential properties, the agreements 1) establish the obligation of one or more associations to maintain property that benefits both an association and the nonresidential properties, and 2) obligate the nonresidential properties to contribute to maintenance costs. The agreements bind residential and nonresidential components and help knit them into the fabric of a community overseen by the council.

The Covenant and the Commission

The community's governance of design requires an equally distinct legal structure, which is embodied

continued

in the covenant—a separate component of the recorded documents—and will be enforced by the covenant commission. The covenant, to which all current and future property owners agree and are bound, maintains the community's character, its landscape, and its environment. It establishes a comprehensive plan for upholding the quality of all future architecture, development, and land use.

The commission—an autonomous, independently funded body—is fully empowered to administer and enforce the covenant's terms, conditions, and standards. Its members consist of both professionals and laypersons, all of whom have demonstrated a mastery of the covenant's vision and concepts before their selection.

Included within the plan for development is the *Community Design Book,* which contains the architectural, development, and design standards and guidelines that govern the placement, installation, and construction of all improvements in the community. The *Community Design Book* was prepared by the developer and is administered by the commission. Either the commission or the developer may modify the *Community Design Book* as deemed necessary to reflect new development forms, different uses, and different geographical areas.

The legal elements of the covenant are carefully selected to initiate and enforce the process. Its terms provide for the full force of state law, from monetary sanctions to injunctions. In addition to legal enforcement, or reactive factors, it contains legal precon-

Each detail of DC Ranch's character and environment, from the designs of the homes and landscaping to the culvert overpass railings, is covered by a comprehensive system that ensures maintenance of quality after the developer passes control to the homeowners.

ditions, or proactive factors, including the following provisions:

- All professionals who submit development plans must be certified in accordance with the design training and familiarization standards of the commission.
- The commission is empowered with the flexibility to encourage design innovation and excellence.
- The commission conducts seminars and juried competitions to create a culture and a value system for sustainable, high-quality development.
- All property owners, through payment of their filing fees, charges for violations, and other charges, ensure adequate funding for the commission's activities.

Although the covenant commission controls *product* and the community council controls *process,* the relationship between the two is direct. An administrative executive officer common to both entities ensures consistency and communication. In addition, the council's board includes a member of the commission.

Realization of a Vision
The community council, the associations, the covenant commission, and their interlocking relationships collectively effect a governance system for the community that provides for excellence in both process and product. Together, these entities create and preserve the values and qualities that distinguish this development and make the developer's vision a reality.

and facilities can all be tailored to smaller groups without losing the overall community concept.

As part of this trend, associations will put a greater emphasis on voluntarism and on multiple use of facilities for special interest groups, including groups from outside the community. The "privatopia" label will be erased by systems, programs, and funds that meet the needs for and strike a balance between inclusivity and exclusivity. Communities can be creators and preservers of value systems, though this will require a new approach to participation and inclusiveness.

The community-building process will be embodied in new approaches to the provision of amenities. This is an area in which much can be accomplished with fewer or no marginal costs. The traditional set of documents, however, will need to change. Rules, assessments, and procedures will all have to adapt. Documentation will be required to deal with minority rights and appellate processes for business as well as governmental decisions.

Design Review Process

The review and approval process for all *new* construction should be removed from the community association and vested in the master developer. This move would do away with the fiction of an association committee as the review authority, remove the potential for legal issues to impede proper design decisions, and eliminate arguments about owners' rights to review. There should be a movement away from the complex book of design standards and guidelines and toward a realistic depiction of what is desired by the developer.

The legal process will be rigorous and will not submerge the new forms of design guidance but support them. There must be a legally enforceable system, and to be truly workable, the system must allow the decision maker a high degree of subjectiveness.

A property owners' committee should deal with building modifications and other postdevelopment construction matters. Associations should elect the committee members rather than the board appoint them, reflecting a move toward segregation of business and governmental duties as well as toward a more representative structure.

Design standards should strive to balance certainty and flexibility and should incorporate

sustainable development features tailored more precisely for particular projects. Because these standards and guidelines will become even more important than they are today, they will need to be prepared with the utmost care.

Neighborhoods within the Community

There will always be a tension between the needs of the individual and the needs of the group. Both must be honored.

—John W. Gardner

Residents' desire to be a part of the large community while at the same time having a neighborhood feeling will cause a growth in neighborhood entities—ideally without generating subassociations, which tend to balkanize communities, increase costs, and polarize attitudes. Alternative structures, more like unified city/county governments, will better meet consumer demands and will permit more cost-effective community government.

These neighborhoods within communities will allow different needs to be met and different attitudes and desires to be reflected. The neighborhood feeling can be kept while retaining the advantage of being part of a comprehensive community structure. Affordability issues can be accommodated by shifting costs around within the community. The potential exists to afford many benefits and to "do good and do well" at the same time.

Affordable Housing

As communities respond to governmental and private pressures and as they assume ultimate responsibility for the obligations imposed upon their developers, more and more projects will include an affordable housing component. Documents will rely upon neighborhood structures, service delivery systems, and alternative assessment systems to integrate affordable housing into the communities.

Maintaining affordability will involve approaches to cap or partially recapture appreciation. It will entail association and 501(c)(3) partnerships to maximize service capacities. Community design regulations will need to address the affordable housing component so that the product cost will meet acceptable limits while maintaining aesthetic integrity. And most important, the governance structure and operation must avoid division and classification.

Security

Whether because of need, misperceptions, or snob appeal, security is a community issue. Gated communities, however, are under attack as enclaves of the well-to-do who are seeking to protect their turf. The community association, its developer, and its document drafter all must look hard at the issues to determine what, if any, security measures will be included; they must accommodate the need and desire for security and privacy while still building a true community.

Then, all parties will need to be creative in dealing with design, education measures, patrols, and coordination with local police so as to achieve the appropriate level of security without gates and walls, which cost so much in both money and acceptability. These steps will require a retooled association.

An Aging Population

The reality of today's demographics will compel master-planned communities—whether age-restricted projects or simply ones with diverse age cohorts—to address the aging of the U.S. population. Striking balances; ensuring proper representation of young and old, working people and retirees; and protecting divergent interests will be among the challenges. The tasks of setting assessment levels, dealing with reserve funds and mechanisms, and providing facilities and services demanded by the market or even required by law to meet the needs of a community's diverse population will challenge existing norms. A mix of ages, needs, and desires will allow cross-service delivery, greater human resource potential, and increased governance participation.

Effects of Changing Technology

Restrictions on antennas, business use of homes, and other outmoded provisions will fall as flexecutives work at home, satellite dishes become smaller, and other advances continue. Other innovations that are coming relate to using technology for the benefit of the association: distributing notices and holding meetings by phone, fax, or computer; instituting community Web pages; holding annual meetings via cable, with voting by computer; and handling assessment collection and service requests online. Documents, budgets, and association operational plans must all be adjusted to take advantage of and not to impede technological realities.

Nonresidential Communities

Perhaps one of the most often overlooked aspects of master-planned communities is that they are not all residential. The nonresidential, the mixed-use, and the special-purpose association all have great utility. Experience indicates great potential for more nonresidential planned communities with more varied uses and structures, but most of the basic premises discussed here apply to nonresidential communities as well.

Increasingly in the future, there will be a marriage of the residential and nonresidential components in mixed-use developments, providing jobs, essential services, and those elements necessary for the residential development to function. The nonresidential association or the commercial development using some of the tools inherent in community association governance will become more and more important, as will ways and means for the residential and nonresidential members to work together on issues of common concern.

Conclusion

The perpetual obstacle to human advancement is custom.

—John Stuart Mill

Community associations have evolved from a seldom-heard concept to one of the most significant factors in real estate development. As governing documents move from the language of rights to a reinstitution of empowerment and judgment, the capacity for future application and evolution is limited only by the imagination of developers and the skill, creativity, and commitment of drafters. The challenge and the opportunity are to redefine the time-honored ways of doing things, to build on them, and to devise new approaches and new applications.

Chapter 5

Mastering Crime in the Master-Planned Community

Brian C. Canin

Mastering crime in a planned community is a broad area of study and involves a tremendous range of opportunities and initiatives. Crime prevention techniques can be as simple and inexpensive as implementing a Neighborhood Watch program or as radical as constructing walls and gates with 24-hour security guards and closed-circuit cameras. Too often, the latter, more radical option has become the tool of choice for residential developers, despite considerable expense, the lack of factual information on benefits to the developer or residents, and the negative consequences for the greater community.

Crime prevention through physical design is a concept that planners and academics have promoted for many years. In the classic book *The Death and Life of Great American Cities*, Jane Jacobs advocates the concept of "the public eye," in the form of pedestrians and others who inhabit the streets and serve as informal protectors.[1] Similarly, William Whyte's *The Social Life of Small Urban Spaces* discusses ways to promote the public use of outdoor spaces as a means to discourage criminal activity.[2] Oscar Newman developed a variation on design-based crime control called "defensible space," also partially based on the notion that the more informal observers on the street, the better.[3] Defensible-space techniques break communities into smaller neighborhoods, promoting a sense of ownership of public spaces. Ownership leads to better maintenance, more surveillance, and a resulting decline in undesirable activity. Often labeled "crime prevention through environmental design," or CPTED, the theory is, again, that community design can facilitate informal surveillance and social activities that deter crime.[4]

Defense as Walled Fortress: The Isolationist Approach

"Defensible space" has been misinterpreted by some developers to include the walling in of neighborhoods. The recent trend toward walled and gated communities does have proponents, who claim that the walls and gates 1) prevent crime, 2) maintain property values, 3) reduce traffic, and 4) help to promote a sense of community. But any evidence for these claims is largely anecdotal and not statistically documented. In their book, *Fortress America: Gated Communities in the United States*, Edward J. Blakely and Mary Gail Snyder explore in depth many of the issues of gated subdivisions.[5] Their findings, and those of others, refute each of the above claims.

First, gating appears to be ineffective in controlling crime. Blakely and Snyder report that "scattered local data on the effectiveness of barricading are anecdotal and inconclusive, with examples of less crime, more crime, and no change at all." Realistically, it would be foolish to believe that a determined criminal could not climb a wall or find a way through a gate. During their research, Blakely and Snyder quickly learned how to enter gated communities easily. Presumably, criminals could do the same. The authors report: "At one development with a remote-control gate, a resident in the exit lane even stopped to tell us the entry code."

Some studies show that residents of gated communities are lulled by a false sense of security into lax habits that actually induce criminal activity. Residents sometimes tempt thieves with unlocked doors and with keys and purses left in cars. Some police departments believe that the walls surrounding these communities offer protection for criminals, who cannot be seen from the outside and, once they are inside, are believed to belong there. And gates cannot protect from the criminals residing within. In some gated communities, most criminal activity is reported to be minor vandalism by insider youth. This pattern, of course, is typical of criminal activity in *all* communities, gated or not. In older communities that have been retrofitted with gates, crime tends to decline at first, then to rise again to pregate levels.

Some residents believe that gates protect property values, but no reliable studies support this notion. It is extremely difficult to study the effect of gating on property values because there are no directly comparable gated and nongated communities to study. The data that do exist tend to be inconclusive. The general consensus among those who have looked at the issue is that there is little or no difference. In some older urban neighborhoods that have been retrofitted with gates, values have increased, but the gating was part of an overall improvement effort. It is thus impossible to credit a single factor with the rise in the property values.

As for traffic, when it is reduced within the walls, it only spills over into the streets of adjacent neighborhoods. This result prompts the question of whether one community has the right to exclude traffic at the expense of another.

Finally, according to Blakely and Snyder, most residents of gated developments report no greater sense of community than do residents of nongated developments.

Considerations for Localities

Privatizing residential spaces and services causes a number of concerns for local governments and residents. Detractors of gated communities use terms like "the balkanization of the suburbs," "ghettoization," and a "medieval" solution to social problems.

Few local governments have begun to consider the full scope of the related social, safety, and fiscal issues. The National Association of Home Builders reports that 62 percent of homebuilders face no restrictions regarding the gating of communities.[6] But several problems do arise for local governments in this connection:

- Financial responsibility for privatized facilities is a major consideration. Responsibility for managing the capital reserves and operating budgets involved, as well as for planning and implementing costly repairs and renewals, is well beyond the expertise of most homeowner associations (HOAs). Further, many homeowners have not been made aware that this responsibility goes along with being a member of a private community. As facilities age and the financial responsibility increases, will HOAs be able to handle the demands? Will the municipality be forced to take over the streets and other facilities, which have often not been designed to code and might have been improperly maintained for years?

- Dade County, Florida, has set up special taxing districts to cover the costs of neighborhoods that are retrofitted with gates. The county's newly built gated communities, however, must rely on HOAs. Many jurisdictions require that private streets conform to the same standards as public streets; Plano, Texas, also requires that the HOA set up a reserve fund for maintenance.
- The perception of double taxation by residents of private communities could lead to an unwillingness to support tax and bond legislation. Because HOA fees presumably cover the costs of most services and facilities within a

walled community, why should a homeowner pay more taxes to provide those same services beyond the walls? Some states have yielded to these complaints and have begun to offer provisions for tax reductions for residents of private communities.

- Obstructed access for city workers—including personnel engaged in police, fire, animal control, and sanitation services—impedes provisions for the health and safety of citizens. Numerous accounts exist of municipal personnel who were unable to respond to emergency calls. At a minimum, delays are caused that can be life threatening in cases of fires or medical emergencies. For convenience, some gated communities have given out codes to public and private service workers who need access, compromising whatever security the locked gates might have offered. Other communities leave gates open during the day and lock them only at night, despite statistics showing that most residential burglaries occur during the day.
- Traffic concerns must be addressed. Privatizing some streets does not promote their

PROTOTYPICAL ACTIVE NEIGHBORHOOD

55

River West Developments

most efficient use and causes greater congestion on the remaining, nonprivate streets. Ideally, neighborhoods should be interconnected to provide for the convenience of residents. However, cut-through traffic and high-volume through traffic are both extremely detrimental to the well-being of residential neighborhoods.

Concerns for Developers

From the developer's standpoint, the expectation is that gated communities yield greater returns, in the form of a faster sales pace and higher prices. In many southern and western parts of the United States, at the higher end of the market or in age-restricted retirement communities, gating is considered necessary. For mid-market communities, however, there is no definitive proof that gating is necessary, and some decidedly negative tradeoffs are involved:

- The guard-gated solution is quite expensive. Well-designed and -landscaped walls with irrigation along collector streets typically cost up to $100 per linear foot. This factor adds capital and maintenance costs to the development.
- Homeowner associations are burdened with the continuing operating and maintenance budgets for 24-hour security, which currently range from $60,000 to $100,000 per guarded entrance per year. Add in the responsibility for street maintenance budgets, and the total represents a considerable financial commitment that must be considered in the home purchase decision.
- In terms of marketing, there are no studies indicating that buyers in the mid-market range prefer gated communities. Blakely and Snyder report that most residents surveyed did not set out to live in a gated community. Most chose their homes based on other factors. It is possible that the trend is not market driven at all but initiated by developers who are following trends in higher-priced communities.
- In some regions, especially in northern states, a gated community is viewed with suspicion, and this kind of security measure is actually a marketing negative. Potential buyers worry that the community is unsafe and that the gating is a response to existing crime problems. Gates are seen by some as a nuisance because they require additional time to enter and exit and make visitor access inconvenient. And there is also the fact that gates break down—both an inconvenience and an expense.

Buyer Factors

Finally, from the homebuyers' perspective, there are tradeoffs and issues to be considered. While a portion of the homebuying public has been conditioned to expect that added security and enhanced property values will be achieved through the use of walls and guard gates, these results have not been realized.

There is a clear distinction between walled and gated communities that are merely card controlled and those with 24-hour, manned security including roving patrols. The latter solution undoubtedly offers much-enhanced security for residents and is typical of higher-end golf club communities in Sunbelt locations, where residents are often seasonal occupants or may travel extensively. Generally, the higher the price points, the more demanding the buyers are with regard to heightened security. Similarly, in the South, retirement villages typically offer their residents 24-hour, manned guard gates with roving patrols as well as electronically wired homes.

A strong buyer motivation in these instances is the "fear of fear" syndrome that exists in contemporary America. People are willing to pay for peace of mind; they want their fear of fear to be eliminated by the reassurance of a fully guarded subdivision, regardless of the reality of how safe a community would be without gates. Their perceptions can sometimes be more powerful than the reality.

Following are some realities about privatized communities:

- It is generally conceded that guard-gated communities do not really deter professional criminals and in fact may make it easier for them to operate within a community, as it is usually assumed that anyone inside the community is authorized to be there. When people living within the walls engage in criminal activity, the gates offer no protection whatsoever. Sophisticated community developers believe that a roving patrol provides more effective security to neighborhood residents than do walled-off streets and a gated entrance.
- According to a 1996 survey by the National Association of Home Builders, the average cost to homeowners in gated communities is an additional $120 per month.[7] This is money that might better be spent on more effective means of security.

- Homeowners will eventually become the proprietors of an aging infrastructure of private streets, walls, and gates with all the associated costs. Annual operating costs alone can be exorbitant. This could have a negative effect on long-term resales, which in turn could cause a neighborhood to decline with age.

There is a growing sentiment in many jurisdictions against guard-gated neighborhoods with private streets. Some residents believe that these solutions do not promote a sense of community and neighborliness and that they foster the perception of enhanced security within the walls at the expense of security outside the gated neighborhood. Also, some jurisdictions are reluctant to permit private streets because of a concern that the jurisdictions themselves will one day inherit the obligation of maintaining these facilities.

With the continuing pressure for affordability and the desire for more livable communities, there may be better ways to spend design, construction, and maintenance dollars. In addition, the option of walled and guard-gated neighborhoods with private streets is not readily available in existing nongated communities served by public streets or in communities where public access is essential, such as those with major arterials or other public facilities.

Crime Prevention through Environmental Design: The Designers' Approach

As has been discussed, there are design solutions to crime that are less extreme and less expensive than walling and gating a community. Planners and designers focus primarily on the integral form and arrangement of a neighborhood, and particularly of its streets, as factors that can contribute significantly to overall neighborhood security. Some general observations on crime and security in residential communities will help to put these issues in context.

- In designing for enhanced security, no simple, one-dimensional solutions work well across the board. Rather, communities can apply solutions from a continuum of conditions and responses to enhancing security. For example, a solution that worked perfectly in a community at one time may not serve as well five years later, as the neighborhood changes and crime increases. When this occurs, anticrime intervention initiatives may need to be escalated.

- The average suburban residential community does not have a serious crime problem, compared with some older, inner-city neighborhoods. Thus, suburban crime does not usually require draconian measures such as walled and gated subdivisions. According to surveys conducted by the U.S. Department of Justice in 1991, 15 percent of central-city households, 4.6 percent of suburban households, and 1.9 percent of rural households identified crime as a neighborhood problem. In general, respondents' assessments reflected how much they were victimized by actual crime.[8] The reality is that very few upper-middle-class whites (those most likely to live in gated communities) have ever had any personal experience with violent crime.

- Numerous articles have been written and much research undertaken on the trend toward the walled and gated communities now proliferating across the United States. Estimates of the number of people nationwide who are living in walled and gated subdivi-

sions vary widely, from 3 million to as many as 8 million. Gating is far more common in the South than in other regions. Based on a 1996 survey by the National Association of Home Builders, 15 percent of new subdivisions in the South, 10 percent in the West, and 3 percent in the Northeast and Midwest are gated.[9]

- According to Blakely and Snyder, "immigration, a growing underclass, and a restructured economy . . . are fueling the drive for separation, distinction, exclusion, and protection. Gated communities are themselves a microcosm of America's larger spatial pattern of segmentation and separation by income, race, and economic opportunity."[10] The authors also point out that while crime rates in gated neighborhoods may be reduced only marginally in comparison with those in ungated neighborhoods, residents' anxieties about crime nevertheless diminish in gated communities. Walls and gates serve as psychological placebos.

- Most solutions to crime involve multiple tradeoffs, particularly relating to the cost

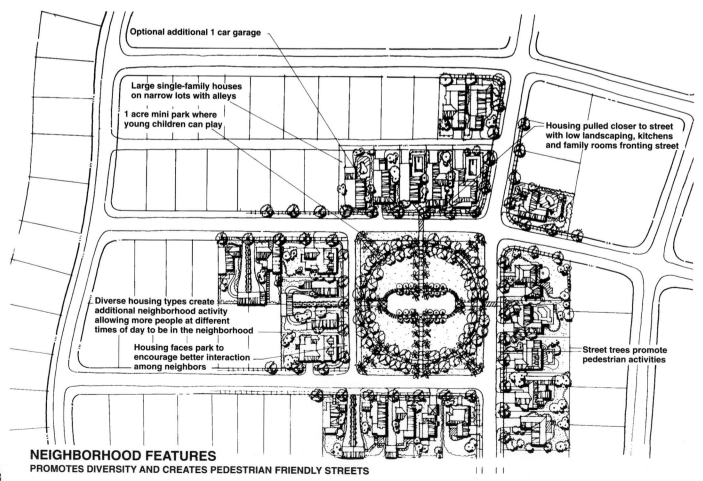

NEIGHBORHOOD FEATURES
PROMOTES DIVERSITY AND CREATES PEDESTRIAN FRIENDLY STREETS

of design elements such as walls and guard-houses and the operation of security systems. Generally, the greater the level of security, the less the neighborhood is a part of the greater community. Typically, residents of walled and gated subdivisions have become isolated from the rest of the community, especially as schools, parks, churches, shops, community centers, and other facilities end up outside the privatized neighborhood and are not readily accessible to residents within the gated community.

As important as, if not more important than, trying to crimeproof a neighborhood physically is creating the *perception* of safety and comfort, which can influence the way in which people behave and use their neighborhood streets. When streets are perceived as a no man's land, they are more inviting to trespassers and criminals. In contrast, when a neighborhood has the feeling and reputation of being "together" and tightly organized, a much lower incidence of crime and vandalism is likely to prevail.

Security is an interactive mixture of perception and reality. Perceptions and realities work to influence each other, and this is one area in which perception definitely affects reality. If people feel secure and safe in the streets, they will use them more, especially if the streets are attractively designed; this greater use in turn will increase safety and security within the whole neighborhood.

Basically, two types of intervention are possible in enhancing neighborhood security. The first is to securitize the individual properties. This option again involves choosing from among a continuum of initiatives, ranging from providing good lighting and clear paths from garages to front doors and good visibility from the street to completely walling off homesites and using the types of security found in penal institutions, such as high walls, electric fences, and armed response teams. These extreme measures are currently employed in many residences in suburban Johannesburg, South Africa, which has become very crime ridden and violent over the last decade. However, these solutions have a dramatic negative effect on the quality of life of the community and generate a fortress mentality in which residents perceive the streets as dangerous places outside the security of the homesite.

The second point of intervention is to securitize the neighborhood as a whole. Again, initiatives can vary, all the way from creating a perception of safety and a high degree of community cohesiveness with very active use of the streets, on the one hand, to walling off and controlling access to the neighborhood through guarded gates with limited access, on the other hand.

Factors Affecting Neighborhood Street Activity

In previous times, when there was a greater percentage of traditional families, moms were at home with their young kids all day. When the older kids returned from school, they played in the front yard with their neighbors while the mother kept an eye on them from inside the house or spent some time socializing with other mothers on the street. On the weekends, dads and kids all over the neighborhood were out working and playing in their yards. The predominant family unit included two parents and two to three children, often supplemented by an extended family of grandparents, aunts, and uncles, all living close by and providing a tight social fabric and network that heightened security.

In contrast, today the traditional family is the exception. Thirty-five percent of U.S. children today live in homes with a single parent, and many households consist of singles without children. In addition, many traditional families now have two working parents. Children's social patterns have gravitated toward more passive indoor activities, like watching television. All of these factors, and others, have tended to reduce the level of street activity in neighborhoods.

Today, the challenge for designers and developers is to create neighborhoods of streets that are more friendly and inviting to pedestrian activity and that can be used by a wide range of residents. Ideally, the neighborhood should be a place where young children can play safely outside, where seniors can enjoy strolling, where young mothers can walk their toddlers to nearby miniparks, and where teenagers can safely bicycle and hang out together. In order to achieve these ends, the streets must be attractive to users, with shaded sidewalks, interesting vistas, and activity nodes such as small parks, neighborhood churches, schools, community centers, and waterways. Ideally, the entire neighborhood should be designed to have a parklike quality,

Key Points in Lowering Crime and Taking Back The Streets in Your Neighborhood

- There are no simple, one-dimensional solutions to the problem of creating safer neighborhoods.
- Perception can supersede and even influence reality in determining a neighborhood's feeling of security.
- Perceptions of security are enhanced in an active, pedestrian-friendly neighborhood where residents make greater use of the streets.
- Security is a combination of many factors and complex interactions, including the physical design of a community.
- Current solutions employed by many builders and developers lead to extremely boring and sterile neighborhood streetscapes that are not conducive to good neighborhood security.
- A much greater emphasis on design and market engineering is needed to integrate residential housing types, lot layouts, and street design in order to increase neighborhood diversity and to generate more active and thus more secure neighborhoods.
- Major savings in infrastructure, and operating and maintenance costs, are made possible by moving away from the concept of walled and guard-gated neighborhoods. The results of designing for an active, diverse neighborhood can be far more cost-effective, visually exciting, and appealing to consumers.

in the sense that it is a pleasant place to be. Commercial activity also has its place within this structure.

To foster this type of neighborhood, the following planning guidelines and design principles should be considered.

Neighborhood Diversity

Developers should encourage neighborhood diversity by planning for a broad range of household types. While the core market profile in each neighborhood will vary and may comprise 70 percent of the total number of households, it is desirable to bracket this group on either end to cover as broad a range as possible. For example, if the core households are two-parent families in 2,000-square-foot (on average) homes on typically designed, 70- to 80-foot-wide lots, the developer should consider adding a few larger homesites in choice locations and some smaller homes for first-time buyers and older, retired couples without children.

Active retirees are home during much of the day and can constitute a good source of "eyes and ears" within the neighborhood. Similarly, older residents, especially single retirees, feel more secure with younger families nearby whom they can call on for help. Elderly neighbors often can interact positively with younger children and enjoy being in the company of younger people, provided they still keep their privacy.

Canin Associates, a planning and landscape architecture firm based in Orlando, Florida, has analyzed existing neighborhoods where a mixture of small and large lot sizes and homes coexist to make for a seamless community. The firm found that a limited number of small homes on wide-frontage lots can exist comfortably across the street from larger homes, as can duplex units that have been designed to blend into the overall neighborhood. This mix provides a range of home prices in the same neighborhood while maintaining compatibility among housing types.

Homes designed for wide-frontage lots have the additional advantage of layouts in which the kitchen and other living areas face directly onto the street, making it easier for neighbors to watch out for each other. This arrangement can be readily perceived by people passing through the neighborhood.

Some large homesites can accommodate "granny flats" that permit younger members of the family to stay in the neighborhood longer or that can be rented to young students or older retirees, both of which groups can add diversity and presence to a neighborhood. In addition, granny flats can serve as small offices for the increasing number of people who are working at home.

An additional benefit of mixing household types is that families with young children and elderly households are more likely to own dogs as pets. Dogs add to the overall security and promote pedestrian activity as people walk with their pets and meet their neighbors.

Pedestrian Activity

Throughout much of the 1980s, the focus in the United States was on providing entry-level housing, with tremendous pressure to contain costs. This focus, in combination with the significant amount of building by national production builders who have taken down large blocks of lots and erected three or four standard home types, has generated many sterile and low-amenity neighborhoods throughout the suburbs. Residential development in the 1990s, while still catering to some of the same pressures for affordable housing for entry-level buyers, is broadening to include many more affluent households with greater discretionary spending power. These homebuyers are more sophisticated and are seeking highly attractive neighborhoods with a full array of amenities.

A key to promoting increased pedestrian activity is the introduction of neighborhood parks. A neighborhood of 500 to 1,000 homesites should have a five- to ten-acre park within ten minutes' walking distance. Each active neighborhood park should have an all-purpose field, a small community center, and basketball and tennis courts. Within two and one-half minutes' walking time of each homesite, a minipark between half an acre and an acre in area should be provided to accommodate the needs of very young children and their mothers, who cannot be expected to walk too far from home. Strategic location of these park systems can make for an active neighborhood environment.

Good urban design should use the opportunity to link these parks with well-landscaped pedestrian promenades or walks along boulevards with homes fronting on the street. These higher-order streets should be designed with larger lots and slightly more generous sidewalks to encourage pedestrian movement and to minimize driveway conflicts between cars and pedestrians. This solution stands in sharp contrast to many contemporary designs, which line collector roads with walls and landscaping designed to screen the rear yards of adjacent homesites. These walled streets are invariably unfriendly to pedestrians and are considerably less well used than neighborhood streets. Pedestrians are much likelier to use a street with houses fronting onto

At Kentlands in Gaithersburg, Maryland, public areas fronting on the streets encourage socializing and discourage criminal activity.

it, where they can greet their neighbors, than to walk down a road bounded by brick walls or blank fences on one side of them and roadway traffic on the other.

Neighborhood parks should be designed for maximum use by surrounding them with streets and by orienting homes to face the park and the street. Other uses that can productively be located near the small parks are neighborhood-scale churches, daycare centers, community buildings, small branch libraries, and community shopping districts, if the neighborhood is large enough to support such endeavors.

Careful Design of Streets

Street design can also markedly affect street activity in a neighborhood. Streets should be hierarchical. Narrow streets promote slow-moving vehicular traffic and enhance a feeling of security and a sense of neighborhood. Short culs-de-sac with no through traffic at all are recognized as the safest and most desirable locations for families with young children. In many of these culs-de-sac, the street itself can safely become a play area.

Higher-order streets like collectors that carry more through traffic should be designed to provide on-street parking and ample sidewalks for pedestrian use. These streets must also be designed to restrict vehicular speed.

Retrofitting the streets in existing neighborhoods can be accomplished by introducing street trees, which act as unifying neighborhood elements and cast inviting shade on sidewalks. In some cases, the use of traffic-calming devices like speed bumps, in combination with stop signs, may be necessary to slow down and reduce through traffic. Residential neighborhoods should be carefully designed to ensure that access points are limited and that cut-through traffic is minimized, as such traffic increases security risks and reaches higher speeds.

Home-Occupancy Businesses

As a greater percentage of Americans engage in part-time or full-time work from their homes, neighborhood security will be enhanced by the additional presence of this group of residents during the workday. The home is now the primary or secondary work location for approximately 44 million workers, according to Link Resources Corporation, a research and consulting firm in the electronic services industry. In addition, 12.8 million persons are classified as part-time self-employed workers (moonlighters). More than 9 million workers bring work home from a conventional job, and more than 8 million workers "telecommute," or work at home at least part time during normal business hours. This latter group is the fastest-growing segment of U.S. workers. All of these segments are projected to grow at rates significantly above that of total employment growth.

A few select homesites in a neighborhood might be zoned for special, limited home-occupancy businesses to form a neighborhood activity center. This grouping of businesses must be carefully located so as not to cause a nuisance within the neighborhood. Typical permitted uses could include a small daycare center, health care

providers and counselors, an accountant, a convenience store, and/or a small restaurant. These businesses should obtain approval from the local homeowner association. While this concept is still experimental and minimally tested, the author envisions these special lots as located at the periphery of the neighborhood, preferably near the entrance, where they would be least intrusive. Reintroducing limited work opportunities into the neighborhood can be a benefit that helps to establish neighborhood character and diversity, if adverse impacts are carefully controlled.

A Sense of Arrival and Accessibility

To enhance neighborhood security, each neighborhood should have no more than two or three external access points, and these entries should be clearly delineated with markers to create a sense of arrival and neighborhood identity. Major through traffic or cut-through traffic must be discouraged. Many design and regulatory means can help to accomplish this goal, including speed restrictions, speed-reduction features, the locations of stop signs, and the widths and layout of the streets themselves.

Neighborhood Amenities And Features

Typically, neighborhood amenities like parks, lakes, and golf courses are surrounded by homesites in order to maximize the builder's lot premiums. Portions of these amenities, however, should be exposed to all residents' view so as to create more pedestrian-friendly streetscapes. This can be done by locating streets around the amenities. When streets are designed to link amenity areas, interesting walks through the neighborhood result. In this way, more "eyes on the street" are encouraged.

Landscape, Streetscape, and Lighting

Front yards should be carefully landscaped to provide privacy as well as harmonious and attractive streetscape treatments throughout the neighborhood. Generally, front yards should provide good visibility of the home and especially of the front door so that passing traffic and adjacent and opposite homesites enjoy direct views, thereby tightening security. In addition, front yards must be designed and landscaped to be integral parts of a generally attractive neighborhood streetscape.

Appropriate street trees should constitute the primary landscape element unifying all properties and adding the shade and visual interest necessary to stimulate pedestrian activity. If properly designed and landscaped, the streets themselves will become attractive neighborhood amenities.

Street lighting is an important aspect of a secure neighborhood. Streetlights should be placed at 60-foot intervals on alternating sides of the street. In addition, yard lights can enhance exterior landscaping and should be placed to illuminate walks, front doors, and entries. Supplemental floodlighting triggered by infrared sensors can also permit safe arrival at a residence after dark.

Neighborhood Caretaker or Concierge

Columbia, Maryland, has successfully experimented with a program of providing home loans for police officers as a way of introducing additional security into tough neighborhoods. This program has reduced crime by 24 percent in certain sections of Columbia. An alternative program could involve the provision of a small lot with a cottage that would be owned by the neighborhood association and be strategically placed to allow a watchman/caretaker to monitor the neighborhood. This unit could be appropriately located near the neighborhood entrance or adjacent to the small neighborhood parks. The unit could be rented at a nominal rate to a retired police officer or security guard, who would function as a neighborhood watch and provide a direct security presence within the neighborhood.

The security person could be hired to patrol the neighborhood, if contracted to do so by the association. In addition, the person could organize and maintain the Neighborhood Watch program and even monitor incoming/outgoing traffic through electronic surveillance, if so desired. Probably, this program would be much more cost effective than the traditional hiring of front-gate security guards and building of walls and guardhouses.

Housing and Lot Design

A significant additional security benefit can be gained through the design of the homes themselves and through adjustments to the site lay-

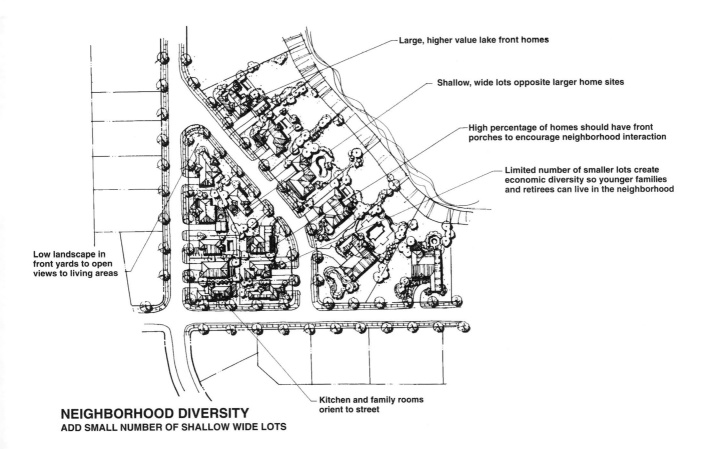

Large, higher value lake front homes

Shallow, wide lots opposite larger home sites

High percentage of homes should have front porches to encourage neighborhood interaction

Limited number of smaller lots create economic diversity so younger families and retirees can live in the neighborhood

Low landscape in front yards to open views to living areas

Kitchen and family rooms orient to street

NEIGHBORHOOD DIVERSITY
ADD SMALL NUMBER OF SHALLOW WIDE LOTS

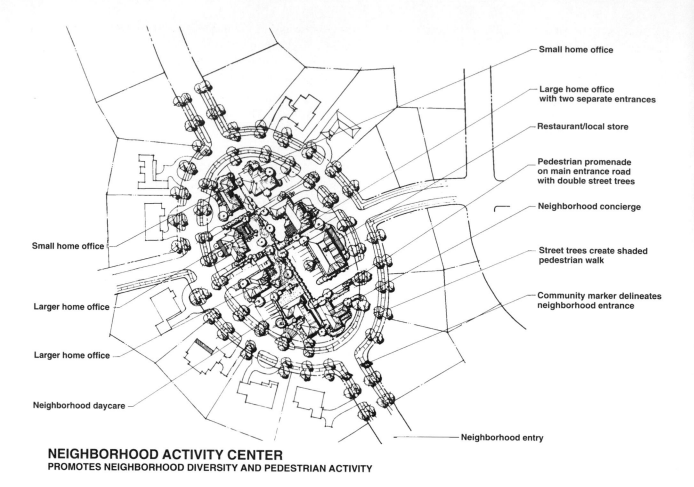

Small home office

Large home office
with two separate entrances

Restaurant/local store

Pedestrian promenade
on main entrance road
with double street trees

Neighborhood concierge

Street trees create shaded
pedestrian walk

Community marker delineates
neighborhood entrance

Neighborhood entry

Small home office

Larger home office

Larger home office

Neighborhood daycare

NEIGHBORHOOD ACTIVITY CENTER
PROMOTES NEIGHBORHOOD DIVERSITY AND PEDESTRIAN ACTIVITY

out employed on each lot. Homes situated on narrow-frontage lots, predominantly with garage doors facing the street, do not make for friendly neighborhoods or improved security. To achieve these goals, a developer can use a variety of means, including one or more of the following approaches:

- Where larger homes with several cars are placed on small lots, the provision of alleys with rear garages removes double-wide garages and driveway parking from the front yard and thus achieves a more attractive street facade with more window frontage and hence enhanced community surveillance. Alleys, however, can afford easy rear access for intruders and thus can pose some additional security risk, unless good surveillance and control are available to offset the additional risk and unless the overall community layout uses built-in security measures.
- An even more efficient solution is to place freestanding garages at the rear of small lots. This arrangement gives the house a greater street presence and more parking space in the driveway than is offered by conventional

front garages. Again, however, there are trade-offs. Some residents will reject separate garages, particularly in colder climates.

- Raised front porches also promote a more interactive street presence, as do clearly visible front doors. Frequently used living areas, like the kitchen and family room, should be oriented toward the street as well. This is a reversal of the current trend toward orienting all living areas to the rear. But with highly amenitized, eye-pleasing streets, living areas can easily face the front yard.

In summary, safer, friendlier neighborhoods are the results of a combination of many factors that all need to be blended carefully together to generate an adequate level of neighborhood vitality and interaction. This vitality in turn will promote a sense of neighborhood identity, which will translate into a perception of a more secure neighborhood that will in turn influence the reality. The enhanced security that is achieved by developing more traditional and more highly amenitized neighborhoods is also likely to exert a very positive impact on consumers' acceptance in the marketplace.

Notes

1. Jane Jacobs, *The Death and Life of Great American Cities* (New York: Random House, 1961).

2. William H. Whyte, *The Social Life of Small Urban Spaces* (Washington, D.C.: Conservation Foundation, 1980).

3. Oscar Newman, *Defensible Space: Crime Prevention through Urban Design* (New York: Macmillan Company, 1972).

4. See Marcus Felson and Richard B. Peiser, eds., *Reducing Crime Through Real Estate Development and Management* (Washington, D.C.: ULI–the Urban Land Institute, 1998).

5. Edward J. Blakely and Mary Gail Snyder, *Fortress America: Gated Communities in the United States* (Washington, D.C.: Brookings Institution Press, 1997).

6. *Builders' Economic Council Survey* (Washington, D.C.: National Association of Home Builders, November 1996).

7. Ibid.

8. U.S. Department of Justice, Bureau of Justice Statistics, *Crime and Neighborhoods* (Washington, D.C.: GPO, June 1994).

9. *Builders' Economic Council Survey* (November 1996).

10. Blakely and Snyder, "Fortress Communities," *LandLines,* Volume 7, Number 5 (Cambridge, Mass.: Lincoln Institute of Land Policy, September 1995).

Chapter 6

Environmentally Responsible Development

Michael Pawlukiewicz

I know that each parcel of land is a precious, distinct, and irreplaceable portion of this distinct and irreplaceable planet. I will treat it with the respect that it deserves, recognizing that I will be judged by the integrity and permanence of my developments, which will survive my lifetime. In attempting to provide adequate staging for decent environments in which people will live, work, and play, I will be ever vigilant toward preserving the quality of the larger environment—the air, the water, and the land.

—Urban Land Institute Code of Ethics

Introduction

Environmental Responsibility

Public opinion polls consistently show that a majority of U.S. citizens are concerned about maintaining the quality of the natural environment. Furthermore, they believe that environmental protection and restoration should be a high priority. The United States is a land of extraordinary natural diversity and magnificent natural beauty. Americans love nature, and accordingly, natural amenities like trees, forests, wildlife, and open space are always popular marketing tools in new development projects.

Pelican Bay, first developed in the 1970s near Naples, Florida, preserved a 570-acre mangrove estuary immediately adjacent to a three-mile stretch of beach. Rather than building on the beachfront, the developers preserved the estuary as a natural amenity for residents.

ULI's Code of Ethics, however, demands a higher standard, a standard that recognizes the need for the long-term well-being of the environment. Understanding the importance of long-term environmental health is a step toward making communities *sustainable,* in other words, to meet the needs of present generations without compromising the ability of future generations to meet their needs.

The urban growth that has spread over North America since World War II has had unexpected consequences in the natural world. The destruction of habitats has caused the population of some species, such as migratory songbirds, to decline sharply. The creation of large areas of homogeneous "suburban habitat," on the other hand, has caused other species, such as deer, to burgeon, bringing the stresses of overpopulation and overgrazing to suburbia. Unique and sensitive environments have been altered or destroyed. Aquatic systems have been degraded by storm runoff from the extensive impervious-

ness that is the hallmark of suburban development. The recognition of these inadvertent and unwanted consequences is now causing land planners, the public, developers, and public officials to look for ways to reduce the negative impacts of necessary and desirable land development. Careful master planning of new communities can reduce these impacts and use nature as an ally so that both the product and the natural systems can be enhanced.

Smart Growth

The dominant pattern of land development in the United States in the past 50 years has been low density, single use, and suburban. This growth pattern has become quite controversial, bringing critics and defenders to debate how it affects local fiscal health, environmental quality, the character of a community, economic growth, and investment in infrastructure. Recently, though, some public officials, developers, and environmentalists have begun promoting the concept of "smart growth." The philosophy accepts that new housing, businesses, and jobs must be accommodated and that the economy, the community, and the environment must be served and fostered in the process. Smart growth may bring the forces that have been described as "progrowth" and "antigrowth" together with a common agenda of community well-being, economic prosperity, and environmental protection.

Both smart growth and sustainable development pursue development that is environmentally sensitive. The interest in smart growth and sustainable development shows that people are concerned about land development practices with broad ecological consequences for us and for our communities. In this case, however, the word "ecological" transcends biology and the relationships among organisms and their environment. When used in the context of smart growth and sustainable development, ecology incorporates other systems that are part of the human environment with the natural environment, including economic systems, community systems, and social systems.

Smart growth promotes growth and land development that build community, protect environmental systems, take full advantage of opportunities in brownfields and the inner city, maximize return on private and public investment, and safeguard human health. Smart growth means that:

- *The community is economically smart.* Economic vitality comes from good jobs and affordable living standards; businesses, including land development businesses, have a reasonable opportunity to succeed financially.
- *The community is environmentally smart.* Water, air, and human health are protected and enhanced, sustainable habitat areas are preserved, and the redevelopment of contaminated properties is encouraged. The community is in balance with its natural resources and can sustain itself without draining local, regional, or global resources.
- *The community is socially smart.* People feel safe, live comfortably, and feel socially connected. New growth does not introduce negative impacts to the community. Local governments are self-sustaining and provide high-quality public services.

Smart growth recognizes the link between quality of life and patterns and practices of development. Smart growth applies a comprehen-

sive approach to accommodating development. Communities that follow the principles of smart growth use new growth to improve environmental quality, enhance economic opportunity, and build community.

Smart growth requires collaboration and partnership. As the private developer proposes and funds development projects and the public sector (usually local government) enforces development regulations and issues permits, the process runs smoother if the private and public sectors share a vision and goals for the project and the community. In the process of collaborating to find a vision all stakeholders can share, each participant can express those values that are most important to him or her and learn from the others what are their most important outcomes.

Sustainability

The President's Council on Sustainable Development, a group of leaders from business and environmental groups, civil rights, labor, and native American organizations, and major business enterprises such as petroleum and chemical companies, defines sustainable development as development designed "to meet the needs of the present without compromising the ability of future generations to meet their own needs."

Sustainable development and smart growth are compatible. Smart growth, in fact, can be seen as a path to sustainable development. True sustainability will not be easy to achieve, especially for a culture as consumptive as ours. For a community to be judged truly sustainable, it must use resources—natural, economic, environmental, and human and intellectual—so as not to deplete them.

Development Principles

Recognizing the need to keep the relationships among economic, environmental, and social systems woven together, some developers of master-planned communities adopt a set of principles to govern a project. The 14 principles, developed by ULI members and staff, can be used to formulate principles for an individual project.[1] All decisions, whether they relate to design, construction, materials, or sales and marketing, filter through the principles so that all parties understand the benefits and consequences upfront, not during the development process.

- *Principle 1. Choose the development site intelligently.* Plan ecosystems ecologically, collaboratively, and decisively to make the best use of existing urban infrastructure and to sustain "green" infrastructure (the land and habitat necessary to maintain the structure and function of the ecosystem). Not all sites are suitable for development. Define the areas to be protected, taking into account local biodiversity and habitat, the larger ecological community, and the regional ecosystem.

- *Principle 2. Respect the uniqueness of the place.* Protect its ecological and cultural resources. Preserve, enhance, and restore natural and biological systems as appropriate.

- *Principle 3. Choose materials to maximize durability, minimize waste, and eliminate the use of toxics.*

- *Principle 4. Design on a human scale.* Help to create a sense of community, and ensure ease of movement and the safety of residents.

- *Principle 5. Make allowance for individual expression, healthy change, and the evolution of a distinctive character of place.*

- *Principle 6. Integrate design, materials, and systems.* Join them to existing site resources with appropriate technology.

- *Principle 7. Factor the local climate and culture into the design.*

- *Principle 8. Minimize disturbance of the site.* Protecting a site's natural environment provides a focus for development.

- *Principle 9. Use materials wisely.* Design buildings to use resources efficiently by minimizing the use of nonrenewables, eliminating toxics, using recycled and recyclable components, recycling construction waste, and adapting older buildings to new uses. Build for durability, adaptability, and decreased maintenance.

- *Principle 10. Optimize the building shell.* Increase energy efficiency by selecting walls, windows, and roofs that minimize energy consumption and increase durability and adaptability.

- *Principle 11. Optimize the efficiency of systems.* Build in energy efficiency to minimize the use of nonrenewable energy sources. Incorporate passive solar principles and natural cooling. Use high-efficiency heating, ventilating, and air-conditioning systems, lighting, appliances, and plumbing systems to reduce waste and pollution from fossil fuels.

- *Principle 12. Plan for water conservation and recycling.* Design and build to reduce water consumption. Use alternative sources of water. Landscape with plants adapted to local climate and moisture conditions.

- *Principle 13. Operate buildings in an environmentally responsible way.* Establish procedures for setting up, managing, and monitoring building operations to ensure environmentally efficient performance.

- *Principle 14. Be a leader in implementing the principles of ecological development.* Proactively and collaboratively find performance-oriented solutions to the environmental impacts of development.

These principles reflect a specific concern with how a development functions in relation to the natural world. Other compilations of principles may stress economic or ethnic diversity or focus more on the design of a community and the social and cultural relationships where people live and work. Examples of principles that are being used in specific projects are included later in the context of those projects.

The following section looks at some of the practices that characterize environmental sensitivity for master-planned communities.

The Practice of Environmental Protection

Understanding "Place"

Each parcel of land is distinctive, the product of physical, biological, and cultural forces that act upon it. The word "place" is used here to mean the distinctive aspect of the landscape or parcel of land. One gets to know and understand a place by becoming familiar with it, studying it, and learning about its characteristics and history. The entire development team must understand the traits peculiar to a site and its natural strengths and weaknesses. Doing so gives greater meaning to the principles, particularly those relating to the environment, as decisions are made that affect a project's design and construction.

Ecological Planning and Design

Becoming familiar with the place begins with identifying the natural systems functioning there through an inventory that forms the database for analysis of natural systems. An ecolog-

ical or natural resource consultant could assist in conducting the inventory.

The inventory might include some or all of the following features:

- *Geology:* physiography, surficial geology, geomorphology, aquifer recharge;
- *Soils:* hydrologic soil groups, hydric soils, suitability and erodibility of soil, suitability for agriculture;
- *Topography:* steep slopes, slope aspect;
- *Hydrology:* surface water, groundwater, floodplains, wetlands;
- *Habitat:* terrestrial, aquatic, forest interior, unusual habitats, threatened and endangered species;
- *Climate:* microclimate, frost pockets, prevailing winds;
- *Living resources:* plants (vegetation associations, vegetation communities, forest stand delineation) and animals (threatened and endangered species).

Ecological land planning seeks to find an appropriate design framework for the planned land uses. Mapping those features that lend themselves to spatial distribution helps with planning. Ideally, information about the site is derived from or entered into a geographic information system (GIS). GIS, a computer-based data management system, permits the display and overlay of diverse forms of geographic information. Use of a GIS greatly facilitates analysis and interpretation of geographical information.

Preparing an inventory allows the development team or ecological designers to become familiar with specific natural features of the place. They can study how the natural features interrelate so that their continued functioning as systems can be accommodated during construction and after completion of the development. Ian McHarg laid the foundation for ecologically sensitive land use planning in the 1960s by mapping site features and resources. He used the best scientific information available, synthesized through map overlays, to determine the areas most suitable for development and to identify those requiring protection.[2]

Nature as Partner

Ecological design recognizes that living and nonliving things interrelate through biological and physical laws. People are no exception to this rule. People and nature must coexist in harmony

71

The Woodlands, near Houston, Texas, is one of the earliest examples of ecological planning in the development of a master-planned community.

and interact in ways that support healthy interdependence. Ecological design incorporates natural principles of using energy and resources efficiently and "substitutes design intelligence for the extravagant use of energy and materials."[3] When designing a community, developers should look for ways to use and enhance natural processes rather than trying to overpower nature with engineering.

One of the earliest examples of the use of ecological planning in the development of a master-planned community is the Woodlands near Houston (see the case study for more details). Ian McHarg conducted the ecological study of the 25,000-acre site. His inventory and analysis led to an ecological plan that was to become the major determinant in preparing the master plan for the Woodlands community.

McHarg discovered that conventional development patterns and practices on that site would alter the natural rates of groundwater recharge and surface water runoff. If that happened, downstream flooding would increase and groundwater levels on and off site would dip significantly lower. To preserve and nurture the forest, avoid land subsidence, and control flooding, McHarg asserted that new development needed to maintain, enhance, and replicate the natural hydrologic cycle. As a result, planning was structured around maximizing groundwater recharge, protecting permeable soils, maintaining the water table, reducing runoff, retarding erosion and siltation, increasing the base flow of streams, and protecting natural vegetation and wildlife habitats.

The Woodlands Corporation first addressed these ecological imperatives in its general plan. Existing stream corridors and other ecologically valuable areas for hydrology, wildlife, and vegetation were preserved as conservation zones within the community's open space system. Arterial and collector roads were sited on ridge lines away from drainage areas. Development was planned to be densest near major roads and intersections and less so away from them. To have the minimum effect on the site's hydrology, development was located on areas of impermeable soils. Minor residential streets were used as embankments perpendicular to the slope of the site to delay flow over highly permeable soils and allow time for maximum infiltration. Design solutions, such as installing permeable paving, were recommended to increase further the on-site percolation of stormwater.

Market studies found that most homebuyers simply did not like the rustic appearance of natural drainage improvements and were willing to pay a premium for conventional engineering techniques that were less obtrusive. To improve marketability, the Woodlands Corporation modified the natural drainage system over time by combining the best elements of natural drainage (for example, preservation of natural stream channels, retention reservoirs, vegetation preserves, and greenbelts) with more conventional engineering practices. The company also has found that some new residents resist clearing for continuing development in the community until they learn about the plan and the safeguards in place to preserve and protect the environment.

Water: A Precious Commodity

In some regions where water is scarce, like the arid Southwest, providing water to serve new development can have significant environmental impacts. As much as one-third to one-half of water consumed in new suburban communities is for irrigating the landscape. Simply reducing such irrigation substantially reduces the impact of new development on water resources.

The most effective means of reducing water consumption for landscaping is the use of drought-tolerant landscaping materials combined with water-efficient irrigation systems. Some jurisdictions in the Southwest require the installation of Xeriscape landscaping plans, which combine limited turf areas, efficient irrigation, soil amendments, mulches, and low-water-use plants for creative landscaping and water management. The San Diego Xeriscape Council and other groups have published useful booklets on the principles of xeriscaping and plant materials.

Water-efficient plumbing fixtures and faucets can reduce indoor water use by more than 50 percent without impinging on the quality of life. When combined with xeriscaping and water-efficient irrigation systems, household water use can be reduced by 80 percent or more without inconvenience to residents.

Another way to manage water ecologically is to find alternative sources of water, for example, "gray water" for irrigation of the landscape. "Gray water" refers to reclaimed household wastewater from sinks and showers, collected in a separate system from the household sanitary waste that must be treated before being discharged. Gray water also refers to the effluent from a sewage treatment plant. Given the advanced treatment requirements imposed on modern sewage treatment plants, the effluent can be of very high quality. Many communities spend millions of dollars treating sanitary wastewater, only to discharge it back into receiving water bodies. Some communities have recognized the value in cleaned-up wastewater effluent and have begun to sell gray water for irrigation of golf courses, farms, and lawns, and for industrial uses. Several jurisdictions, including some in California, have enacted code provisions to allow the use of gray water for irrigation of the landscape.

Stormwater Management to Prevent Pollution

When rainwater flows over lawns, sidewalks, streets, and parking lots, it collects pollutants—heavy metals, petroleum compounds, nutrients, pet wastes, sediment—and the rainwater itself may contain atmospheric pollutants like acid compounds and automobile-generated nitrogen oxides. Called "non-point-source pollution," these pollutants are transported in runoff to contaminate rivers, streams, and lakes. By adding impervious surfaces, development increases the quantity and velocity of runoff, leading to more erosion and flooding.

Developers should encourage the use of systems designed to manage stormwater on site and to replicate the runoff of the site in its natural state. Natural stormwater drainage minimizes degradation of water quality, prevents downstream erosion and flooding, and recharges groundwater reserves. Natural drainage uses permeable surface materials, surface drainage, and infiltration instead of conventional drainage through a storm sewer. Permeable paving materials allow rainwater to pass through them into the ground, reducing the volume of runoff and potentially recharging underground aquifers. A secondary benefit is that light-colored pervious materials reflect sunlight rather than absorb its heat, helping to reduce the buildup of heat. Swales and retention ponds, in addition to controlling stormwater, create attractive site features and save money by reducing the costs of infrastructure.

The stormwater management strategy at Prairie Crossing, a 667-acre conservation community 40 miles north of downtown Chicago, incorporates natural systems to purify runoff and allow it to infiltrate the ground naturally. Runoff flows through a natural, sequential system of stormwater swales, restored upland prairies, created wetlands, and lakes. This train of treatment reduces the rate and volume of runoff and increases lag time, allowing greater water infiltration and evaporation. Swales and prairies remove 60 to 90 percent of the suspended solids, phosphorus, and metals. Wetlands play the principal role in denitrification of the runoff, thus preventing excess nitrogen from reaching the lake and nearby creeks and marshes. In addition to improved water quality, this natural stormwater management system reduced costs of infrastructure by more than $1 million over a conventional curb, gutter, and storm sewer system.

Advantageous Use of Solar Energy

Because subdivision lots seldom change after they are mapped, land planning and site design may have more impact on a building's energy efficiency over the long term than the design and construction of the building itself. Land development and construction must be integrated to achieve optimum energy efficiency, but often they are not. In California, for example, residential lots are typically created by a land developer who is not involved in designing or constructing houses and whose concern is how many lots can be mapped on the site. The homebuilder buys finished lots with no input in their layout or design. Decisions about building design must accommodate the restrictions imposed by the land plan, based on the developer's best guess of what builders will build. This fragmentation inhibits optimizing energy efficiency through solar orientation—or virtually anything else.

Optimizing site design for solar and passive energy focuses primarily on buildings' orientation. A typical residential plan with culs-de-sac results in about 20 percent of the lots' being usable for passive solar energy; minor revisions to the street plan and layout can increase that figure to 70 or 80 percent. Orientation varies depending on latitude and other factors, but in general the ideal orientation in the northern hemisphere places the main living areas of a building facing slightly east of south. To boost energy efficiency, land planning, building design, and building components must be integrated rather than subjected to fragmented design and development.

Landscape Design

Landscaping is the single most humanizing and softening element in the built environment, creating a context for structures. It can greatly ameliorate the detrimental effects of the built environment by reducing heat gain, absorbing carbon dioxide and air pollution, offering shelter from the prevailing wind, and reducing dust. On the negative side, landscaping that is not carefully planned can waste energy, time, water, and light. Landscaping changes and grows over time and must be designed as a changing, adaptable part of the physical environment to optimize planning and costs.

Conventional suburban landscaping, with wide, treeless streets and large lawns, raises the ambient temperature as much as 10 degrees above that of surrounding areas, while narrower streets lined with shade trees cool the area, reduce noise levels, and absorb particulate air pollution. The proper placement of trees around buildings reduces the amount of energy used for heating and cooling. According to an EPA publication, *Cooling Our Communities*, trees use solar radiation to turn water into water vapor, and a single tree can transpire 100 gallons of water per day, which is the equivalent of five air conditioners each running for 20 hours. In winter, trees can block cold winds and retain solar warming.

The following guidelines provide a framework for sustainable landscape design:

- Understand the site's historic and regional landscape characteristics.
- Respect the existing natural landforms and landscape. To the degree possible, preserve existing landforms and vegetation that define the site's natural structure and character.
- Restore the site's landscape character and palette. For portions of the site that will remain undeveloped or be designated as natural open space, use native plant species to establish a permanent, sustainable landscape.
- Create landscaping that can be sustained as a permanent, ongoing environment. Landscape improvements should enhance the environment for residents and require little or no water and maintenance.
- Use landscaping to define spaces, to create places for varied activities, and to reinforce the expression of relationships between buildings.

Infrastructure Planning to Protect the Habitat

To support a community's ecological system, the critical system elements must be identified and preserved. The conventional approach to protection of the habitat has been to preserve habitat piecemeal, project by project. This approach does not always work, as clearly indicated by the well-documented precipitous decline of many species of migratory songbirds in North America that can be attributed to the destruction and fragmentation of habitat caused by the extensive urbanization of the past 50 years. These birds, among them warblers, vireos, thrushes, and tanagers, are woven into our continent's web of life. They also connect us, through their migratory patterns, with tropical and rain forest ecosystems in Central and South America.

Viewing these species as indicators of an ecosystem's health, we can see that they and we are in trouble. They need large, sustainable sections of habitat to be able to successfully resist predators, parasites, and other ecological pressures. Less habitat in smaller pieces makes them more vulnerable and less likely to survive. Thus, good stewardship asks that we examine our land development habits and how we protect ecosystems and habitat.

A new approach views protection of habitat and the ecosystem, by virtue of their importance to our ecological well-being, as part of the community's infrastructure. Because communities are already comfortable with the concept of planning for water and sewer systems, and for transportation and roads, it should be easy to see the value of planning to sustain a living, healthy ecosystem. Identifying critical habitats also serves to define areas that, by virtue of being outside the protected area, are appropriate for development.

In southern California, the habitats of federally listed endangered species blanket the entire landscape. The developer of a proposed development must prepare a habitat conservation plan (HCP) to protect any endangered species likely to be affected. The Endangered Species Act, however, focuses on the protection of individual species. In many cases, several endangered species may be affected by one project, making the preparation of HCPs extremely complex. To untie the knot of complexity, California developed a process to protect appropriate habitat for endangered species. Called the natural communities conservation plan (NCCP), it requires a collaborative effort among federal, state, and local governments, landowners, and environmental groups to protect many species and sensitive natural habitats and to prevent the need to list other species as endangered. Using the NCCP, communities can develop larger plans to identify the best habitat areas to preserve while allowing development to proceed in other, more appropriate areas. Under this system, as projects are reviewed for development approvals, the developer can meet any obligations that arise under the Endangered Species Act by dedicating land from the development site if that land has been identified in the NCCP. If none of the proposed development site is in the NCCP, the developer can contribute elsewhere to land preservation. As of this writing, NCCPs have been negotiated successfully in Orange County and in San Diego County.

The Collaborative Process of the Watershed Approach

Watershed planning has generated considerable enthusiasm around the country. It is viewed as a way to organize politically and institutionally to solve environmental problems, protect eco-

The environmentally sensitive landscape design of Fairview Village included replanting 4,000 native trees and shrubs, which will help establish a permanent, sustainable landscape.

logical systems, and accommodate growth, while honoring the interests of economic, cultural, and environmental stakeholders. The watershed approach starts at the grass roots to make environmental decisions and investments that will achieve the most environmental protection and economic security for the least cost. By replacing the outmoded "top down/command-and-control" environmental regulatory process, it could become a mainstay of regional ecological development.

Conclusion

While in the past developers were concerned with preserving trees, green space, or wildlife corridors, today we understand that the way to protect the environment is to try to protect sustainable areas of ecological systems. It is not always possible, particularly for individual projects, but communities, local governments, and regions must find ways to identify and acquire sustainable ecosystems.

Environmentally Innovative Master-Planned Communities

Prairie Crossing, Grayslake, Illinois

Prairie Crossing is a 667-acre master-planned community 40 miles north of downtown Chicago dedicated to environmental preservation and sustainability. The project is being developed at 20 percent of the permitted density, and the 317 houses in the development are being constructed with energy- and resource-efficient technologies. More than 350 acres are protected from any future development. Two hundred of these acres are restored prairie, and 150 acres are dedicated to wetlands and working farm fields. Portions of this preserved area are linked to the community, including the village green, a trail system, a lake, and community-supported gardens.

The Prairie Holdings development team wants to prove that small-scale suburban development, planned and built in harmony with the environment, can be environmentally and economically successful. Rather than development to the maximum allowable density, the vision for Prairie Crossing consists of a thriving community within a sensitive natural environment. "We want to be stewards of this abundant ecological heritage," says Susan Meyer, coordinator of the Liberty Prairie Conservancy, one of the groups working with Prairie Holdings to protect the prairie, farmland, wetland, and habitat.

The restoration and re-creation of 200 acres of native prairies and wetlands has added critical habitat for native plant species in a region where habitat has been typically destroyed by development and farming. The grasslands attract native and migratory birds and wildlife. A lake, ponds, and restored wetlands are designed to appeal to a variety of waterfowl, wildlife, and plant species. Easements permanently protect these areas and were donated to the Conservation Fund and the Liberty Prairie Conservancy.

The Liberty Prairie Conservancy, founded in 1994, manages a distinctive 2,500-acre natural

Prairie Crossing, about 40 miles outside Chicago, is characterized by more than 350 acres of open space, which is over half the total site. This dedicated open space includes an extensive trail system to encourage walking and biking throughout the development.

area in this part of Illinois called the Liberty Prairie Reserve. The reserve combines agricultural and natural areas with row crops, organic farming, pastures, wetlands, prairies, and oak savannas. Its size and configuration make the reserve an effective, sustainable conservation unit encompassing enough topographic diversity and habitats to maintain viable populations of species that require large, diverse areas. The reserve contains six dedicated Illinois Nature Preserves and is habitat for at least three state-endangered species.

One-half of 1 percent of each home sale and resale goes to the Liberty Prairie Foundation, which supports environmental education and programs in the region. Based on an agreement with Prairie Crossing, the foundation also receives $300,000 per year from a portion of landfill tipping fees from a nearby landfill company, USA Waste Services.

To ensure effective environmental conservation and energy efficiency, Prairie Holdings initiated partnerships with numerous organizations and agencies, including the Liberty Prairie Conservancy, the Conservation Fund, USA Waste Services, and Sieben Energy Associates. Building successful community partnerships has been a key feature of the Prairie Crossing project.

These partnerships have in turn helped to win acceptance in the community and to knit Prairie Crossing into the existing community fabric.

Ten principles guide development at Prairie Crossing: 1) environmental protection and enhancement, 2) a healthy lifestyle, 3) a sense of place, 4) a sense of community, 5) economic and racial diversity, 6) convenient and efficient transportation, 7) energy conservation, 8) lifelong learning and education, 9) aesthetic design and high-quality construction, and 10) economic viability. Architectural techniques like porches, large windows, and shallow setbacks, for example, encourage community interaction. Building a sense of community is achieved with amenities that include a 12-stall animal barn, a farm market, a community center, tennis courts, a fitness center, and gardens. Two types of gardens serve the community. First, garden plots are available to residents to grow fruit, vegetables, and flowers in an ecologically sound manner. Second, a 150-member community-supported garden entitles subscribers to freshly picked organic fruits, vegetables, and flowers for each of the 20 weeks the farm is in production. Subscriptions can be bought for $200, $300, or $400, with each subscriber entitled to that amount of produce plus 10 percent.

Energy-efficient construction, a community recycling program, and trails to encourage biking and walking have been integrated into the development. Rail service to Chicago is now available within a five-minute drive, and a new station serving stops at O'Hare International Airport and Chicago will open adjacent to the development soon.

The founders of Prairie Crossing believe that a mix of incomes and races is essential to the future of our society. A range of housing prices is offered, including affordable housing. An aggressive marketing and lending program encourages minority homeownership and ensures diversity in age, race, occupation, and household income.

Dewees Island, South Carolina

Dewees Island is a 1,206-acre oceanfront island just north of Charleston, South Carolina. The residential development at Dewees Island is notable because of the developer's adherence to a strict environmental master plan based on a set of integrated, sustainable development principles. The use of that plan and those principles in the design, marketing, and construction of the project makes it an excellent model for master-planned communities.

The overarching principle for Dewees Island is based on Aldo Leopold's assertion that "conservation is a state of harmony between man and nature." Based on that maxim, the following principles guide Dewees's development:

1. Development and the environment are natural allies.
2. All development and building occur in the context that all resources are limited.
3. Communities and buildings can be resource providers, not just resource users.
4. Land is held in stewardship for future generations.
5. It is less expensive in the short and long term to build in harmony with the environment.
6. Communities are planned for people.
7. Technologies are to be supportive, not dominant.

Development began in June 1991 by the Island Preservation Partnership, a South Carolina general partnership formed by the original landowners and a group of equity investors. Development is being guided by John L. Knott, Jr., Dewees's CEO and managing director, who helped craft the island's sustainable development environmental master plan. The community dedicated more than 65 percent of the island to permanent conservation. Development is limited to a maximum of 150 homesites, which average over two acres each. Houses are restricted to a maximum of 5,000 square feet, with no minimum. In addition, houses may not disturb more than 7,500 surface square feet, that is, on average less than 9 percent of a lot.

Only community docks exist on Dewees Island. All roads on the island are a natural sand base, and only electric vehicles are allowed on the island. Among the project's many amenities are 2¾ miles of beach, boat access, a fully staffed environmental education center, a system of interactive nature trails, a 200-acre tidal lake, and a 120-acre impoundment. Dewees Island boasts a swimming pool, two tennis courts, a community pavilion, and fishing docks—but no golf course or clubhouse.

Dewees Island's development principles have been expressed in several ways:

- Houses are sensitively placed within the habitat, designed to take advantage of winter sun and summer shade, the prevailing breezes, and natural lighting.
- Recycled and nontoxic building products are used, among them recycled cotton insulation, hydra-stop roofing systems to simulate metal roofs, recycled decking, and nontoxic interior products.

- An architectural resource board guides homeowners through all sustainable development practices. The board also helps establish a variety of low-country architectural styles.
- The South Carolina Energy Center is conducting research for a self-sustaining energy source for the island to harness wind, sun, and ocean tides to provide electric power in the hope of making the island energy independent. Energy independence is possible for Dewees because the design of housing uses passive heating and cooling techniques. As a result, homeowners consume 50 to 60 percent less electricity than normal.
- No impervious surfaces exist on the island, ensuring maximum infiltration of water to the underground aquifer.
- Only vegetation indigenous to the South Carolina coastal plain is permitted at Dewees, removing the need for irrigation, fertilizers, and pesticides.
- Houses must use water conservation fixtures, reducing water consumption by as much as 60 percent.
- Source reduction, and reuse, recycling, and composting of solid waste reduce construction

The Island Preservation Partnership, developer of Dewees Island, South Carolina, has placed 65 percent of the island in permanent conservation to preserve the environmentally sensitive setting.

Plants that are native to the South Carolina coastal plain are the only plants and vegetation allowed to be planted on Dewees Island, making the use of irrigation, fertilizers, and pesticides unnecessary.

waste by more than 70 percent and household waste by more than 50 percent.

• Pilings and lumber are recycled for use as landscaping features, mulch, paths, walkways, and other uses on the island.

The island developed a wastewater treatment system that has no impact on the environment. Each residence has a system of three septic tanks that provide for anaerobic and aerobic treatment of the waste. The liquid effluent from the septic system is piped to a large community drainfield, which is cycled so that one-fourth of the field is used at a time while the other three-fourths rests. This centralized system is a biologically based, closed-loop operation that creates no discharge into local waterways.

Spiritual well-being is also a concern at Dewees. An outdoor chapel provides an area for reflection, prayer, and meditation. Dewees's owners, because of their commitment to working as a resource provider, pledge to preserve

natural resources for children, grandchildren, and future generations.

Community of Civano, Tucson, Arizona

Civano is a master-planned community currently under construction that uses the principles of sustainable development and traditional neighborhood design. Planned for 820 acres within the city of Tucson, Civano intends to be an exemplary demonstration of cost-effective, resource-efficient development where use of energy and waste will be reduced while the level of economic activity is maintained or increased. The Civano project is planned to demonstrate the marketability of sustainable community design on a large scale at affordable prices. The master plan envisions construction of 2,300 houses and apartments and creation of 1,200 jobs on the site. In eight to 12 years, Civano expects to become home to more than 5,000 people and the location of light industry, offices, and retail businesses.

Commercial, cultural, and civic activity clustered in the village core will foster a small-town ambience. Businesses in Civano will provide jobs for some of the residents, reducing their need for automobile travel and its attendant air pollution. Half the population and two-thirds of the jobs will be within a five-minute walk of Civano's town center. Residents and employees alike will have access to active recreational facilities and natural desert open space.

Case Enterprises, the developer of Civano, plans to showcase techniques that conserve natural resources without sacrificing quality of life. It hopes that a pedestrian-friendly environment, reduced energy demand, alternative energy supply, lower use of potable water, and increased recycling will create a comfortable community with less impact on the environment. Ultimately, the successful development of Civano will demonstrate methods of design and construction that will enable Tucson and other cities to meet the demands of growth without straining available natural resources.

The underlying goal and fundamental principle guiding the developer of Civano is to build a real community—a real place for people to live, work, and play. Other goals are to use proven, available technology to measurably reduce the use of natural resources below current levels; to build a strong sense of community among the people who live and work in Civano, ensuring that it evolves positively to meet the needs and concerns of the future; to enable people to meet their economic needs yet maintain social values and ecological harmony; and to become a world-leading solar energy center, attracting businesses engaged in solar power and other renewable resources.

The initial construction plan is to reduce energy demand by using the best available technology, including passive solar design. As photovoltaic electric generation and similar technologies become economical, Civano expects to incorporate them to provide electric power to the community.

Harvested rainwater or reclaimed gray water will be used to irrigate vegetation and conserve potable water. Improved collection and disposal methods will facilitate solid waste recycling. It is hoped that pedestrian-friendly streets, together with walking and biking paths, will reduce the use of autos for internal circulation.

The village is planned around a compact core with a full mix of employment opportunities, shops, services, and recreational activities. Both detached houses and multifamily dwellings will be built to accommodate residents with a wide range of incomes.

Notes

1. The group includes George Brewster, executive director, California Center for Land Recycling; Frank Martin, president, Hidden Springs Community; Marianna Leuschel, principal, L Studio; Michael Pawlukiewicz, director of environmental policy, ULI; and some members of the conservation community.

2. Ian L. McHarg, *Design with Nature* (New York: John Wiley & Sons, 1992) .

3. Sim Van der Ryn and Stuart Cowan, *Ecological Design* (Washington, D.C.: Island Press, 1995), p. 55.

Chapter 7

New Visions in Community Design

Adrienne Schmitz

Design is about solving problems. Community design seeks to address a complex set of problems concerning how people live and work, how they interact, what kinds of housing they choose, and how changes over time can be accommodated in the community. Like any kind of design, community design goes through fashions, but unlike trends in clothing, music, or restaurants, which might change every season, trends in community design evolve gradually over decades.

The Importance of Design

All too often, design takes a back seat to other aspects of development. Frequently, little concern is evidenced for aesthetics or for how well the community addresses its residents' lifestyles. Many of the key elements that make up a community plan are dictated, not by designers, but by traffic engineers, whose interest is in accommodating vehicles, not residents. Zoning approvals are based on rules that are formulated to accommodate vehicles and are often a hindrance to good design. The result can be visual blight and diminished livability.

At Magee Ranch in Danville, California, the Broadmore Group was careful to maintain the natural landscape. The 259 homes are clustered, leaving 80 percent of the 600-acre site untouched.

Community design is also dictated by the market. Most homebuyers view a home as an investment as well as a purchase that meets needs and lifestyle. Some homebuyers show little indication that they care about design; their primary concern is buying the most square footage for their dollar to maximize the potential return on investment. Some homebuyers seek ever larger houses, with interiors featuring every possible amenity and exteriors that turn their backs on the community. Dubbed "McMansions," these large tract houses are often 5,000 square feet or more.

Often, consumers are afraid to buy a different or new concept because they have been conditioned to believe that anything other than the tried and true will not retain its value. So they settle for the same old floorplan in the same old community plan, whether or not it suits their tastes or needs. Developers buy into this thinking, believing that if it sold well in the past, it will continue to sell in the future.

Conventional Master-Planned Communities

The suburbs had their roots in the 1920s and 1930s but really burgeoned after World War II. At that time, cheap land, cheap gasoline, and plentiful mortgage money became the major determinants of the suburban form. Viewed as revolutionary at the time, the Levittown developments, by William Levitt & Sons, exemplified postwar suburbanization and were in fact masterplanned communities. Between 1947 and 1951, sprouting from potato fields on Long Island, the first Levittown grew into more than 17,000 Cape Cod and ranch houses on uniform 60- by 100-foot lots. The houses were not prefabricated, but they were among the first built using mass production techniques. The land plan was a network of sidewalk-lined curving drives linked to arterials called parkways. The plan developed in stages determined by the pace of sales (which averaged about 300 per month!). The community included scattered convenience retail stores, school sites, swimming pools, and playgrounds, all providing for residents' daily needs. Levitt developed a second Levittown in Pennsylvania, outside Philadelphia.

The "new town" movement of the 1960s was a major step forward from the Levittowns in the evolution of master-planned communities. New towns were based on comprehensive plans that sought to consider every element of community design. The plans addressed environmental and aesthetic concerns as well as issues of how people lived and worked, what kinds of people would

live in the community, and how to include a broad demographic mix. Some of the most notable master-planned new towns include Reston, Virginia, Columbia, Maryland, Las Colinas, Texas, and Irvine, California. These communities were built on the concept of self-contained villages in which residents could live, work, and play. All types of housing were incorporated and all types of land uses included, separated from one another by landscaped buffers.

The physical form is suburban in character. Roadways form hierarchies: residential access, collectors, and arterials, with transportation consisting primarily of private vehicles. Open green space is emphasized over urban convenience. And low densities with separate land uses prevail.

Changing Paradigms

A number of forces relating to changing lifestyles and public opinions are causing designers and developers to rethink the future of community design. A few of these key factors will illustrate change and how designers are responding.

- *Public reaction to growth is increasingly negative.* Developers recognize the power of NIMBYism (the "not in my back yard" syndrome) as the major obstacle to new development. They are responding with communities designed to appease public opinion. Important factors are environmental sensitivity and minimizing impacts on the existing community with better aesthetics and amenities. Educating the public will become increasingly important.

- *Home values have stabilized.* While a home will always be considered an investment, resale values are stabilizing, and homes are being purchased less for their investment potential and more for livability. As this phenomenon occurs, a community's design and amenities and the lifestyle it provides are becoming increasingly important to buyers.

- *Lifestyles are changing with technological innovations.* Home-based workers are more common than ever. With people spending more time at home and in their communities, the quality of the community and amenities provided gains importance.

- *In many regions, the best development sites are no longer available.* Developers are turning to infill and redevelopment sites, which often have locational and other advantages over raw land but pose a new set of challenges, including public outcry.

- *Social problems, including crime, urban decay, and segregation of the underclass, are becoming everyone's problems.* Communities must serve more diverse populations and must provide social infrastructure to meet needs beyond housing.

- *Traffic congestion has become an epidemic and is the leading cause of antigrowth sentiment.* Land planners must consider alternatives to private vehicles, including accessibility for pedestrians and public transportation.

While the issues appear to be diverse and unrelated, the solutions all hinge on using planning and design to create livable communities rather than just real estate projects. Community design today is about much more than buildings and lots. It is about building real towns, villages, and neighborhoods.

No Growth, Slow Growth, Smart Growth

In the past, new development had a positive connotation. Growth spelled more jobs, better communities, and greater opportunities for all residents. This image has completely turned around, and today, citizens' reaction to new development is negative, even hostile. Antigrowth policies are unrealistic, however. The population continues to increase and must be supplied with new housing, jobs, and services. The slow-growth movement of the past sought to minimize the impact of growth by controlling its timing. But slowing the *pace* of growth fails to address the *nature* of growth and development. Some regions are experimenting with "urban growth boundaries"—lines beyond which no development may occur. But, on its own, this sledgehammer approach is often arbitrary, and it still fails to address *how* to develop or *what kind* of development works best.

Smart growth is an attempt to realistically and comprehensively control growth, with practices that are environmentally sound and economically vital, and encourage livable communities. It seeks to identify a common ground where developers, environmentalists, public officials, citizens, and financiers can find ways to accommodate growth that is acceptable to each entity. Smart-growth policies recognize the crucial role that development plays in maintaining and improving communities, and promote development that enhances existing communities, is compatible with the natural environment, uses tax dollars efficiently, and is profitable for private investors.

Unfortunately, smart growth is often the path of greatest resistance for the developer. Lenders' underwriting criteria often prohibit mixed-use buildings and reward single-use zoning. Public policies are designed to reinforce prevailing development patterns. In many instances, smart growth is simply illegal. For example, standard zoning practices often forbid mixing land uses and require unnecessarily wide streets, excessive amounts of parking, large setbacks, and large lots.

Traditional Neighborhood Development

Developer Robert Davis notes that "it is only in the last 50 years that developers engaged in the radical experiment that tears towns and cities apart. New urbanism is an attempt to pick up the threads so recently abandoned of this 5,000-year-old craft of building towns and cities."[1] Traditional neighborhood development, also called "new urbanism" and "neotraditionalism," is a concept of land planning based on the most desirable and livable towns and neighborhoods of the pre–World War II era, before automobiles became the primary consideration of community design. Traditional neighborhood development is a smart-growth approach to design. It presents solutions, or at least compromises, for many of the smart-growth issues and other issues facing community developers.

In 1981, on Florida's panhandle, an 80-acre development began the new urbanist movement. Seaside, developed by Robert S. Davis and designed by the team of Andres Duany and Elizabeth Plater-Zyberk, was a revolutionary concept of looking back, not for superficial architectural elements, but for the framework of the plan and for how people would live within the community. Seaside's planners believed that developments before World War II provided better living environments than the automobile-based communities of the latter part of the century. What the Seaside model proposed was the ambience of a small town, where residents could walk to obtain daily needs and interact with other members of the community. Since 1981, designers of new urbanist communities have expanded and refined that vision.

At the heart of planning for traditional neighborhood development is alleviating traffic to ensure better livability. Through good planning, walking and bicycling can again become viable and even pleasurable means of transportation for many destinations. The companion goal is to reduce traffic by minimizing the number and shortening the distance of auto trips by better integrating residential and commercial land uses and designing more effective and convenient street patterns.

Five elements define a neotraditional community:

1. It has a center and an edge. The center includes a public space, such as a square, a green, or an important street intersection, usually located near the middle of the project. The center is the focus of the neighborhood's public buildings. Shops and workplaces are usually there, especially in a village (which is a neighborhood in the country).

2. It is compact, ideally a five-minute walk from center to edge.

3. It includes a mix of activities, for example, residences, shops, a school, workplaces, and parks. A variety of housing types—single-family houses, townhouses, apartments, and often variations within these categories—are included.

4. It consists of an interconnected network of streets and blocks, generally laid out in a modified grid pattern.

5. It gives priority to public space. Civic buildings are offered prominent locations. Open space is provided in the form of squares, parks, and plazas. Streets are designed to be part of the public realm.[2]

These broad, simple elements allow for much interpretation. Features such as small lots, rear alleys, detached garages, and retro architectural designs are not proscribed, but they have evolved as responses to specific problems. For example, if walkability is a key issue, how can the plan reduce walking distances? Denser development is one solution. Because an appealing streetscape is essential for encouraging walking and rows of front-loaded garages create an unappealing streetscape, putting garages in the rear is a common practice for traditional neighborhood development. The key elements make no mention of a quality or style of architecture or of materials to be used for sidewalks or public facilities. None of these items are necessary for a good plan.

Traditional Neighborhood Development as a Design Solution

Traditional neighborhood development came about because some developers and designers were dissatisfied with the lifestyle imposed by conventional suburban development. They rejected the sprawl, dependence on automobiles, and lack of character and sense of place. While other solutions could address the issues facing

Seaside's walkable residential streets all lead to the beach. This well-known vista includes the beach pavilion, one of many focal points throughout the community.

Duany Plater-Zyberk/Steven Brooke

community designers, neotraditionalism is thus far the only design movement in the forefront.

Sprawl

Sprawl began with the post–World War II housing boom, when suburbanization was rapid and the automobile became the common mode of transportation. Sprawl results in underuse of land and infrastructure and forces dependence on the automobile over more efficient modes of transportation. Even short walking trips are often impossible, with barriers, lack of sidewalks, and the dangers of crossing heavily trafficked roads. Sprawl breeds sprawl. Because dependence on automobiles is necessary, increasingly more land is required for roads and parking,

Urban-style streets and squares have been created in the downtown core of Reston, Virginia, where the public spaces of Reston Town Center have become popular gathering places for workers, shoppers, and area residents.

pushing development even farther out and onto ever larger spaces.

By prescribing compact development, traditional neighborhood development uses land more efficiently, potentially allowing for more open space. Mixed uses further improve efficiency. For example, shared parking becomes more feasible. But the public needs to be educated about what sprawl really is. Much of the public equates sprawl with density, when in fact the two are opposites.

Portland, Oregon, has used the concepts of traditional neighborhood development and urban growth boundaries citywide to control sprawl. Portland's primary intent is to preserve farmland beyond the city limits, but other benefits have resulted. While Portland is sometimes criticized for some of the negative effects of this planning, the city ranks among the most livable and desirable in the country. Most traditional neighborhood developments on their own are not large enough to have an effect on sprawl. Real change will occur only when clusters of traditional neighborhood developments form whole regions.

Auto Dependence and Traffic

A byproduct of sprawl is dependency on automobiles. Because destinations are so dispersed, people have no choice but to drive from home to work, from work to lunch, from home to the store, from the restaurant to the theater, and so on. Every trip made by every person requires a vehicle.

The poor, who cannot afford to own cars, are relegated to declining and increasingly poorer inner urban areas, where public transit still exists. Children and the elderly are held hostage in their own homes because they lack the means of transportation required for independence. The auto culture will not go away. Busy lives mandate flexible, independent transportation options. Realistically, community design must accommodate the automobile, not ignore it.

Traditional neighborhood development proposes not to eliminate automobiles, but to tame them. Community streets are scaled to be shared with pedestrians. They are narrowed and speeds are slowed for pedestrians' safety and convenience. Parking is made less prominent for better aesthetics. Traditional neighborhood development provides options besides auto use. No one wants to walk to the supermarket for a week's worth of groceries. But a walk to the convenience store is made possible. Most people will not be able to walk to work, but walking to a meeting in another building or to lunch at a nearby restaurant is viable if pedestrians are properly accommodated. Thus, with many auto trips eliminated, traffic is minimized.

Reston Town Center illustrates how, even on a 20-acre site, the principles of traditional neighborhood development can create a walkable downtown. Phase I of Reston Town Center is an urban-style commercial core at the center of a conventional 460-acre suburban commercial district. The urban core includes 240,000 square feet of street retail stores, 530,000 square feet of mid-rise office buildings, and a 430,000-square-foot full-service hotel, for a total of 1.2 million square feet of mixed-use development at a floor/area ratio of 1.3. The retail component is a careful blend of shops, restaurants, and entertainment, enhanced with public spaces that include a skating rink, fountains, and outdoor seating areas. Office workers most likely drive to work, but once there, they dine, shop, and take care of most daily needs without using their cars while enjoying a very pleasant environment. In addition, Reston Town Center draws shoppers and diners from a regional market, evidence of the large market potential for such urban-style spaces.

With demand for urban-style town centers expanding, developers are now integrating them into many conventional suburbs as additions or replacements for older-style strip centers and enclosed malls. With their mix of shops, restaurants, theaters, and outdoor gathering spaces, town centers are often viewed by market analysts as retail entertainment centers because they create synergies beyond those of a typical shopping center. Shoppers are drawn for the complete experience, rather than just to purchase goods.

Character and Sense of Place

With their emphasis on the public realm over private spaces, plans for traditional neighborhood development create a stronger sense of place than do conventional plans. Landmark buildings and public squares provide markers that identify places in the community and the community as a whole. The common practice of using regional architectural styles in traditional neighborhood developments further promotes sense of place.

Two distinctly different neo-traditional towns in Florida. Tin roofs and picket fences instantly identify Seaside, while Robert Venturi's movie theater is an unmistakable image of Celebration.

The street system facilitates sense of place by its relatively rectangular orientation. A grid, especially if street names follow a logical pattern, makes it easy to find one's way, while a street that curves around and back on itself, as found in conventional suburbs, can be disorienting.

Probably no community exemplifies sense of place better than Seaside, with its modern adaptations of indigenous Florida architecture. The dense jumble of tin roofs, latticework, and sun-drenched pastel colors spells instant recognition for this community. And at Celebration, in Orlando, Florida, landmarks exist at every turn, creating an indelible, Disneyesque identity. Celebration's downtown is a catalog of architectural

Historic Kirkwood is located within walking distance of downtown Kirkland. Most homes feature rear garages with access from alleys.

trophies. Marking one entrance is a water tower with no function other than being a memorable entrance feature.

Revitalizing Urban Areas and Small Towns

Traditional neighborhood development can be an ideal form of development for reinvestment in declining inner cities, inner-ring suburbs, and older small towns. In these cases, the new development melds with and enhances the community that is already in place. Sometimes land prices are depressed in these older areas, allowing developers to build a more affordable product than they could in suburban areas.

Historic Kirkwood, in Kirkland, Illinois, is a traditional neighborhood development located 60 miles west of Chicago. The existing small-town framework was extended for development of a 90-unit community on a 20-acre parcel adjacent to the historic town. The developer, Vintage Properties, knew the project had to be affordably priced because of its remote location. Vintage was able to price housing well below that in neighboring areas: single-family houses begin at $119,000, compared with typical starting prices of $145,000 in the region.

Defining Clear Edges

The concept of an edge should not be misinterpreted. The edge of a traditional neighborhood development is not a wall separating it from the next neighborhood or necessarily the line on the tax map that defines the real estate parcel.

Rather, it is the connection that *links* a neighborhood to its surroundings. The edge is an opportunity for development and should be employed at its highest and best use.

Edges can take several forms. According to John Fregonese, of Portland, Oregon–based Fregonese, Calthorpe & Associates, an edge might be a lake, parkland, or other natural feature to be maximized as a community amenity rather than privatized for individual lots. The edge might be an arterial road, in which case the edge should be used for intense commercial development to take advantage of the higher traffic levels. Or an edge might be more subtle, as in a change in the character or intensity of development. An edge is a wasted opportunity if it is lined with backyards and walls rather than productive development that generates activity and increased value.

Edges might also be considered in terms of activity. An edge is the limit of a five- or ten-minute walk; it is the boundary defining where most daily activities can be accomplished. The neighborhood retail shops, elementary school, and basic recreation should be within this boundary. The importance of the edge is to prevent the neighborhood from losing its identity. Edges should not be confused with buffers. With good design, buffers should never be necessary. All uses and development patterns should be compatible with one another.

Laguna West, in Sacramento, California, uses its edges appropriately. The western edge, which borders I-5, is used for commercial development. Sites fronting the interstate are occupied by highway-serving commercial uses, while the sites facing inward are local-serving businesses. The northern edge of the community is industrial; it has attracted major manufacturers, such as Apple Computers, Intel, and JVC. The town center is a link between the industrial edge and the residential neighborhoods.

Architecture

To the casual observer, the most obvious element of traditional neighborhood developments is their retro architectural styling. While styling is relatively unimportant for the success of the plan, architectural quality and cohesiveness add to the appeal of a community and should be part of the plan. Most traditional neighborhood developments incorporate a theme based on the historic architecture of the region.

One way to establish the design criteria for a community is to create "pattern books." Historically, pattern books served builders as easily understood guides to building houses. They also were used as marketing brochures. Pattern books include elevation drawings, floorplans, and detailing but do not dictate the specific plans as would blueprints. They allow for individual interpretation, enabling a builder to maintain the local character without necessarily replicating the same house over and over.

Local character is the key. Ray Gindroz, of Urban Design Associates in Pittsburgh, says, "We believe you should always know what town you're in." His firm prepares pattern books for communities by first surveying the best local architecture in an area. Some of the features that are important are the windows, roof pitches, front doors, and special features such as porches, lanterns, turrets, or other ornamental elements. A community's builders use the pattern book to guide them in developing specific models; thus, each builder is free to build on its own terms and express its own style while maintaining an overall character for the community. Builders report that design costs are reduced with pattern books.

Historic architecture and materials are preferred for several reasons. They are less likely to look outdated over time. They facilitate later renovations, because traditional building materials are less likely to become obsolete and unavailable. And homebuyers tend to prefer traditional styling. Unfortunately, decades of amateur designs implemented with cheap materials have given contemporary residential architecture a bad image among most homebuyers.

Open Space

Drew Brown, president of DMB Associates in Phoenix, says, "Open spaces matter. They need to be meaningfully integrated into the places where we live, into the community." Open space should not be about more space, but about better, more usable space in the form of urban parks, playgrounds, and squares.

The very best views and design features should be open to the entire community, spreading the premiums among all residents. Additional value can be created with small "pocket parks" and squares throughout the community, allowing residences in several locations to have attractive views. Thus, public spaces are integrated throughout the community, making them more easily accessible for more residents and safer because they are not in isolated areas.

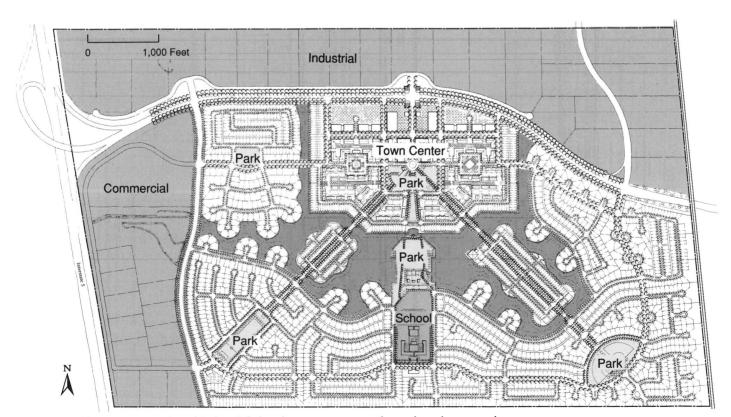

At Laguna West, commercial and industrial development occupy edges along busy roads.

Harbor Town, Tennessee

Developed by the Henry Turley Company, Harbor Town, on Mud Island in Memphis, is one of the earliest and best-known traditional neighborhood developments. The 135-acre development maintains a strong orientation toward both the Mississippi River and the downtown Memphis skyline, and exemplifies the features found in today's traditional town planning, including grid street patterns, a strong pedestrian orientation, village squares, and architectural styles based on historical prototypes.

Planned by RTKL Associates of Baltimore, Harbor Town will include 891 units of mixed residential products. A town square features multifamily residential units, retail and office space, a private school, a yacht club, and an inn. While the project was attractive to renters from the start, the unproven location of Harbor Town initially made it difficult to attract buyers, necessitating a marketing budget several times larger than what would be considered typical. Development of the private school and special promotions appealing to traditional families improved the community's marketability.

Development of the town square was difficult. An unproven

Harbor Town, looking west with the Mississippi River at the top. The developing town square is to the left.

Henry Turley Company

The Pros and Cons of Traditional Neighborhood Development

At ULI's 1998 Spring Council Forum, a panel debated the pros and cons of the new urbanism, including the costs and marketability of this type of development, and how to reconcile some of the difficulties relating to the retail component, parking, and open space.

Cost, Price, and Value

Critics claim that traditional neighborhood development is expensive to build and must command high selling prices, citing projects like Seaside and Kentlands. But these projects were not developed as high-priced projects. Seaside began as a community of inexpensive beach cottages; as the town gained notoriety and status,

however, prices escalated dramatically to meet demand. Seaside ultimately drew high-income buyers, who naturally build high-end houses.

Kentlands was initially positioned to be competitive with surrounding new subdivisions. Prices climbed only after development was far enough along that buyers could begin to understand the concept and demand increased. Proponents of traditional neighborhood development explain that prices escalate to meet market demand and that if enough traditional neighborhood developments entered the market to meet demand, prices would become comparable to conventional forms of development.

Historic Kirkwood, described earlier, is another example of how market forces have moved a development into higher price brackets. While Kirkwood maintains its affordable starting prices in the original section, the project has become so popular for its small-town charm and attrac-

market was a concern for prospective tenants, especially grocery store operators targeted by the developer. The Turley Company decided to originate its own grocery store for the development. A hybrid grocery store and corner market targeted to serve the specific needs of the community, Miss Cordelia's Grocery & Picnic, quickly became a central element in the Harbor Town community.

The grocery store anchors the first commercial building in the village center, a one-story structure built by the developer that also contains a café, a laundry, a bookstore and coffeehouse, and a bank. The success of this commercial block has prompted interest by others to continue development of the town square. Across the street, a two-story retail/office structure is currently under construction, the design of which will begin to enclose the town square, further completing the vision of Harbor Town.

The Harbor Town Square commercial center is adjacent to apartment buildings. Entrance to the grocery store is at the side of the building, adjacent to rear parking.

Streetscapes in Harbor Town are guided by design standards for porches, windows, balconies, and rooflines, using regional architectural elements as the basis.

tive houses that the developer added a section of custom homes priced in the mid $200s.

Opponents of traditional neighborhood development cite the expensive design elements, such as brick sidewalks and period street furniture and architectural detailing. But, as proponents point out, these elements are not crucial to the plan's success. And the smaller lots and street areas of traditional neighborhood development reduce development costs over conventional plans. Jay Parker of Parker Rodriguez, a planning firm in Alexandria, Virginia, estimates that the development costs for traditional neighborhood development are about 20 percent higher than for conventional development but that a parcel will yield 20 percent more lots, effectively negating the extra costs.

Some proponents believe that traditional neighborhood development is a better way to increase land values than conventional building patterns. Public amenities such as parkland are sited to increase the value of the entire community rather than to generate a handful of premium lots. The town becomes increasingly valuable as it matures, and gains texture and diversity. Robert Davis, developer of Seaside and chair of the Congress for New Urbanism, observes, "If this kind of community development is done correctly, with each new increment of development you're actually adding to the value of what you haven't yet developed. Where you're primarily trying to sell privacy and exclusivity, each net increment of development actually detracts from the value of what you're creating."[3]

Market Appeal

The marketability of traditional neighborhood developments has been widely debated, but little hard data exist because of limited experience from which to draw. In 1993, Market Perspectives of Roseville, California, analyzed questionnaires from 311 residents of Kentlands, Harbor Town, and Laguna West (Seaside results were tabulated separately, because residents tend not to be full time) concerning their opinions of traditional neighborhood development. Eighty-four percent of respondents preferred traditional neighborhood development over a conventional community. Readers should recognize, however, that this small, biased sample does not reveal views of the general homebuying public.

In 1996, American LIVES of San Francisco conducted a national survey of homebuyers and found that two-thirds of those polled preferred at least parts of the concept of traditional neighborhood development:

- 20.8 percent like the whole concept;
- 48.4 percent like the concept but want larger lots; they like the town center but not high density;
- 30.8 percent like suburbs the way they are and reject the new urbanism.

The largest segment (48.4 percent) is the one to watch. This group wants to buy into traditional neighborhood developments, but the concept needs some work. Generally, respondents want towns but not the density of towns. They want walkability but prefer to live on culs-de-sac. Reconciling these conflicts and others is the challenge for designers of new communities.

Analysts need to reassess the way market research is conducted. Todd Zimmerman, of the market research firm Zimmerman/Volk, points out that the research does not yield useful answers if the wrong questions are asked. The majority of homebuyers purchase existing houses, not new houses. Large percentages of people with high incomes and the ability to live where they want choose to live in classic 1920s neighborhoods. These are the market comparables for traditional neighborhood developments. Yet conventional market research surveys only buyers of new houses and their preferences.

The Commercial Component

The retail spaces in traditional neighborhood developments can be problematic. A typical development with a small-scale town center may not have enough of a market on site to draw retailers. The limited size of the center also makes it difficult to achieve synergistic relationships.

The shops might be too small for most retailers. Small local retailers that are suitable for the spaces cannot afford the rents dictated by new construction. And the larger retailers, such as supermarkets, do not fit the aesthetics of neo-traditional development. But solutions to these problems are being found.

A residential community of only 280 dwellings, Seaside is home to about 40 small shops, restaurants, and other businesses. Because Seaside retailers cater to a niche not served outside the community, and do so with style, the businesses are able to attract not only residents and guests of Seaside, but also patrons from surrounding resorts.

At Harbor Town, in Memphis, Tennessee, developer Henry Turley could not find a tenant for a grocery store, so he established his own store. A 6,000-square-foot hybrid between a supermarket and a convenience store occupies a building that is designed to visually minimize the bulk of the store. A row of small storefronts lines two sides of the building, with the grocery store opening onto a third side. Thus, three sides of the building are faced with activity-generating storefronts. Early indications are that the stores are quite successful.

Parking in a Walking Environment

Both residential and commercial parking must be accommodated in communities. Solutions to residential parking in traditional neighborhood developments include alleys with rear garages, long front driveways with rear parking, and recessed garages that minimize the visual effect of front-loaded garages.

Two objectives in providing commercial parking are to minimize the number of required spaces and to minimize the visual impact. Curbside parking can add considerably to the inventory of parking spaces without adding parking lots. Curbside parking has the added value of creating a buffer between traffic and pedestrians. Time-of-day sharing is one way to minimize the number of spaces required, and it is facilitated in a mixed-use environment. Shared parking is also enabled by a shopping area's walkability. If a shopper can park, then walk to several stores, only one parking space is required, rather than one space for each store. The appearance of parking lots can be improved by wrapping buildings around a rear lot and breaking lots into smaller groups of spaces. It is important to ensure that

Three Ways to Integrate Large Stores into Streetfront Retail Areas

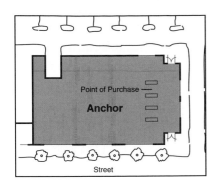

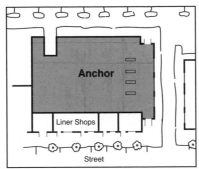

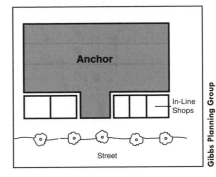

This diagram shows a streetfront entrance. A rear entrance can be used by those who park in the rear. Because both entrances are at the far end of the store and outside the checkout area, security is not compromised. Large windows along the street allow for displays of merchandise.

The small shops along the streetfront can be individual retailers or specialty departments of the large retailer. Entry to the small shops can be from inside the anchor store or from the street. With the small shops at the front, the building has a more comfortable scale. The entrance to the large store is the same configuration as that in the first diagram.

This layout creates a true "main street" character. The large store has a prominent streetfront entrance, and small shops add variety to the facade while benefiting from traffic created by the larger store.

---

curbside parking counts as part of the development's zoning requirements for parking.

The Street System for a Traditional Neighborhood Development

One failing of new towns of the 1960s was that they separated pedestrian trails from all other uses. Paths often cut through wooded areas and led nowhere. While nature paths are aesthetically pleasing, many residents view them as isolated and dangerous. They also do not suit the practical needs of pedestrians using walking as a form of transportation rather than recreation.

Plans for traditional neighborhood development are designed to promote pedestrian activity and lessen dependency on automobiles. Plans emphasize streets that connect. Grid or modified grid street patterns facilitate both pedestrian and vehicular access. Without the conventional hierarchy of streets, traffic is evenly dispersed throughout the community rather than funneled onto collectors and arterials while residential streets sit empty. The most important element of the street pattern is not the rigidity of straight streets and uniform blocks, but the connection between streets that go somewhere.

When sidewalks run parallel to streets, traffic must be slowed for pedestrians' perceived and actual safety. Narrower streets, especially with parking on both sides, accomplish this goal. Such streets also discourage cut-through traffic, because nothing is to be gained by a shortcut that takes longer.

The problem with the grid is that it discourages culs-de-sac, the most marketable location for residences. Some communities, including Laguna West, however, have devised modified grids that incorporate culs-de-sac.

Traditional Neighborhood Developments Don't Work Everywhere

Neotraditional concepts work better for some products than for others. One homebuilder at Belmont Forest, a traditional neighborhood development in Loudoun County, Virginia, found that the concept is ideal for townhouses. The buyer gains the option of a two-car garage, and because the garage is detached at the rear of the lot, the townhouse includes more square footage than with a front-loaded garage that would take up the entire lower level. The buyer gains privacy in the rear because of the separation created by the garage. Street frontage is more appealing than the usual parking lot frontage of conventional townhouse subdivisions. And townhouses are integrated into the same community with single-family houses—a plus for townhouse owners although not necessarily for owners of single-family houses.

The concept also works well for multifamily housing, because the sense of neighborhood is enhanced by buildings fronting on streets rather than on parking lots. The advantages become harder to justify for large, high-end, single-family suburban houses, where buyers are used to having a large lot, often in a cul-de-sac, that affords a sense of privacy. Privacy might be further eroded by rear alleys, depending on their design. Buyers who are used to the convenience of a front-loaded, attached garage might resist the rear garage. For many buyers, features such as attached garages, private lots, and location on a cul-de-sac have great appeal, while the negative social and fiscal impacts of conventional suburbia are more intangible and harder to justify as reasons against the purchase of a home.

The dense development that embodies most traditional neighborhood developments is inappropriate for most rural areas. It is also difficult to integrate into some kinds of suburban areas. The urban form upon which traditional neighborhood development is based is a foreign concept in many areas of the country that were developed after World War II, particularly in the Southwest. Many people in the United States today have never lived or worked in a city or town, and there are parts of the country where "traditional" means a gated suburban enclave of culs-de-sac. In these regions, the concept of neotraditionalism is difficult to understand, much less embrace.

Another potential difficulty is the degree of regulation and conformity required for the density of traditional neighborhood developments to function. Strict covenants guide most of these communities, controlling every architectural element, landscaping, and sometimes even interior features like the type of curtains permitted. For those unaccustomed to such rigid controls, they might be an unacceptable way of life.

While traditional neighborhood development offers solutions to some of the problems of modern living, it creates new problems for developers. Municipalities entrenched in the old ways of doing things are reluctant to revise zoning to permit traditional neighborhood developments. The public's no-growth stand is typically focused on issues of density rather than on seeking realistic solutions to traffic and disappearing open space. Lenders resist unfamiliar forms of development. Developers and designers must educate and work with all these players to enable change.

How Influential Is the New Urbanism?

Despite nearly two decades of new urbanism, only a handful of projects have reached a stage of near completion. According to Chris Leinberger, of Robert Charles Lesser & Co., only about 10 or 15 percent of all new master-planned communities are based on the concept of traditional neighborhood development.[4] If this is the major trend of the current era, why has it generated so little in the way of actual development?

The first reason relates to the evolutionary nature of real estate development. Because the process involves such a great deal of time, trends unfold very slowly. Developments may spend years on the drawing board and in the approval process, only to take even more years for sales and development.

Moreover, changing the shape of development is extremely difficult. A developer seeking to buck convention must fight zoning regulations, underwriting requirements, and outcry from citizens, all of which cost time and money. Many developers may find being a pioneer not worth the cost. Other reasons have to do with misconceptions. Some developers believe that there is no market for traditional neighborhood developments. Some believe that the plans are more costly to develop, or that new urbanism is a radical, short-lived trend.

Reaching Common Ground

Not all buyers will want to live in traditional neighborhood developments, and certainly not all developers will want to build them. Rather than continue the debate over neotraditional versus conventional, however, planners and developers should initiate a dialogue concern-

Street trees make a major difference in the look and feel of a community. Eventually these oak trees at Disney's Celebration will form a canopy of shade over the sidewalks and streets. Some developers plant on-site tree nurseries at the start of development so that larger specimens will be available at a minimal cost.

ing points of agreement. Much can be gained in numerous areas through coordinated efforts. Jay Parker of Parker Rodriguez cites some of the points that both camps tend to agree on:

- *Reduce road standards.* Most developers complain of overly generous road standards. In fact, ULI has been arguing against them since its first *Community Builders' Handbook* was published in 1947. They are costly and unnecessary, and promote unsafe driving speeds in residential areas. Localities must be convinced to reduce road standards for everyone's benefit.
- *Include a variety of housing types and densities close to each other.* A mix of housing types and prices is socially desirable and broadens the market for a development. Zoning should allow for mixed densities and housing types within a community.
- *Include shopping close to residential areas.* Shopping is a desirable amenity for residents. Zoning should accommodate mixed uses so that

neighborhood-scale shopping can be integrated into residential communities.

- *Combine rights-of-way to minimize wasted land.* In some jurisdictions, shared rights-of-way are prohibited, by the government, the utilities, or both. Separate rights-of-way for a road, utilities, and a pathway have been known to result in 150-foot cleared rights-of-way for 40-foot-wide streets. State or local governments can legislate changes in these regulations if pushed to do so.
- *Clear trees only where necessary.* Trees are a valuable aesthetic and environmental asset for a development, and they are an aid in marketing. Preserving them should be a priority.
- *Include street trees.* No single element of community design has more impact than street trees. A row of shade trees arching over a street forms a haven for both drivers and pedestrians. Trees soften and unify the look of a neighborhood, no matter what the built environment looks like. But street trees are

often prohibited by codes written to encourage safe, high-speed traffic.

- *Overcome NIMBYism.* Public protest has become the greatest problem for developers. No-growth attitudes affect government approvals. Smart growth and good design are ways to overcome NIMBYism. Educating and working with the public can help.
- *Promote efficient use of land.* Zoning that allows mixed uses, higher densities, and reduced requirements for infrastructure can facilitate better land use.
- *Promote quality over quantity in open space.* Make the space accessible and usable.

The Next Generation of Community Design

Designers of new communities must address the weaknesses of traditional neighborhood developments: the lack of market-proven building lots on culs-de-sac, less privacy in exchange for the greater public good, the public's negative perception of density, and the viability of commercial components. Many conventional developments are starting to integrate elements of the new urbanism into their plans without buying the whole package. Modified town centers are being planned at Summerlin, near Las Vegas, and Valencia, north of Los Angeles, both well-established, conventional master-planned communities. The Woodlands, outside Houston, is developing a traditional neighborhood residential village (see the accompanying case study).

Design elements such as street trees, front porches, narrower lots, and less prominent garages are all creeping into the plans of otherwise conventional suburban developments. The long-term trend will most likely lead to a refinement and evolution of the neotraditional form. This will appeal to the large market segment that likes the concept but questions some of its current failings.

Coving is one alternative design trend to watch. Most appropriate for lower densities, coving creates a parklike streetscape of meandering lanes with staggered setbacks and varying lot sizes. Development is determined by natural contours and other land features.

One major contribution of the new urbanism is that it has caused planners and developers to think about livability, social values, and community design rather than continue on the narrow path defined by engineers and zoning regulators. What livability will mean for future communities has yet to be determined, but it most likely will include elements from both neotraditional and conventional suburban plans, along with new concepts yet to be explored.

Notes

1. "Critiquing the New Urbanism: A Hard Look at the Design, Marketing, and Financial Realities," ULI 1998 Spring Council Forum, May 1, 1998, Denver, Colorado.

2. Robert Steuteville, "The Elements of a (Neo)Traditional Neighborhood," *New Urban News,* July/August 1996, p. 2.

3. "Critiquing the New Urbanism," May 1, 1998, Denver, Colorado.

4. Ibid.

Chapter 8

The Business of Master-Planned Communities

Ehud Mouchly, Pike Oliver, and Larry Netherton

The future of master-planned communities as a rational business investment is open to question. Master-planned communities typically require a tremendous capital commitment over an extended period of time—often a decade or more. Because master-planned communities epitomize large-scale change to the status quo, this immovable asset can be a large target of hostile activism.

Like all real estate, especially undeveloped land, master-planned communities are subject to the shifting legal and political interpretations of public and private interests and obligations. Generally, these changes have brought developers of master-planned communities greater uncertainty about regulations and increased financial obligations for community facilities and off-site improvements.

As an investment, a master-planned community is analogous to a zero-coupon junk bond, with little economic performance and financial return until late in the investment cycle. The long-term, "back-ended" nature of an investment in a master-planned community should command extraordinary returns when compared to other investments that typically offer more consistent returns over a shorter period of time.

Increased regulatory risk and uncertainty have become permanent features of master-planned communities.

The business of developing master-planned communities involves understanding and balancing several factors:

- Capital market demands and cyclical economics: Where does the money come from, how much does it cost, and how long will it stay?
- Market demand: What shall we build? If we build it, will they come? What will they pay?
- Public policy and public opinion trends: How long will it take, who pays, and how secure is the plan?
- Demographic and social changes: What will it look like?
- Technological changes: How will it be served?

These considerations are not new. They have shaped land use patterns throughout history. Their expression in the 1930s gave form to the first greenbelt communities.

The future holds several possibilities:

- The master-planned community may give way to a less ambitious form of community development, with projects ranging from 500 to 5,000 acres;
- The business of the master-planned community itself may be restructured so as to shift some of the regulatory and financial uncertainties into the public and/or not-for-profit sectors;
- Master-planned communities may be feasible only under rare combinations of locations that offer less regulation as well as regional economic growth strong enough to provide sufficient absorption and the resulting revenues necessary to offset the large initial investment.

It is unlikely that all forms of master-planned communities will disappear entirely. Master-planned communities are, after all, the result of an evolutionary process that endeavors to capture a profit premium through providing communities instead of merely creating subdivisions.

Capital and Returns

Capital Markets and Land Investment

In 1879, Henry George proposed a land tax that would attain utopian goals for land use, including the containment of sprawl, by taxing land at rates disproportionate to improvements. One of the philosophical underpinnings of the tax was the idea that land value stems from population growth and community improvements rather than individual initiative.

The land tax has long been disregarded, but in a sense, it echoes faintly in investment in a master-planned community. An increasing proportion of the returns that once accrued to the landowner or the developer are siphoned off to finance community interests, such as off-site infrastructure, schools, and environmental preservation. Indirectly, the potential profit in a master-planned community may be further reduced by community demands for lower densities, affordable housing, or other modifications.

As community interests command more of the traditional profit, less is available to the investor. And as the return decreases, master-planned communities will be less attractive to long-term capital. To the extent that returns are even more unpredictable, the economic profile of master-planned communities will begin to diverge from other real estate products. This divergence is counter to other real estate finance trends. The key elements of standardization, uniformity, quantifiable risk, and liquidity are not present in current or foreseeable master-planned communities.

As they bring master-planned communities to the market in the next century, developers will be faced with several paradoxes:

Paradox 1: Capital markets will be broader, but fewer sources of financing will be available.

An emerging global economy will create increasingly efficient capital markets. Money will more rapidly seek out a wider range of economic opportunities, funds will rapidly shift from one asset class to another, sometimes in a matter of seconds, and a wide range of financing vehicles will be available to channel those funds.

Financial engineering has become a refined art. Many vehicles have been created to bring increasingly diverse sources of capital to real estate. Permutations on mortgage-backed securities, new forms of legal vehicles, and increasingly varied domestic and offshore sources have enabled the transformation of financing for income properties and residential mortgages into investments that can be securitized.

These changes have several common features, however: 1) they address huge markets; 2) the underlying assets can be grouped according to product type, geography, and underwriting

Visitacion Associates

The San Bruno Mountain habitat conservation plan provides for conservation of ecosystems and wildlife while integrating 600 acres of homesites on 3,300 acres near San Francisco. Illustrative of the trend in land use regulation, the plan requires a collaborative planning process involving the landowners and developer, and city, county, state, and federal agencies.

characteristics; 3) standardized documentation, procedures, and even institutions can be created around the financial profiles; and 4) financing instruments can be tailored to conform to common dimensions of the capital market. Much of real estate has become a fungible product.

The enabling factors in real estate investment are expectations of return, perceived risk, and time. Real estate financing instruments can be described or quantified in all three dimensions, so that third-party investors, removed from the underlying assets and often unable to under-

stand their economics, can examine the offered package and determine wheher it fits their portfolio. The performance of the assets can be continuously monitored and the instruments traded as appropriate.

Developers of master-planned communities, however, are becoming a nonentity in the capital markets. There is no consistent source of financing for master-planned communities, the size of the overall market for master-planned communities is not large enough to command widespread attention, the nature of the business is not understood, and master-planned communities usually attract attention only when too much capital and too few opportunities are available elsewhere. Each master-planned community is usually individually financed, and few opportunities exist to spread risk by access to secondary markets.

Moreover, traditional financing sources have withdrawn. Publicly traded corporations, especially transportation and resource companies, have withdrawn to core businesses. Local financial institutions, such as savings and loans, are gone. Only major landowners remain, and, if they are starting raw without a history of cash flow and market performance, problems with financing are formidable.

Paradox 2: Master-planned communities will face increasing levels of risk but offer lower rates of return.

Investors expect to be compensated for perceived risk. Historically, the achieved rates of return on successful master-planned communities have ranged from negative to 20 or 25 percent. Some investors would assert that the returns have been inadequate to compensate for the perceived risks.

Traditionally, the risks have been those confined to the business plan, and success has rested on the optimal mixing and phasing of land uses. The business plan began with market forecasts and the balancing of capital improvements against reasonable expectations of cash flow. Perceived risk was based on uncertainties of costs and revenues, and the absorption rate of land parcels. But these factors could be measured, if not mitigated, depending on the skill and experience of the developer.

Increasingly, however, the developer must face four new factors:

Upfront investment is increasing. Developing master-planned communities is not getting any easier or cheaper.

The first barrier is entitlements. The cost can run into millions of dollars for a typical master-planned community in most West Coast or East Coast markets. These funds are at risk because the entitlement process can—and probably will —be stopped or delayed at any point for any rational or capricious reason. Community affairs, public relations, or litigation constitute significant cost items in the predevelopment budget. Enormous amounts of money are committed before there is a hint of even a return of capital,

much less a return on investment. Public finance deficits and philosophies of "self-financing growth" or "development must pay for itself" add to the burden.

Expectations for returns are increasing. The returns demanded to offset the perceived risk are increasing. Typical expectations must be higher than those from stabilized income properties where risk and return are more easily quantified and understood. They probably should be higher than the stock market, where an investor has the advantage of immediate liquidity.

The survivability of cycles is more challenging. The average life cycle of a full-service master-planned community is 15 to 20 years, encompassing a full cycle for an economic enterprise: initial capitalization, development, operations, and orderly disposition.

Master-planned communities as business enterprises must wait years before it is certain that the product will even be introduced. And once the product is available, inventory control or phasing requires the economic equivalent of a capital investment, rather than an operating cost. In addition to normal supply and demand, the product is vulnerable to interest rates, which cannot be predicted during the shelf life of the inventory and are seldom in sync with other cycles for the master-planned community.

Added to this problem is immobility. The venture is tied to local economic growth, and it is vulnerable to regional recessions derived from shifts in the local economic base, sector-specific changes in the national economy, or local dependence on a single employer.

Risk is increasing. Increased risk has weakened the utility of the traditional business plan for the manager of a master-planned community.

The business plan for a typical master-planned community reflects traditional concepts of risk, factors that can be controlled or reasonably quantified. Using the definition of risk as the degree of deviation from an expected outcome, it is relatively easy to determine the sensitivities surrounding changes in market and other measurable factors.

The dimensions of entitlement risk for a master-planned community, however, have far outstripped the boundaries of the business plan. A land project can be delayed or can fail for factors beyond anyone's reasonable ability to predict, much less control. The degrees of reasonable variation are so huge that sensitivities are sometimes rendered meaningless.

Uncontrolled catastrophic variables, such as environmental and political risks, can wipe out an entire project. These variables are totally unpredictable, and they bear no correlation to rational variables within the economic model. They are increasing in frequency and have an obvious impact on local and investment decision making.

Paradox 3: Land is expensive but worth little.

The experience of the past two decades has laid the groundwork for a reevaluation of the concepts of land valuation. The traditional appraisal concept of comparable sales method of valuation is nearly dead. The experience of the late 1980s proved that comparable sales are a chronicle of the activities of "greater fools."

The idea of land residuals derived from discounted cash flows has become dominant, especially with the ease of spreadsheet analysis. This procedure has the advantage of putting an apparently finer point on land values, as future revenue streams and development costs can be quantified with relative ease.

Over the past cycles, a new realism has emerged—the idea of "negative residual land values." It arose when the estimates of future revenue streams of an existing project would not justify its replacement cost, and the resulting residual land value became a negative number.

The reasons for a negative residual land value are twofold. First, the costs of development get out of control as a result of entitlement issues, site-specific conditions, or carrying costs. Second, changes in the revenue stream arise from structural economic and demographic changes.

Negative residual land value suggests that at a specific point, *no* land use would justify development. The interesting aspect is that negative land residuals are often applied to properties that were in the mainstream market during the previous cycle and had been put into play by knowledgeable developers and investors. Lands considered valuable at one point in the cycle may be deemed worthless in the next. Such short-term dramatic swings suggest the concept of land as a commodity. But this kind of valuation is contrary to the long-term capital commitments required of a master-planned community.

Thus, as master-planned communities enter the next century, they will face capital markets where land can be valued highly in one phase of the cycle and negatively valued in the next. This short-term view of a long-term asset will obviously affect the ability of the master-planned community to survive business cycles and secure financing for ongoing operations.

Paradox 4: Master-planned communities demand a lengthy commitment, but capital will be impatient.

From the earliest master-planned communities, it has been well documented that their long life spans are their major vulnerability. At the same time, capital is more impatient. As financial markets increase in efficiency, funds will seek out incrementally higher returns and move rapidly from one class of assets to another. Separation between the motivation for investment and the objectives of the master-planned community will be greater. The last vestiges of other reasons to invest in a master-planned community—ego, social good, commitment to a philosophy or concept—will disappear. The developer of a master-planned community will have "hot-money" partners willing to jump ship at the earliest opportunity for alternative, short-term returns.

Master-Planned Communities and The New Economic Realities

Although windfalls from the development of master-planned communities are still quite possible, there is little likelihood that global structural changes in the economy will embrace an investment that is so contrarian, unique, and obtuse compared to all other opportunities.

To attract money, developers of master-planned communities or their financial intermediaries must begin to find ways to adapt to the new world. They face several challenges.

Develop new ways to package financing.

Opportunities will always exist to craft local, custom ventures with landowners. They will not be enough, however, because:
- Descendants of original landowners often want to cash out immediately.
- Some of the new institutional owners want speculative liquidity and do not want to engage in development.
- Funds for predevelopment and due diligence work are entirely at risk. Once small and manageable within a developer's budget, their magnitude is increasing.

Rarely can a master-planned community be financed by a single source. It must be broken

into financing pieces that conform to the demands and appetite of the players in the capital
market. One opportunity is to address timing.
Much as permanent financing replaces construction loans, the different phases of a master-
planned community can be broken down according to perceived risk. It is conceivable that an
entire succession of financing packages could
be required, matched to perceived risks and
anticipated investment horizons.

Acquisition financing could be a permanent,
high-risk "tranche" or an interim phase. Predevelopment financing could be added on top and
then replaced by entitlement financing, which
could be followed by land development financing. Development phases would be self-sufficient,
almost self-contained minicommunities, so as
to shorten the investment cycles to four to
seven years.

This practice has been common when landowners carry property through an option period,
with new equity funded only when major risks
are removed. Institutions now commonly fund
site improvements if some evidence exists of
significantly reduced entitlement risk. The next
step is to institutionalize the process, so that
portfolio managers, rather than local sources or
partners, can easily invest in master-planned
communities and trade the underlying paper.

To make staged financing more widely available, sophisticated and consistent breakdowns
of the individual stages must be described and
standardized documentation attached to each.
This process, in turn, requires a massive effort
to quantify risk and educate passive investors
about the significant differences between investments in land and land development versus investment in traditional income projects
or homebuilding.

Develop new ways to quantify risk.

Assured financing will be found if and when
financing for a master-planned community follows the evolutionary path that other forms of
real estate took toward the secondary markets.
The most difficult step will be to reach consensus on universal measures of risk. Too few
master-planned communities are in the market
at any one time to obtain the benefits of risk
management through diversification of a portfolio. Single-entity financing will demand more
specificity and less generalization in underwriting and will not benefit from secondary
or securitized financing.

At the same time, the nature of the risks
themselves cannot be easily generalized. No
standard way exists to effectively quantify—
for purposes of financial markets—the risks of

denial or reduced approvals that will make the project infeasible.

Singular, catastrophic risks to a master-planned community can be environmental, political, or economic:

- Endangered species lists, tighter definitions of wetlands, broader definitions of habitat.
- Unforeseen changes in elected councils, boards, or commissions; shifts in position by elected officials; the emergence of hostile community action groups.
- Withdrawal of capital, loss of major employers, collapse of market values.

In hindsight, such risks are usually foreseeable and controllable. In reality, they are encountered time after time and always deemed manageable by the victims, who often are sophisticated principals. As a class, they represent a major barrier to financing master-planned communities, because they cannot be statistically controlled and they require intensive on-site involvement to understand.

Develop common ways to describe risk.

If risk cannot be easily quantified, then at least it can be described. Financing sources have little patience or need for understanding details of a local entitlement saga. Certain common elements of the entitlement process, however, can be better communicated and understood.

Entitlement processing. Part of the problem stems from the lack of a common language to describe geographically disparate entitlement terminology. The significance of unfamiliar local terms can often be discounted or overlooked during underwriting.

Detailed entitlement budgeting. Development regulations are fast becoming one of the most costly line items in the predevelopment budget, and also one of the riskiest. Pressure from the addition of exactions, proffers, impact fees, and other processing costs to the cost of for-sale housing and income properties is well known at the local level. Less documented are the costs of delays in processing and the higher returns demanded by capital for assuming processing risk.

Separation from for-sale housing and income property analysis. It is necessary to separate land development from other forms of real estate investment in vertical construction. Although the analytical tools are sometimes similar, the concepts are different. The variables in a land development project are more likely to be determined through local negotiations. Uncorrelated variables can be assumed for timing, capital commitments, staged liquidations, development alternatives, and price points. Unlike an income project, no market analogies exist to determine occupancy and rent-up rates.

Anticipate the policy, social, and technological changes that will affect master-planned communities.

The risks associated with the long-term exposure of capital in a master-planned community can be mitigated by superior positioning of the product. The master-planned community of the late 20th and early 21st centuries, however, will address smaller market segments. Real growth of personal income, changing demographics, greater regulatory risks, and changing technology will require the developer of a master-planned community to change the product to meet the market and to alter the process through which that product is brought to market.

Social and Technological Change

Public Policy

Ancient real estate textbooks define real estate as a "bundle of rights" and define the income to land by the "quality and quantity" of rights found in the property.

More than any other form of real estate, master-planned communities are on the leading edge of the reallocation of the quality and quantity of rights associated with land. Several major trends are discernible:

- Preemption of local governmental land use by state and national regulations, especially in environmental matters;
- A dramatic increase in the number of regulatory issues and a corresponding decrease in absolute property "rights";
- An increase in the number and type of participants in the process through which land use entitlements are obtained; and
- Evolving societal values that support these trends.

The basis for more land use regulation

It is difficult to accept the notion that a landowner with significant property rights and assets at stake should be dependent on the whims of uninvolved third parties having no responsibility

The Developer as Political Campaigner

A developer should view rezoning by initiative or referendum as the final roll of the dice. Not only is it expensive to mount a campaign, but also the loss of an election provides decision-making bodies with all the ammunition they need to turn down any future rezoning simply because "the people have spoken." In certain situations, however, an election is a viable alternative for a developer seeking to rezone a parcel of land.

While every jurisdiction and circumstance are different, some key elements must exist for a developer to consider rezoning through the ballot box. The risk and expense of running such a campaign make it imperative that certain conditions exist:

- The existing zoning is marginally economical.
- Opposition is limited.
- A significant "carrot" can be dangled before the jurisdiction and the voters.

In the end, the developer must create a win/win situation.

Koelbel and Company of Denver, Colorado, was extensively involved over seven years in modifying the zoning for a 550-acre parcel of land. Ultimately, a large portion of the parcel was rezoned from one dwelling unit per two and one-half acres to one per acre, a significant increase in density. Residents from the surrounding area immediately placed an initiative on the ballot to reject the new zoning, which would have prevented the firm from developing the site at the newly approved density and precluded any meaningful development. At this point, the firm decided to take its case directly to the electorate.

Rather than merely mounting a defensive strategy aimed at reaching a compromise or defeating the NIMBY-based initiative, a developer should respond proactively. Koelbel's response was to develop

a creative new master plan that would better appeal to voters yet allow enough density to be profitable. The test of the ballot box is so crucial and so risky that rethinking the project, even though it might mean going beyond the restrictions of permissible zoning, is paramount.

The provision of a carrot that appeals to a broad base of voters is crucial to gain support for the project and ensure victory. The carrot used most often is dedication of environmentally sensitive open space that is accessible to the entire public. Amenities such as private golf courses or swimming pools may be appealing for the overall plan, but to appeal to a broad constituency, the developer should consider providing a public benefit that is open to all and that voters otherwise would not receive. Koelbel was able to provide enough dedicated open space in a new master plan for

for the financial or social impacts that result from their participation in decision making. Long-standing principles of the free enterprise system appear irrelevant, however, given the magnitude of the trend toward increased participation and greater land use regulation.

It is not hard to understand how this situation came about. Population has continued to increase at a far faster rate than the inventory of developable land. Economic and technological factors have led to dramatic increases in the proportion of households that can afford lower-density development. More people able to compete for less land inevitably creates conflict. With widely varying degrees of success, this conflict has been institutionalized in a rapidly expanding body of environmental and land use regulations, and increasingly complex development requirements for planning and processing.

The original premise of the new town and later the master-planned community suggested some expediency in the entitlement process.

The master-planned community was an opportunity to engage in true comprehensive planning, achieve economies of scale, and ensure that all elements of the community were technically balanced. The empirical benefit of a superior land project has long since been lost to the political outrage arising from off-site impacts and resistance to growth.

The reality is that the formal regulatory process is almost irrelevant. The average master-planned community is of such a size that its approval has become a political issue, and the regulatory process has become merely a device to ensure avenues exist to deny or delay the project.

The master-planned community lies at the intersection of public and private interests. The first tier of support or opposition is from those who will be directly affected by the development through traffic, taxes, crowding, or direct environmental impacts. A second tier lies with those who are not directly affected but who have a local

the site that voters defeated the initiative, thereby approving the new master plan.

A developer who decides to use the ballot box to change existing zoning must address some key issues. Four ingredients are necessary to win an election:
1. A professional campaign team;
2. A campaign strategy oriented toward grass-roots support;
3. Focus, discipline, resources, organization, and political support from voters as well as elected officials; and
4. Fragmented, disorganized, and underfunded opposition.

A professional campaign team should include a campaign manager, a pollster, an advertising and public relations firm, graphic designers, legal advisers, in-house support staff, and a facilitator or expediter to keep the project moving. The campaign manager's responsibility is to devise the strategy and to monitor polling and marketing for the campaign. Hiring a good pollster to measure community support is crucial. The facilitator should take care of the day-to-day details of running an election campaign.

The campaign strategy must be based on information about voters' sentiments from extensive surveys and polls. The strategy must be clearly defined and closely followed. The campaign that stays on course has a better chance of winning than a campaign that allows itself to be defined by the opposition. The message should be simple and continuously repeated throughout the campaign, building to a peak just before the election.

To communicate effectively with voters, the team should employ strategic public relations based on the results of polling, the characteristics of the jurisdiction, and the type of project to be developed. The developer should work with the campaign team to devise a direct mail campaign.

Grass roots are the key to local elections, and the public relations campaign and advertising must be oriented toward the voters. The developer should meet with community groups, speak before homeowners associations, walk through the community, share morning coffee with citizens, and speak with residents at every opportunity. Gaining the support of elected officials lends more legitimacy to the proposal.

Creating the "fear of loss" among voters is key to the strategy. The developer's goal is to convince voters that approval of the new development will gain them something they otherwise would not get—that the proposed project includes positive benefits that future development might not.

Walter A. Koelbel, Jr.
President, Koelbel and Company
Denver, Colorado

---

vision of how the urban area should develop. A third tier lies with those having private agendas who generate irrational and capricious opposition. Finally, some are more concerned with specific issues common to a wide geographic area, such as endangered species.

These four groups and others will command more power during the development process. People are newly aware that the system can be influenced by local participation, and new communications technology makes it far easier to mobilize the public and monitor how elected representatives vote. And the deeply ingrained concern about quality of life can be invoked by almost any development proposal.

The origins of land use regulation

Managers of master-planned communities must recognize that much of their projects' destiny will rest in regulatory arenas far away from the local community. While the ability to track regulatory issues decreases sharply with distance, the impact of a new federally listed endangered species or changes to wetlands regulations can be just as profound as a local school or water issue.

The federal level. Land development is no longer the concern of only local government. Federal legislation has addressed specific environmental issues that in turn have become effective levers for influencing virtually all aspects of a proposed master-planned community. Now the developer of a master-planned community must devote considerable resources not only to emerging national issues, but also to the considerable and varied interpretations given existing laws through regional regulatory agencies.

The state level. In a sense, cities in major metropolitan areas have abdicated their responsibility to address growth. Their inability to effectively work across a patchwork of 19th century local governmental entities and a purely reactionary response to growth have resulted in enabling legislation for regional governmental agencies and for statewide growth management.

And as state and regional entities become more engaged in land use issues, the developer of a master-planned community will be faced with more stops to make on the road toward entitlement.

The local level. While ceding power in certain areas to higher levels of government, local land use regulation will continue to grow stronger. Few cities can afford to pay their own way, and, as a result, more efforts will try to force growth to pay for itself. Cities will do so by increasing fiscal revenues through development exactions and by decreasing expenditures for municipal services through tighter control of land uses with perceived attendant costs.

The nature of future land use regulation

The new nature of land use regulation is the transfer of decision-making responsibility from the private to the public sector. Current trends suggest that future regulatory control will center on several key areas.

Growth management. "Urban limit lines" have emerged in California and other western states, particularly Oregon, as a principal device for the control of sprawl. In this model, growth is directed toward infill parcels in urban areas.

In most cases, such urban limit lines discourage master-planned communities, as most large contiguous landholdings that could accommodate master-planned communities are outside urban limit lines. To the extent that owners of these rural parcels will be driven to sell at the highest and best use under existing land use regulations, opportunities for future master-planned communities will disappear. If these lands are converted to the lowest parcel size allowable under existing zoning (say, five- to 20-acre estates), assembly will be infeasible.

Environmental issues. Nearly 30 years of increasing environmental awareness and sensitivity have resulted in increasing command and control at all levels of government. Federal agencies, in particular the U.S. Fish and Wildlife Service and the Army Corps of Engineers, are directly involved in the review of development plans for master-planned communities.

Most of the regulation has been reactive to specific projects, and long-term permitting processes have been difficult to engage.[1]

Financing infrastructure. The high cost and front-end burden of infrastructure has always been a problem for the developer of a master-planned community. More recently, master-planned communities have been required to shoulder an increasing share of off-site and regional facilities, such as interchanges, sewage treatment plants, and major stormwater structures. When the costs of such community facilities, along with schools and parks, are passed on to homebuilders and homebuyers, they will further reduce revenues from land sales.

Various special district financing devices have been created to provide these community facilities,[2] but they usually represent a shift in the timing of the payment for the facilities and the cost remains attached to the property within the master-planned community.

In the final analysis, infrastructure is not free. Somewhere between the local tax base and the private developer, the burden must be borne. The debate will focus on who will pay the costs of growth and when. And as long as the question is unresolved, the politically expedient solution will be to force more of the burden back to the master-planned community, thus further reducing the residual land value.

The process of future land use regulation

The notion of participatory planning of the 1960s found its place in the development process of the 1980s. The underlying theory is local determination of local events, even though there is no direct investment in the issue other than a political position. A single individual, armed with a full arsenal of regulatory devices and carried forward by politicians anxious to serve existing and future constituents, has the power to stop major development.

The developer of a master-planned community needs to anticipate social changes that will give rise to greater public participation in the planning process. Among them are a perception that the quality of life is adversely affected by growth and the trend to empower community groups to determine the shape of their own neighborhoods. The use of initiatives and referendums gives increasing frequency to "ballot box planning," with isolated issues being decided out of context of the overall regional picture.

On the other side are often groups in favor of growth, and with similar organization and lobbying tactics, they can be effective proponents of projects. The business plan for a master-planned community must include surveys of the community's attitude, efforts to identify issues, and grass-roots communications and organization.

Social Changes

Development managers of master-planned communities face a difficult problem. They must create a product—at enormous capital cost—to meet a prospective demand over a period of 15 to 20 years of demographic and social change. Unlike the homebuilder, who has considerable flexibility to meet consumers' tastes and needs, the developer of a master-planned community is locked into overall density, off-site commitments, and planning concepts.

Predictable change

The statistical elements of demand are known: the baby boom, followed by the baby bust, followed by the baby boomlet. But the link between these elements and master-planned communities is local. A mobile society and differing regional economic strength make master-planned communities more dependent on local job growth, income, regional patterns of growth, and other usual factors.

The size of the traditional market for a master-planned community will shrink. The size of the traditional homebuying cohort in the next two decades will shrink considerably as a percentage of population, compared with the group that entered the market in the 1970s and 1980s. Depending on housing choices available and local dynamics, developers of master-planned communities may have to broaden their product mix to maintain market share.

Income available for housing will be redistributed. Levels of income determine market position, amount of discretionary community features, and ultimately the feasibility of master-planned communities. Very large segments of the population must reside in the middle and upper-middle brackets to support the prices and sales rates necessary for a profitable traditional master-planned community.

Several kinds of redistribution will affect housing purchases. Household income will be more volatile as the employment base shifts to a more fluid workforce. Discontinuous employment and job mobility may reduce the percentage of overall household expenditures on housing. Finally, inherited wealth could make more capital available for housing downpayments.

Household composition will change. The suburban market of the postwar years was oriented toward the single-family house purchased by a single wage earner with children. In the 1990 census, 30 percent of all households consisted of two wage earners, and 12 percent were single-parent households.

A major advantage of the master-planned community is its ability to address, through site planning and product mix, those facilities and conveniences to assist households that have less time and fewer connections to accomplish ordinary chores and responsibilities.

Market diversity will increase. The diversity of master-planned communities has increased over the past two decades, but the economic characteristics of households residing in master-planned communities have remained about the same. While ethnic diversity brings different storefronts and sometimes different housing types, the impact on decisions faced by the developer of a master-planned community is relatively minor.

Speculative change

Part of the market share for master-planned communities will be determined by forces that can be measured today but could veer off current trends over the next 25 years.

Regional economic growth. Local real estate cycles are extremely pronounced, with very large capital investments made on the basis of assumed stability and growth. Such stability is illusory in the current global economy, where major segments of business are moved off shore, combined, relocated, or eliminated. Based on events of the past two decades, it seems foolish to assume stability in banking, communications, manufacturing, and services. Nevertheless, real estate decisions have been made on the basis of such stability.

Job distribution. Few central cities have been able to retain and enjoy the increase in regional employment. The move of back-office operations and even headquarters facilities to suburban areas has redefined employment patterns and the resulting commuting time demands on transportation systems.

Some large master-planned communities have been able to capture some of this job growth, and others have benefited by locating near it. In some cases, issues of the balance between jobs and housing and affordable housing arise as the result of perceived imbalances in planning for a master-planned community.

The potential location of future master-planned communities may be an issue. Each urban region is distinctive, but in some areas the extent of outward growth has reached a limit imposed by growth management, reasonable commuting patterns, or physical resources.

Income levels and housing budgets. Aside from issues of redistribution of income and potential market segments, master-planned communities will have to face the possibility of stagnant disposable income. Private sector restructuring and taxation policies at all levels of government could erode the amount of funds available for housing. If the proportion of move-up housing in master-planned communities drops significantly or people are unable to pay the price of a typical house in a master-planned community, the impact will eventually be felt on land residuals at the point of sale, eventually on land residuals at the point of acquisition.

Unpredictable change

A case can be made that suburbs exist because they have been perceived as more desirable than the city. The earliest commuter suburbs offered land, single-family housing, less crime, better schools, and many other characteristics deemed desirable for family life. These same qualities have been embodied in successive waves of suburban development, ending with today's master-planned communities.

Now, however, two things have happened. Master-planned communities have not proved immune from urban problems, and the value structure of suburbia is being seriously questioned.

The developer of a master-planned community is in the education business. The reputation of schools has been a historical draw of households to the suburbs, and master-planned communities traditionally have exploited the top of the market. Many master-planned communities have volunteered or been forced to play a major role in the provision of school facilities and even programs.

The question for the future is how the developer of a master-planned community can provide the impetus for a quality school system and at the same time negotiate an equitable funding system, all in the context of complex local, state and federal initiatives.

The issue of crime is different. No longer confined to the inner city, crime is now an everyday part of life in suburbia and the master-planned community. The obvious opportunity for the manager of a master-planned community is to increase sensitivity to security in planning a project without turning areas of the project into fortresses. Other areas, such as the conditions that give rise to neighborhood stability, are more subtle and unresearched, and are probably beyond the developer's immediate tools.

Technology

The rate of change

The issue of technological change and master-planned communities is seductive. The rate of change over the past two decades has been enormous. In general, the impact of faster and cheaper transportation and communication will lead to changes in the ways that residents of master-planned communities work and shop. The most frequently invoked images of this future usually involve bicycles, coffee kiosks, and fiber-optic and cellular technology.

The most significant impact on master-planned communities will be indirect, however. How retailers and employers use new technologies will determine the behavior of residents of master-planned communities. The developer will sell land to the retailer but does not have the expertise or the position to dictate how much of the retailer's business will be in store. Work patterns and employment practices will continue in flux, and it will be up to the employer to determine working hours and work sites. Leisure activities will be more varied, but the income-producing opportunities will be provided by real estate specialists other than the developer.

Areas of change

The most immediate impact of technological change will probably affect the individual house and the workplace. Redefinition of spaces, wiring for communications, lighting and other "smart" household and office features, and energy-saving devices are all within the builder's sphere.

The next level of impact is the infrastructure that will be necessary to deliver services to the household, with the most immediate the wiring to deliver various forms of services: power, telephone, television, Internet, fax, and so on. It is impossible to bet on any specific technology. It is perhaps easiest to imagine a large buried conduit through which the wire du jour can be frequently rethreaded and plugged in. The developer of a master-planned community should think less in terms of the specific hardware and more about how the installation and maintenance can be negotiated with the service providers, especially in light of deregulation.

Amended ordinances in Yardley, Pennsylvania, allowed developers of Farmview flexibility in site design in return for preservation of substantial farmland, resulting in a reduction in street and utility costs and an advantage in marketing.

The longest-term and most significant level of technological change is transportation. No other force has had a greater long-term impact on urban land use and the master-planned community, and few others have such a long cycle. Moreover, the issue is the most troublesome for the developer of a master-planned community. Public opinion and the planning staff's predispositions often require setasides or specific infrastructure for transportation technologies that may not arrive for decades.

The negotiating problem has no specific solutions beyond an enlightened constituency. As congestion of existing transportation corridors increases, however, so will demands on the developer of a master-planned community to preserve those corridors for those who arrived first.

Conclusion

Master-planned communities have always held the promise of a better life. Whether idealism or marketing hype, the thread is always there, and to varying degrees master-planned communities have delivered. The key components are singular vision and decision making, private capitalization, and unifying components that extend beyond the individual house.

Some master-planned communities may continue to be developed in their traditional form well into the 21st century. Such projects will be located in extraordinarily high-growth, limited-supply areas, and they will be favored by extremely patient financial sponsors.

Other master-planned communities that compete for funds in the open market, however, must find ways to restructure their financing to conform to the risk/return profiles of alternate investment opportunities. In a broader context, the development, regulatory, and financial communities must understand the challenges and changes necessary for this real estate product to continue as a viable component of the urban fabric. As never before, all participants in the land use process must be prepared to master the qualities of understanding, cooperation, compromise, and patience if this unique form of land use is to continue to serve the needs of the market.

Notes

1. The problem has been recognized, but solutions are still far in the future. The effectiveness of cutting-edge concepts like California's Natural Communities Conservation Program has yet to be proved.

2. "Special district" is a generic term for various forms of infrastructure debt financing, where users or subsequent developers pay the debt service for the debt instruments, for example, assessment districts, community facilities districts, land improvement districts, municipal utility districts, and metropolitan districts.

Case Studies

The Woodlands

The Woodlands, Texas
The Woodlands Corporation

The Woodlands is an example of a large-scale master-planned community with a conventional plan derived from the concept of new towns in the 1960s. It provides a complete living and working environment, drawing both residents and businesses from a national market. The Woodlands's developers have striven to create excellence in every facet of the community, concentrating on developing a superior quality of life through social infrastructure, comprehensive governance, and physical planning.

Opened in 1974, the Woodlands is situated on a densely wooded 25,000-acre site in Montgomery County, Texas, 27 miles north of downtown Houston. The project was developed by the Woodlands Corporation (TWC), a subsidiary of the Mitchell Energy & Development Corporation founded by George P. Mitchell.

Since its inception, the Woodlands's planners have paid careful attention to the natural environment, with an emphasis on preserving the natural vegetation. Approximately 25 percent of the acreage will be retained in forest preserves, parks, golf courses, and lakes. Stringent design controls encourage the preservation and restoration of native vegetation along drainage courses and roadways, and in residential and commercial areas. The plan consists of seven residential villages, commercial and institutional districts, and an extensive open-space network. The community also features an open-air performing arts pavilion, regional mall, hospital, community college, and university center for undergraduate and graduate studies.

Area Description

The Woodlands abuts I-45, the principal north/south expressway connecting Houston and Dallas. When the Woodlands opened, conventional scattered-site suburban development was already occurring all along the I-45 corridor north of Houston, and the area has continued to grow at a strong rate. By 2000, 1 million people are expected to live within 20 miles of the Woodlands Town Center. To accommodate this population, TWC is developing the Town Center and surrounding business districts not only as a downtown for the community but also as the major employment, commercial, entertainment, and cultural center for the entire north corridor of the Houston metropolitan area.

Project History

In the late 1950s, George Mitchell, the Woodlands's founder, became interested in the concept of new towns as used in Irvine Ranch, California, Columbia, Maryland, and Reston, Virginia. New towns called for a mix of housing in all price ranges, employment centers, public facilities such as schools, parks, shopping, libraries, and health services, and other amenities. Mitchell decided that the Houston metropolitan area, with its dynamic growth, needed such a place.

On May 11, 1964, Mitchell acquired 49,000 acres in Montgomery County from the Grogan-Cochran Lumber Company, including nearly 3,000 acres that were to become part of the Woodlands. It took Mitchell another 11 years and 300 transactions to assemble the 19,000 acres that made up the Woodlands site in 1975. Through an additional 200 transactions, Mitchell expanded the Woodlands to more than 25,000 acres, an area one and one-half times the size of New York City's Manhattan.

While acquiring land, Mitchell commissioned studies on how to develop the property and still protect the ecological integrity of the forest. He met with noted architects, engineers, hydrologists, ecologists, and urban planners and traveled extensively to study the best features of both new towns and older cities. In 1970, Mitchell selected Gladstone Associates as economic and marketing consultants, William L. Pereira Associates as master planning and design consultants, and Wallace McHarg Roberts and Todd as environmental planning consultants. Mitchell's wife Cynthia is credited with naming the Woodlands.

The Woodlands was one of 13 new towns nationwide to qualify for federal loan guarantees under Title VII of the Urban Growth and New Community Act of 1970, administered by the U.S. Department of Housing and Urban Development (HUD). In 1972, HUD issued $50 million in 7.1 percent New Community Debentures guarantees. This loan guarantee imposed burdensome reporting requirements on the development, requiring a large on-site staff and adding to development costs. The original $50 million HUD-guaranteed debentures were retired in 1992. As the only Title VII new town to succeed in making good its debentures as issued, the Woodlands demonstrated that it could manage to weather a sometimes inhospitable real estate

environment by adjusting the pace of development to fluctuations in the market.

Construction in the first village, Grogan's Mill, began in 1972 on 1,937 acres in the southern portion of the landholding just west of I-45. Heavy rains, three snowstorms, and remnants of a hurricane turned the construction site into a sea of mud, but work continued. Early development included a public elementary school, a golf course, a country club, an inn, a village center, and an information center. The first office building, One Timberloch Place, was occupied by Mitchell Development Corporation, forerunner of TWC. In January 1974, a decade after the first land purchase, the first residents moved to the Woodlands.

During the mid-1970s, the Arab oil embargo, high interest rates, and tight money kept the pace of development slow. In the late 1970s, however, the pace increased impressively, and in 1979, the Woodlands reached a population of

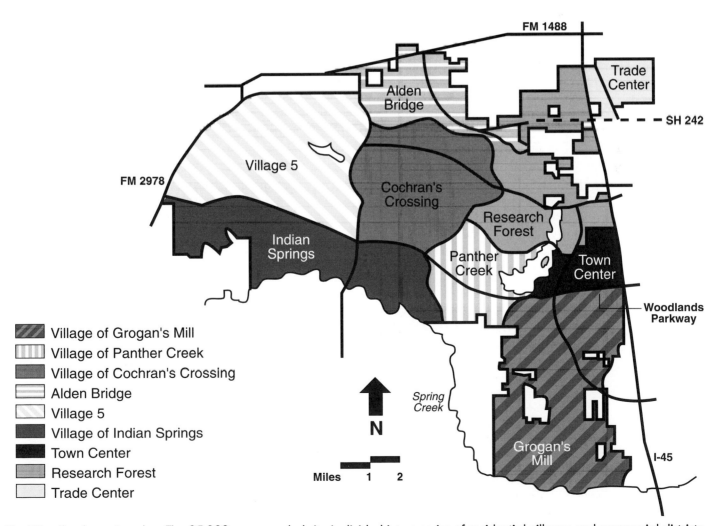

The Woodlands master plan. The 25,000-acre wooded site is divided into a series of residential villages and commercial districts.

approximately 8,000. Development was then started in the second village, Panther Creek, and a fire station, more stores, and offices were added.

The third village, Cochran's Crossing, began in 1981, and the first section of the Village of Indian Springs was initiated soon thereafter. In 1981, plans were announced for a regional shopping mall, Research Forest, and its key facility, the Houston Advanced Research Center (HARC). By 1983, construction had begun on the Woodlands Community Hospital (now Memorial Hospital–The Woodlands) and a second golf course, which would become the Tournament Players Course. That fall, the Panther Creek Village Center opened for business.

By late 1989, the population of the Woodlands reached 27,400. The multipurpose trail network had grown into a 53-mile system, and the development included 18 churches, eight schools, 144 miles of streets, and over 5 million square feet of commercial space.

The highlight of 1990 was the opening of the Cynthia Woods Mitchell Pavilion, a $10 million, 13,000-seat performing arts center, now the summer home of the Houston Symphony. Plans for the Town Center were announced in 1993. The Village of Alden Bridge and the Woodlands Mall opened in 1994. In 1995, Montgomery College, part of the North Harris Montgomery Community College District, opened its new facilities on a 100-acre campus in the Woodlands. Also in 1995, Tenneco Business Systems chose the Woodlands as the location of its world headquarters.

Since 1990, the Woodlands has ranked first every year in sales of new homes among new communities in the Houston region, with units currently priced from under $90,000 to over $1 million. Sales average 1,000 to 1,200 new homes per year. Based on the current pace of sales, the Woodlands will reach completion around 2030.

Master Planning and Design

For the most part, development in the Woodlands has held true to the general master-planning principles articulated for the community in the early 1970s. Each village incorporates a mix of housing products, but within villages, neighborhoods comprise a single type of housing. Neighborhoods are separated from one another by vegetated buffer zones. Access to most neighborhoods is through a single vehicular entrance. Residential streets are generally curvilinear, and culs-de-sac are highly valued.

The master plan for the community identifies the general location of major arterial roads and major utilities but little else. The Woodlands has required relatively few local regulatory approvals for land development as a result of its location in the Houston area, where land use regulations are minimal compared to other parts of the country. No local zoning regulations apply, giving TWC complete flexibility to determine land uses and densities. As a result, TWC is able to respond quickly and cost effectively to market changes while maintaining self-established standards for high quality.

Mistakes were made in planning and design of the first village center, Grogan's Mill Shopping Center. The original shopping center opened in 1974 but never reached its potential because of a market area that was too small, too much competition, and poor design. It lacked a large anchor grocery store, had poor access and visibility, and used a dated architectural style. Most retail tenant spaces were located inside the shopping mall component, an inefficient arrangement.

TWC is renewing and repositioning the center. The updated center will have a new 56,754-square-foot supermarket, better signage, and a new architectural style. Tenants will be configured in a conventional strip center, with freestanding pad sites on the perimeter. The Woodlands Information Center, originally located adjacent to the shopping center, has been relocated to a prominent site in the Town Center. The Shell Learning Center, which opened in 1996, now occupies a portion of the former mall structure linked to the Woodlands Executive Conference Center.

A modified neotraditional plan is being implemented for the first time in the Woodlands. In Alden Bridge, the newest village, the concept is a pedestrian-oriented neighborhood anchored by a village center near a village green, surrounded by housing for seniors, a daycare center, recreation facilities, civic facilities, multifamily housing, and cottages.

The 138-unit cottage neighborhood is reached via a single vehicular entrance. The cottages face curved, tree-lined streets with sidewalks; garages face either the street or rear alleys. Front-facing garages are set back ten feet from house facades. Alleys have a 30-foot-wide right-of-way with 12-foot-wide pavements bounded by rolled curbs; garage doors are set back at least 18 feet from the alley curb to allow for parking in the

An 80-mile system of paved multipurpose trails meanders through the community, linking parks, commercial areas, and residential enclaves.

The Woodlands Corporation

driveway, as garages are often used primarily for storage rather than parking in the Houston area. Interior lots are generally 46 by 110 feet when served by an alley and 60 by 110 feet when front loaded.

The 800-acre Town Center is envisioned as the downtown of the Woodlands and the commercial, entertainment, and cultural focal point for the entire north Houston/Montgomery County region. It is intended to be an exciting and productive place day and night, seven days a week. The Town Center will ultimately include 18 million square feet of office and commercial space supporting 40,000 employees. The mix of existing and planned land uses in the Town Center includes retail, office, service, cultural, entertainment, recreation, a convention center, hotels, and multifamily residential.

The ambience of the Town Center is characterized by ornamental streetlamps, sculptures, colorful awnings, banners, gardens, and fountains. Combined with traffic thoroughfares, a pedestrian pathway system, and light transit, these elements are intended to create a vibrant, state-of-the-art business and commerce center.

The Town Center currently contains a regional mall, a variety of freestanding restaurants and retail facilities, 1.5 million square feet of office space, a 17-screen movie theater, and an out-

door performing arts center. The Cynthia Woods Mitchell Pavilion, a 13,000-capacity outdoor amphitheater, is the cornerstone of the entertainment district in the Town Center.

The Woodlands Mall was developed by a partnership between Homart and TWC. The recently expanded center covers 1.2 million square feet with over 140 tenants, including five anchor stores. TWC set high architectural standards for the project to guarantee that it would enhance the community.

The Woodlands Waterway, a 1.25-mile-long landscaped water feature, which should be completed by early 2000, is planned to be a centerpiece of the Town Center. The Waterway is envisioned as a linear park lined with pathways, restaurants, and gardens for the office buildings, hotels, and entertainment areas along its course. Water taxis along the waterway will become part of the transportation options within the Town Center.

Express commuter bus service operated by the state transit agency runs between the Woodlands and downtown Houston. The bus stops at a 1,000-space park-and-ride lot in the southern part of the community. The fenced park-and-ride lot opened in the mid-1980s and has on-site security, a waiting room, restrooms, concessions, and an adjacent 200-space lot for private vanpools. A second 650-space park-and-ride lot opened in 1997 in the northern part of the community. TWC helped obtain public funds for improvements and provided the required local share of costs.

No public bus service operates within the community, and past proposals for such service have generated controversy. Many residents associate public transportation with urban problems and think that bus service is likely to bring crime and other problems to the community.

Recreational and Cultural Amenities

The Woodlands's extensive array of recreational and cultural amenities is intended to provide something for everyone. Amenities include a multipurpose pathway system, neighborhood and community parks, a county-operated activities center for seniors, a community association–operated recreation center, a private athletic center, a YMCA, a private country club, an executive conference center, and an outdoor performing arts center.

The pathway system is over 80 miles long. Grants from HUD provided initial funding for

the system. Pathways were originally unpaved, suitable only for hiking and horseback riding, but a decision was made early on to pave them. All pathways are eight feet wide and suitable for walking, jogging, in-line skating, biking, and use by electric golf cars. Many of the original pathways are not visible from roads or developed areas, and some problems with safety have occurred. Users are advised to take reasonable safety precautions. In general, however, residents highly value the pathway system, and it is an important marketing feature for the community.

The two major residential community associations own, operate, and maintain the park system. The parks include community swimming pools, playgrounds, playfields, picnic pavilions, tennis courts, and other recreational facilities. Lake Woodlands, a 200-acre manmade lake, is stocked for recreational fishing and can be used for sailing and other nonmotorized boating.

The South County Community Center serves as headquarters for the local YMCA and the Friendship Center, a United Way agency that provides services and activities for senior citizens. It was built by TWC and is now owned by Montgomery County.

A regional YMCA is located in the Village of Cochran's Crossing. TWC leases land to the Y

Four golf courses provide recreation as well as desirable settings for residential neighborhoods.

for $1.00 per year; it is funded through donations to a capital campaign and membership fees. The YMCA offers fitness programs, operates a child development center, and features a cardiovascular equipment room, an aerobics room, two gymnasiums, and swimming facilities.

The Woodlands Athletic Center, a private swim, tennis, and athletic club in the Village of Grogan's Mill, features Olympic-class swimming and diving facilities and has been the site for national and international competitions.

The Woodlands Country Club, a membership facility, is a for-profit adjunct business venture of TWC. The club was one of the first structures built in the Woodlands, sharing some facilities with the Woodlands Executive Conference Center and Resort. Facilities include a pool, exercise center, health spa, and tennis facilities. The club currently has 45 holes of golf, including the original 18-hole course and a newer 27-hole course designed by Arnold Palmer.

The Woodlands Executive Conference Center and Resort, operated by TWC as a for-profit venture, has repeatedly been voted one of the top ten such centers in the nation. More than 150,000 conferees attend annually. The resort includes 360 guest rooms and suites and over 60,000 square feet of meeting space, as well as its own 18-hole golf course.

The PGA Tournament Players Course is a public 18-hole course that is home to the annual Shell Houston Open. The tournament, televised nationally, has helped give the Woodlands national name recognition. TWC and the Houston Golf Association built the Texas Golf Hall of Fame, which opened in 1992 adjacent to the Tournament Players Club.

The $14 million Cynthia Woods Mitchell Pavilion, located in the Town Center, is a cultural focal point for the entire north Houston area. The amphitheater, which can accommodate 13,000 people, hosts Houston's major performing arts organizations and national tours.

Community Operations And Governance

The Woodlands's operations and governance are administered by a network of public and quasi-public entities. Municipal utility districts (MUDs) provide water, sewer, and drainage services to all homes and businesses in the Woodlands. MUDs, provided for by Texas law, have taxing

The Woodlands Executive Conference Center and Resort is part of a complex that includes the Woodlands Inn, an athletic center, a country club, and a village center.

authority. Montgomery County provides a basic level of police protection, emergency medical services, a branch library, and road maintenance. TWC-constructed roadways are built to county standards, and the county participates in the cost of major roadways and most installations of traffic signals.

Because the Woodlands is located in an unincorporated area, community associations serve as the de facto local level of government, providing a forum for residents' involvement in management of the community. Community associations are initially controlled and nurtured by the developer, then transferred to community control as development is completed. During this transition, associations evolve into representative bodies that are able to interact with other public bodies and serve as community forums. The first community association in the Woodlands was transferred to residents' control in 1992.

The Woodlands has five distinct but interrelated community associations representing both residents and businesses within the community. All community associations are nonprofit corporations. Each association has its own board of directors and holds monthly meetings. The boards have final authority for financial and policy issues. All residents in good standing who are at least 18 years of age are entitled to vote on the affairs brought before the associations.

The resident-based community associations fund fire protection and emergency medical and

119

The wetlands mitigation program designates areas along stream corridors to be protected as natural open space.

rescue services; contract for enhanced police protection; own, operate, and maintain community parks and trails; contract for residential trash collection; maintain street lights and the streetscape; and provide a place for storage of recreational vehicles. Through the residential design review committees, they enforce the covenants and review proposed changes to residential exteriors and lots. They also sponsor the Woodlands Watch, a volunteer, neighborhood-based program of fire, police, and medical education and support.

The associations are supported principally by annual property assessments, with rates established by the boards of directors during annual budget approval. The covenants create a permanent first lien on every piece of taxable property subject to the covenants and obligate each owner to pay the assessment. The associations also aggressively pursue, and have obtained, federal and state grants to construct many of the community facilities.

The associations contribute funds to the county government and contract with the sheriff's department to provide additional deputies beyond the normal level of service, who are assigned specifically to the Woodlands. This special branch of the sheriff's department provides 24-hour police

protection. Within the Town Center, augmented public safety services are provided by the Town Center Improvement District, a community association of business owners.

Safety and Security

A major contributor to residents' sense of safety and security within the community is the Woodlands Watch, an expanded neighborhood watch program sponsored by the resident associations in conjunction with the Woodlands fire department and the county sheriff's department. Going beyond basic crime prevention, the Woodlands Watch established an organized system for reporting suspicious activity to the police. It also offers education about fire prevention, fire safety, and medical emergencies. Neighborhood parties are held periodically to help residents get to know each other. The central theme of the program is concern for each resident and for the overall safety of the community.

In addition to the Woodlands Watch, many residents credit the single-entry neighborhoods and maze-like street patterns in the Woodlands with keeping crime rates low. None of the Woodlands's neighborhoods are currently gated, and the question of whether to gate all or portions of the community is a constant subject of debate. An increasing segment of the market appears to want gates, but the social division gating would enforce is not consistent with the strong community concept that the Woodlands was founded on. Individuals are permitted to gate their own homes if they choose, and several residents have done so. All homes are wired for security, and some are tied into local security monitoring services.

Before the opening of the regional mall, The Woodlands Corporation formed a team to study security initiatives to augment public safety services already provided by the state, county, and municipal governments. As a result, the Texas legislature created the Town Center Improvement District as an independent unit of government to develop, improve, and maintain the public elements of the Town Center. The improvement district contracts with a private security firm to provide patrols on horseback to monitor the parking areas. Wearing bright red jackets, the "mounties" also provide information and assistance to visitors and serve as highly visible marketing symbols for the Town Center. The improvement district also pays for ten additional sheriff's deputies, whose primary beat is the public areas surrounding the Town Center. The improvement district pays for these services with revenue generated from a one-cent sales tax on businesses in the Town Center.

Soft Infrastructure and Social Programming

TWC recognizes the importance of a community's social aspects. In the early years of the community, the company had a director of institutional development responsible for creating soft infrastructure and social programs. As time went on, the company decided that the best approach was to be a catalyst in creating this infrastructure rather than attempting to take full responsibility for its planning and implementation. This approach is consistent with TWC's guiding principle that a developer should not provide services that can be provided by others and should ideally tap grass-roots support from within the community.

According to this principle, community support helps ensure that neither the government nor the developer becomes an omnipresent force in the community. The community is more qual-

ified to identify needs within the community and is better able to pull together a constituency to make the undertaking successful. Several social institutions in the Woodlands received corporate support from TWC until they were up and running, including schools, health care facilities, churches, libraries, and daycare facilities. Once established, many of these institutions and services are run by the county. TWC encouraged the county to recognize the need for community centers and facilities for seniors in the Woodlands; it has worked closely with the county to identify locations for such facilities and has served as a project manager for the county to design and build them.

TWC believes that churches help to form the fabric of the community and works closely with an ecumenical coalition, Interfaith, to identify needs for new churches, to locate appropriate sites, and to sell these sites to churches at below-market prices. Interfaith also coordinates religious activities in the Woodlands. Twenty-nine congregations meet in the Woodlands, with new churches forming at a rate of about four each year. Interfaith was incorporated in 1975 as a nonprofit, tax-exempt charity. It is governed by an 18-member board of directors and has a staff of approximately 150 employees. Social services provided by Interfaith include visits to new residents, publication of a community directory, a full-time information and referral service, a child development program, family services programs, advocacy for senior citizens, and assistance for dislocated workers.

The Interfaith Child Development Center, established in 1976, is the oldest and largest child care facility in the Woodlands. The center serves 500 children with a variety of daycare and preschool programs. In addition to the Interfaith Child Development Center, about 15 private and nonprofit child care facilities operate in the Woodlands. TWC publishes a list of child care facilities for informational purposes only but does not endorse or recommend particular facilities.

Education

TWC recognizes that the quality of public schools is critical to the success of the community. Originally, the site straddled two school districts, one of which appeared to be more capable of serving the rapidly growing population of the Woodlands. TWC negotiated a change in school district boundaries so that all of the Woodlands's residential land would be in one district. The company works closely with the school district to determine the need for new facilities, providing advice on the pace and type of new development and demographic changes in older neighborhoods. It also works with the school district to locate school sites within the community and either donates the sites or sells them at an institutional price.

TWC was instrumental in creating a private day school in the Woodlands for kindergarten through grade 12. The John Cooper School was established in 1988 to meet the need for a coeducational, nonsectarian school that provides a superior education to a diverse population of academically able students. TWC recognized the need for this type of school based on the interest of companies and executives moving to the community and those who already lived there, and assembled a group to make the school a reality.

TWC encouraged the development of a community college and university center within the Woodlands, selling 100 acres to the college at an institutional price, contributing $2 million to help fund the college's initial 70,000-square-foot building, and donating ten acres of land for the university center.

The Environment

The Woodlands proudly advertises that it was the first community to voluntarily prepare an environmental impact statement, in 1973 before such studies were required. An exhibit in the information center states that the environmental objective of the Woodlands is to understand and work with nature, to preserve the natural beauty, to encourage retaining the natural vegetation, and to foster wildlife habitats in a community setting. TWC executives point out that because of this commitment to the environment, residents of the Woodlands enjoy living in a wooded environment with an abundance of parks and wildlife habitats, a drainage system that retains natural streams, and commercial zones that do not infringe on residential areas.

Maintaining the integrity of the forested environment is a challenge during development and after residents move in. New homebuyers from outside the community often require some education to prevent them from removing the preserved forest understory in their yards to create larger lawns or other high-maintenance landscapes. TWC publishes and distributes "A Resident's Guide to Landscaping in the Woodlands," which encourages residents to preserve

The Woodlands Mall, opened in 1994, has been expanded to 1.2 million square feet with more than 140 tenants, including five anchor stores.

existing vegetation and to use native plants, which are more adaptable to the local climate and require less maintenance. The guide provides helpful information on the natural life cycle of the forest and the benefits of natural landscaping.

Natural drainage was an innovative feature of the original master plan. To the extent possible, existing stream corridors were preserved in their natural state, with drainage improvements in developed areas directing storm runoff to these streams through open manmade channels, swales, and stormwater retention ponds where groundwater could be recharged. The benefits of using this natural approach to drainage are twofold compared with conventional engineering techniques employing curbs, concrete gutters, and underground pipes: it is ecologically sounder and less expensive to construct and maintain. Natural drainage was strictly used in the first neighborhoods but was later modified to incorporate conventional engineering practices within neighborhoods when it was determined that most homebuyers did not like the rustic appearance of natural drainage improvements and were willing to pay a premium for conventional engineering.

Wetlands permitting under the requirements of the federal Clean Water Act became a prominent issue for the Woodlands in 1989, when revised wetlands delineation and permitting guidelines focused attention on isolated wetlands. Because the eastern portion of the site, where most development was then taking place, was characterized by the presence of scattered small ponds meeting the definition of isolated wetlands, TWC began to work closely with the U.S. Army Corps of Engineers to prepare a mitigation program to deal comprehensively with unavoidable losses of these isolated wetlands. Potential mitigation areas were designated along stream corridors in the open-space network so that as permit requirements were determined section by section, mitigation strategies could be implemented to compensate for actual losses of wetlands. Mitigation strategies included the establishment of natural area preserves that include uplands, natural wetlands, and created wetlands. This program proved to be successful and continues to guide the wetlands permitting process in the Woodlands.

TWC is proud of its track record on environmental protection, and other Houston-area developers are beginning to emulate its approach.

A typical residential neighborhood illustrates how the developer could build housing in the forest without destroying the environment.

The Woodlands Corporation

TWC has found that as a result of this approach, the community is more desirable and hence more profitable. This increased profitability more than covers the increased costs of development and land preservation.

Housing Products

Recognizing that diversity in housing is very important, TWC is constantly searching for new product lines. At this writing, 22 custom builders and seven production builders are working in the Woodlands. TWC establishes development criteria for each new residential neighborhood, and builders' plans are subject to architectural review by the development review committees.

Affordable housing in the Woodlands has a broad market base, including both young and old. It is difficult to build housing in the Woodlands that sells for less than $100,000 per unit, but some successes have occurred. Ryland Homes has met the demand for affordable housing, with townhouses starting in the $90s. Lennar Homes built a very successful duplex product that sold in the $70s.

Approximately 2,500 rental apartment units are located in the Woodlands; the average occupancy rate is 95 percent. TWC manages all six rental apartment complexes in the community. It prefers to control management of rental apartments, believing that outside management firms might not have the same long-term interest in the community's viability.

The community offers a variety of options for senior citizens of all incomes, ages, and life-

123

Office parks take advantage of the natural setting at the Woodlands.

The Woodlands Corporation

styles, including congregate facilities providing a continuum of care. Most housing for seniors is conveniently located near shopping centers, medical facilities, churches, and community centers whose social activities and services help to ensure the independence and well-being of senior residents. An effort is made to integrate seniors into the mainstream of community life. The county and several of the community's senior housing providers operate on-demand transportation services for senior citizens.

The Woodlands includes 660 assisted-living rental apartments for individuals who are aged 62 or older or who are physically challenged and must support themselves on limited incomes. These apartments, rent for which is based on income, are located in three separate neighborhoods. Two are owned and managed by the National Corporation of Housing Partnerships and are subsidized under the Federal Housing Administration Section 8 program. A third is owned and managed by Volunteers of America and is subsidized under the FHA Section 202 program.

Another option for seniors is the Woodlands Health Care Center, a 206-bed luxury retirement living and nursing center opened in 1986. The Woodlands Health Care Center provides health care by on-call physicians and on-site registered nurses.

The Forum at the Woodlands Retirement Living Community is a congregate care and assisted-living facility owned and managed by the Marriott Corporation. It consists of 303 rental apartments and single-family cottages with 27 assisted-living units.

Marketing and Sales Strategy

The Woodlands is advertised as "a real hometown for people and companies." The marketing program consists of two parallel efforts: attracting new residents and attracting new businesses. Both efforts sell the Woodlands as a place where people can live, work, play, and learn.

The marketing program has evolved over time in response to changing perceptions of the community in the marketplace. Hosting the Houston Open and the opening of the Tournament Players Course, the third in the nation, have provided national exposure for the Woodlands since 1976. The opening of the hospital in 1985 is credited with enhancing the perception that the Woodlands is a complete community. The relocation of Hughes Tool Corporation to the Woodlands in 1991 increased the level of interest in the Woodlands as a corporate location. The opening of the regional mall and plans for the Town Center in 1994 greatly enhanced the image of the community as a dynamic place to be.

The homebuying market primarily comprises relocations to the Houston area and local move-up buyers. Half of all new homebuyers in the Woodlands come from outside the Houston market. Of these buyers, 85 percent are brought into the community by realtors. TWC therefore is active in promoting the community to realtors, relocating corporations, and relocation firms.

With approximately 25 percent of new home sales to existing residents of the community, TWC recognizes the importance of community relations. When a resident contacts the company for information or resolution of a problem, the company works hard to be responsive and to treat the individual with respect and courtesy, knowing that every resident is also a potential customer.

TWC maximizes the pace of development and sales by catering to niche markets. TWC's ability to do so is enhanced by its capabilities in database management. As niche markets wax and wane, the challenge is to be responsive and flexible enough to accommodate the shifts. The decision to build upscale patio homes, for example, responded to the needs of a niche market. Research indicated that an untapped market existed for low-maintenance, zero-lot-line patio homes priced from the low $100s into the $400s. This type of product was previously unavailable in the Woodlands or in any other community in the Houston metropolitan area.

TWC uses a variety of methods to track the interests and concerns of consumers. Prospective residents are asked to fill out survey cards at sales centers and the information center, and the cards are then collected and tabulated. New residents are surveyed several months after they move in. A random survey of all community residents is undertaken every two years. Past surveys have indicated that trees rank first as the reason people chose to live in the Woodlands, but the quality of schools and public safety also rank high on the list. When post-move-in surveys indicated that some new residents were dissatisfied with the builders of their homes, TWC followed up with the offending builders. Surveys show that residents are currently interested in controlling growth in the community and region, bringing new upscale shopping, dining, and entertainment venues to the community, and bringing more services such as car washes and self-storage facilities to the community.

The Woodlands is marketed to the widest possible spectrum of potential buyers. TWC's objective is to appeal to all income levels with housing products that sell in all price ranges.

Preserving trees is a primary goal at the Woodlands.

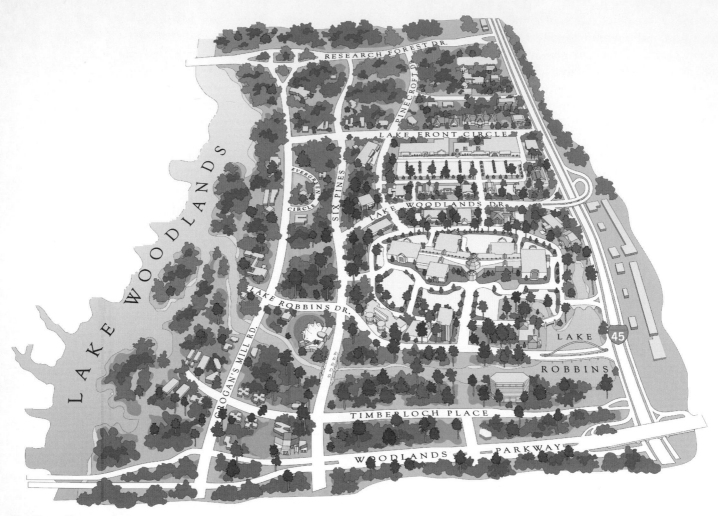

The Town Center plan.

Most of the company's marketing budget is spent on advertising in the weekend "Home" section of metropolitan Houston's newspaper. TWC subscribes to requirements for equal opportunity and is committed to attracting a diverse population to the community to give it vitality. At one time, TWC advertised in ethnically targeted publications to appeal to specific ethnic groups, but the strategy proved unsuccessful and the company prefers to concentrate on media with overall public appeal.

Direct-mail promotions are an important part of the marketing program, used to promote the annual Showcase of Homes in addition to several special events per year geared to specific housing price ranges. Direct mail is also used to advertise open houses held in the community every other week. The annual Showcase of Homes is a tool to generate a mailing list database for the special promotions and open houses. TWC maintains an Internet site to provide information to prospective residents from

other parts of the country. The site generates two to three E-mail inquiries per week, typically from high-quality prospects.

The Woodlands Information Center has been in operation since 1974, providing visitors with information about housing and other aspects of the community. The center contains no sales areas. Realtors are encouraged to bring their prospects to the information center, and existing residents are encouraged to bring their guests to the center for an introduction to the community.

TWC increasingly has focused attention on marketing the Woodlands to senior citizens. Although most marketing to seniors has a local focus, TWC recognizes that the senior market is in fact a national one, with prime prospects being those seniors whose adult children live in the Woodlands. In fact, two-thirds of the seniors living in the Woodlands have adult children who also live there. TWC sees a trend for extended families' reuniting in a place like the Woodlands and stresses the importance of accommodating their needs with a variety of housing products and services that appeal to the wide range of ages, incomes, and lifestyles represented. The marketing challenge is to communicate this advantage.

General Business Strategy

The Woodlands Corporation is a multifaceted real estate development company engaged in the development, ownership, and management of residential, commercial, hospitality, and resort properties with a principal focus on large-scale community development. The company's mission is prescribed by long-term strategic thinking, professional management, creative problem solving, and environmental stewardship.

The publicly held company is smaller, more compact, and more focused in its activities than it once was. It contracts for nearly all maintenance, construction, engineering, and planning functions. Increasingly, TWC is establishing strategic alliances with financial partners, retaining an ownership interest and roles in management and leasing but involving financial partners to spread the risk and free capital. Mitchell Mortgage Company, a subsidiary of TWC, services over $600 million in loans. TWC also has an ownership interest in Stewart Title Company of Montgomery County.

During the 1990s, TWC disposed of most real estate assets outside the Woodlands to focus on those within the community. TWC owns and manages the conference center, country club, and four golf courses. It owns an interest in and operates the three village shopping centers, a strip shopping center, and the regional mall. TWC develops residential lots and sells them to homebuilders. The production builders each have their own sales office. Homes constructed by custom builders are sold through a central sales office, the Woodlands Custom Homes. TWC implements an umbrella advertising program for the Woodlands.

Enhancing the value of land for future development is one of the company's primary objectives. Land may be set aside for a proposed residential village or a commercial site. Meanwhile, ongoing infrastructure development increases the value of these lands. The Woodlands Town Center is an example of this type of planning. Land surrounding the mall site was set aside in the 1970s for future development of the Town Center. As the landowner, TWC will benefit greatly from its development for retail, restaurant, hotel, office, and high-density residential uses.

TWC carefully avoids overbuilding beyond the market. The company was able to survive the economic downturns of 1972 to 1976 and 1983 to 1987 by building only what the market could absorb. As the community has gained prestige, both residents and businesses have been willing to pay higher rents and prices to become a part of it. Office space in the Woodlands leases for higher rates than comparable space in downtown Houston, and residential lot prices in the Woodlands are in the top tier for the Houston region.

TWC seeks to build and maintain good relations with both local government and the local community. As a result of good relations with local government, it is often able to facilitate tax abatements to encourage new businesses to locate in the Woodlands. TWC is sensitive to the opinions of community residents and actively encourages community involvement in problem solving.

The use of public funding is a strategic part of the company's financial plan, and $350 million in public funds has been invested in the community to date. The Woodlands has been the most proactive development in the Houston area in seeking government funding for facilities and programs. It has used public money to create special districts, such as the Town Center Improvement District, to obtain road improvements and to build water and sewer infrastructure. The company tries to leverage public funds through public/private partnerships whenever possible. During the initial road-building phase, Road District No. 1 and TWC provided the local seed capital required to attract state funding for overpasses, interchanges, and other improvements. The Woodlands was the first development in Houston to get ISTEA commitments, Section 8 tax credits for affordable elderly and family housing, and park grants.

The company sees the Woodlands as a model for other planned communities and a model for planned growth. The Houston region has more master-planned communities than any other metropolitan area in the United States, accounting for 25 to 40 percent of new home sales. The Woodlands demonstrates how, in the absence of comprehensive land use regulations, high standards for development are maintained, ensuring that the product is competitive in the market.

Summerlin

Las Vegas, Nevada
Howard Hughes Corporation

Summerlin is one of the largest and fastest-growing master-planned communities in the nation, with the notable distinction of having ranked as the best-selling master-planned community in this country for five years since 1992. Located on the western edge of the city of Las Vegas in Clark County, the community is intended to be a place where people live, work, and play. The center of the community is approximately ten miles northwest of both the airport and the stretch of Las Vegas Boulevard known as "the Strip." The community's T-shaped site covers 22,500 acres, spanning five miles east to west and more than nine miles north to south.

Summerlin is projected to be completed by 2015, with 60,000 residences and a population of 160,000. The completed community will include approximately 30 residential villages, a mixed-use town center, three mixed-use village centers, four business parks, approximately 15 golf courses, six resort hotels, a network of parks and open space, public and private schools, churches, and other community facilities.

The first phase of Summerlin, comprising approximately 7,900 acres, is annexed to the city of Las Vegas and will contain approximately 25,000 residences when completed around 2000. Of this total, 7,700 residences will be part of Sun City Summerlin, a 2,475-acre, age-restricted enclave for adults over 55. In addition to Sun City, plans for Phase I include approximately 17,300 dwellings in seven family-oriented villages. Plans for Phase I also include a mixed-use village center, a business park, a resort hotel, and community amenities.

Summerlin's master developer is the Howard Hughes Corporation, which became a subsidiary of the Rouse Company in 1996. To date, Hughes's investment in the infrastructure of the community includes the 3.5-mile first phase of Summerlin Parkway (the primary entrance to the community), a trilevel freeway interchange connecting

Summerlin Parkway to U.S. Highway 95, the community's arterial and residential roads, two championship golf courses, four village parks, and the initial segments of a communitywide trail system that is planned to be 160 miles long upon completion.

The Area

The Las Vegas metropolitan area is one of the fastest-growing regions in the country, with a year-round population of more than 1 million people. It attracts approximately 6,000 new residents each month and approximately 30 million tourists annually. Gambling was legalized in Nevada in 1931, and money, water, and power began to flow into the city with the end of the Great Depression and completion of Hoover Dam in 1935. Most public revenue is derived from taxes on sales and the gambling industry. Personal and corporate income taxes are banned by Nevada's constitution.

In the late 1980s, during the deep recession that struck neighboring California, Las Vegas received a large influx of young job seekers as well as many older Californians who sold their homes and retired to larger houses for less in Las Vegas. This in-migration helped to raise local standards for quality development.

Summerlin came along at the right time in relation to Las Vegas's growth. In the 1970s and 1980s, the city continued to expand westward, typically in the form of custom-lot residential subdivisions known as "sections," accompanied by a hodgepodge of retail development along the major arterial roads. Mostly situated beyond the suburban sprawl, Summerlin's site was attractive but relatively inaccessible. To overcome this disadvantage, the Hughes Corporation decided to finance the construction of the initial 3.5-mile segment of Summerlin Parkway through the formation of a special improvement district. The

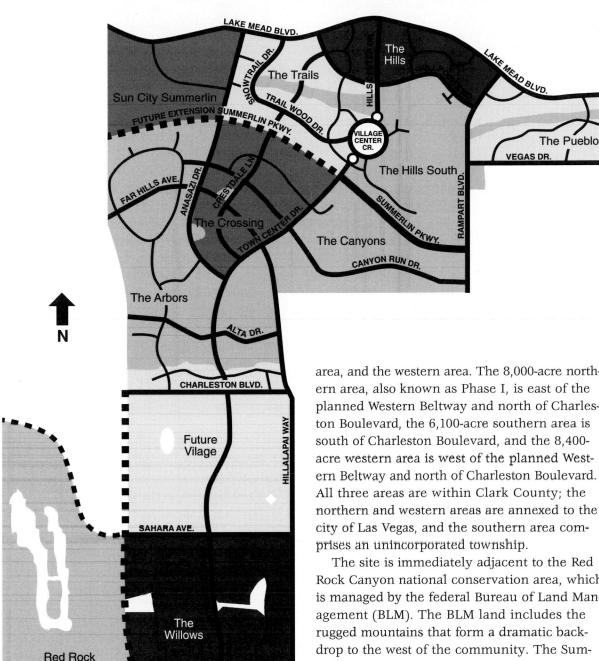

The map shows the Summerlin master plan with areas labeled: LAKE MEAD BLVD., The Trails, The Hills, Sun City Summerlin, FUTURE EXTENSION SUMMERLIN PKWY., SNOWTRAIL DR., TRAIL WOOD DR., HILLS CENTER DR., LAKE MEAD BLVD., VILLAGE CENTER CR., The Pueblo, VEGAS DR., The Hills South, FAR HILLS AVE., ANASAZI DR., CRESTDALE LN., The Crossing, TOWN CENTER DR., SUMMERLIN PKWY., RAMPART BLVD., The Canyons, CANYON RUN DR., The Arbors, ALTA DR., N, CHARLESTON BLVD., Future Village, HILLALAPAI WAY, SAHARA AVE., The Willows, Red Rock

parkway provides convenient access to U.S. 95, the region's major east/west route, putting Summerlin ten minutes from downtown Las Vegas and 15 minutes from the Strip. Summerlin Parkway is planned to be extended westward to the Western Beltway, a proposed regional circumferential route.

Description of the Site

For planning, the Summerlin site is divided into three areas: the northern area, the southern area, and the western area. The 8,000-acre northern area, also known as Phase I, is east of the planned Western Beltway and north of Charleston Boulevard, the 6,100-acre southern area is south of Charleston Boulevard, and the 8,400-acre western area is west of the planned Western Beltway and north of Charleston Boulevard. All three areas are within Clark County; the northern and western areas are annexed to the city of Las Vegas, and the southern area comprises an unincorporated township.

The site is immediately adjacent to the Red Rock Canyon national conservation area, which is managed by the federal Bureau of Land Management (BLM). The BLM land includes the rugged mountains that form a dramatic backdrop to the west of the community. The Summerlin site commands a broad view of the Las Vegas Valley.

History of the Project

The land was acquired in the early 1950s by Howard R. Hughes, Jr., the legendary industrialist, aviator, and visionary, from the federal government through a land exchange just as the Korean War was beginning. Hughes's plan was to build a research laboratory for Hughes Aircraft Company, which was quickly outgrowing its Culver City, California, facilities. Under pressure from company advisers, Hughes instead expanded the Culver City location, and the Summerlin site became one of many vacant parcels in Hughes's vast inventory.

129

When completed, Summerlin's trail system will extend for 160 miles through landscaped and natural areas, connecting schools, residential areas, and community amenities.

The Hughes Corporation began to seriously consider the development potential of the site in the early 1980s, naming the property for the Summerlin branch of the Hughes family tree. Hughes recognized that the project represented a huge financial risk, and, rather than encumber the project with debt, the company decided to use bulk sales of land to generate the capital required for constructing infrastructure and services. The configuration of the property lent itself to carving out two parcels for bulk sale without compromising the integrity of the master-planned community. The ensuing two sales, 1,300 acres to the southeast in 1983 and 1,000 acres to the north in 1984, raised about $50 million in capital and had the added benefit of bringing infrastructure closer to the remaining land, as the new owners developed the parcels as amenity-oriented residential subdivisions.

Also during the early 1980s, the company worked with the BLM and the Nature Conservancy to exchange land to protect the Red Rock Canyon from encroaching development. The company transferred 5,000 acres on the western edge of the property to the BLM and received 3,000 acres on the southern end in return.

In 1987, the Hughes Corporation agreed to a bulk sale of approximately 1,000 acres to the Del Webb Corporation for Sun City Summerlin

for a retirement community; in subsequent years, Del Webb purchased two adjacent parcels from Hughes of approximately 800 and 600 acres each, bringing its total to 2,530 acres. These land sales helped bring more utilities, access, and critical mass to the remaining land, while helping to raise capital of more than $75 million. Ground was broken at Sun City Summerlin in March 1988, and the first residents moved in in March 1989.

During the late 1980s, the company focused on the construction of Summerlin Parkway and other major infrastructure, as well as prepared a master plan for the remaining land. The master plan was completed in 1990 and revised in 1991 to accommodate a westward shift of the alignment for the Western Beltway. The company made arrangements with the PGA (Professional Golfers Association) in the late 1980s to construct a Tournament Players Club (TPC) within the community, and sponsored an advisory panel through the Urban Land Institute to obtain advice from other developers about the company's plans.

As a result of the panel, the company decided to become more proactive in developing the project. Hughes developed two private schools, two public schools, a large public park with an outdoor amphitheater, and the TPC golf course

by the time that the first residents moved in in February 1991; a major library and performing arts center opened in 1993.

The Hughes Corporation considered an initial public offering in 1994, but the market was not receptive. According to president and CEO John Goolsby, some of the company's owners, heirs of Hughes, were eager to liquidate a significant portion of their holdings. The company subsequently solicited bids from possible investors, including the Rouse Company, a large publicly held real estate development company based in Columbia, Maryland. Rouse acquired the company in 1996 in a deal valued at $520 million in stock, cash, and credit. As a wholly owned Rouse subsidiary, the Hughes Corporation's real estate portfolio complements Rouse's, which includes a mix of retail complexes, office buildings, and master-planned residential communities. Through the deal, Rouse and Hughes's owners became equal partners in Summerlin. Recognizing that the community's undeveloped land was difficult to value, the Hughes owners were willing to accept a smaller initial investment from Rouse, $65.4 million out of the $520 million total, in return for a share of Summerlin's future profits.

Hughes updated the community's master plan in 1996 and by January 1997 had obtained all city and county entitlements necessary to complete the community; a development agreement was obtained from Clark County in 1996 for the 6,100-acre southern area, another in 1997 for the 8,400-acre western area. These development agreements permit development of an additional 38,000 dwelling units, 180 holes of golf, 12 million square feet of commercial space, and five hotel/gaming sites on the remaining 14,500 acres in the southern and western areas. The agreements also commit the city and county to provide infrastructure and improvements, including an interim eight-mile segment of the Western Beltway through Summerlin by 2000 and a two-mile westward extension of Summerlin Parkway by 1998.

Master Planning and Design

Summerlin's master plan is based on a village structure. At buildout, the community will include approximately 30 distinct villages in addition to Sun City. A typical village will contain 1,700 to 2,500 residences in 12 to 15 neighborhoods; a typical neighborhood will contain 100 to 200 dwellings of a similar product type. Except for custom-lot neighborhoods, each neighborhood is defined as a single development parcel, averaging 18 to 35 acres, to be developed by a single homebuilder.

Each village will feature an individual character and integrity of design. Housing type and design, density, street landscaping and character of the surrounding wall, street plan, price range, and amenities will differ. Even the topography and view corridors will vary widely from village to village. Some villages will be primarily residential in context; others will be mixed use. The essence of the concept is that each village will have a personality all its own while enjoying access to the range of amenities the community provides and reflecting design elements consistent with the community at large.

The master plan for the community defines the general location and character of each village, as well as the location of other major land uses and major road alignments. As development proceeds, the Hughes Corporation will prepare a more detailed plan for each village, defining neighborhoods and sites for community parks, schools, and other land uses. Specific plans for individual neighborhoods are prepared by homebuilders in conformance with requirements specified by Hughes.

The master plan designates three types of villages: primary, amenity, and low density. Primary villages are intended to have a full range of housing products, from entry level through deluxe, and a village center, typically consisting of a park, school, and/or worship site. Amenity villages have mostly high-end housing products and at least one public or private golf course. Low-density villages, located in the highest elevations, will have modest to high-end housing products on larger lots; three of the five proposed low-density villages are planned to include at least one golf course and a resort and/or hotel, and a fourth is planned for a village focus. Building sites in these large-lot areas are to be narrowly defined so as to preserve natural drainage, vegetation, and topography.

The master plan includes a mixed-use town center, which is intended to become the centerpiece of the master-planned community as well as the retail, employment, entertainment, and cultural focus for the west side of the Las Vegas metropolitan area. The town center is still in the conceptual stages.

The master plan includes three mixed-use village centers, one each in the northern, southern, and western areas, equidistant from the proposed town center. Business parks are planned near these village centers. The first village center, in the northern area, is under construction, with completion of a major retail component, the Trail Center, a 175,000-square-foot retail center.

Outside the town center and village centers, sites within Summerlin for retail, office, and service uses are limited, and selection of such sites is guided by a communitywide retail strategy whose goal is to aggregate these uses in fewer locations to strengthen viability and to create a greater sense of place. In addition to Summerlin's first retail center, Pueblo Shopping Center, Summerlin residents are served by a number of strip centers located just outside the community.

Sites for six resort hotels have been designated in Summerlin. Construction of the first, The Resort at Summerlin, is to be completed by spring 1999. The casino/resort is owned by Seven Circle Resorts of Switzerland.

Parkland and open space in Summerlin include a network of community and neighborhood parks, a trail system, and public and private golf courses. The master plan dedicates 250 acres for recreation centers, libraries, houses of worship, health care centers, fire and police stations, and arts and cultural facilities. Land allocated for these sites is generally located on or near open-space areas and close to schools.

While promoting diversity in design and development, protective covenants, restrictions, and design guidelines ensure that standards of quality are maintained in every aspect of the community during development and construction. A complete set of design guidelines is created for each village to deal with such specifics as landscaping, wall construction, facade treatment, and setbacks.

A detailed set of overall landscape and engineering standards is used throughout the community. The street system is designed to provide a strong sense of orientation; traffic circles are frequently used to make the system more consumer friendly by eliminating some traffic signals, and standard road widths are narrowed in lower-density areas. The major entrance to the community, Summerlin Parkway, is landscaped with drought-tolerant plants suited to the arid climate.

Recreational and Cultural Amenities

Summerlin offers a full array of recreational and cultural amenities. The community's major cultural facility to date is the Summerlin Library and Performing Arts Center. The 38,500-square-foot facility, designed by architect Robert A. Fielden, opened in August 1993. It will house more than 100,000 volumes when its collection is complete. Its 291-seat theater hosts local and regional theater productions nearly every weekend throughout the year. The library is home to an art gallery, conference and meeting rooms, an audiovisual department, a literacy center, a used book store, and a large marine aquarium. The Hughes Corporation built the facility and deeded it to the county.

Four houses of worship hold services in Summerlin's first phase of family-oriented villages, and four more worship center sites have been designated for Phase I. Another six sites for worship centers are located in Sun City Summerlin.

Approximately 20 percent of the community's land area is designated as "community space," including passive and active open space, recreational facilities, golf courses, a comprehensive pathway system, and landscaped areas. Both the amount and percentage of preserved acreage for parks and nature trails are higher in Summerlin than in any other community in Nevada.

Parks vary in size from pocket parks serving individual neighborhoods to larger village parks serving the entire community. The miniparks are designed to meet the specific needs of the neighborhoods they serve. For example, a park may include tot lots or be specifically designed for senior citizens. Others may feature sculpture or special landscape treatment. Most parks are located near schools and pedestrian pathways, and serve as part of the village focus areas.

Each primary village has a park with a different recreational focus, such as baseball, tennis, or soccer. The demand is great for active recreation facilities, particularly for organized sports activities. Distributing recreation facilities among villages has several advantages, among them providing critical mass for the facilities, helping to distinguish each village, and helping to promote a communitywide spirit by giving residents a reason to visit other villages.

The first completed park in the community was Hills Park, a 6.7-acre park in Hills Village, which includes a large central pavilion, outdoor amphitheater, children's play area, and sport courts. The amphitheater offers performances and a year-round schedule of events. The park quickly gained a reputation as a place for concerts, family reunions, company picnics, and other special events shortly after its completion in 1991, and it has often been voted the most popular park in Las Vegas in the *Las Vegas Review-Journal*'s poll.

In addition to Hills Park, Summerlin currently contains three other village parks. Pueblo Park is a 68-acre linear park that meanders throughout Pueblo Village. One of Las Vegas's most distinctive parks, Pueblo Park features a "desert interpretive garden," two active play areas, pathways, and extensive natural desert areas. Trails Park, a 28-acre linear park in Trails Village, includes three lit baseball fields, a community center and swimming pool, a children's play area, a meadow area, and picnic pavilions. Crossing Park, in Crossing Village, is a 12.5-acre amenity with two full-size lit soccer fields; it will include a children's play area and picnic pavilions.

Hills Park, a 6.7-acre park that includes a central pavilion, outdoor amphitheater, children's play area, and sport courts, is among the most popular parks in Las Vegas.

Roundabouts are used as part of the roadway system to minimize the use of traffic signals.

The Summerlin Division works closely with the city park agency and the local school district to link the recreational facilities of the schools and the park to allow for shared use. For example, the park in Willows Village, south of the planned town center in the southern area, includes a water park and aquatic recreation facility as well as baseball and soccer fields.

The custom-lot neighborhood of Eagle Hills is home to Eagle Park, a six-acre neighborhood park for the exclusive use of Eagle Hills residents. The park's family-oriented amenities include lit tennis courts, half-court basketball, shuffleboard, and barbecue and children's play areas. Mountain Trails Park, in the custom-lot neighborhood of Mountain Trails, features a children's play area, picnic areas, two tennis courts, and half-court basketball. These facilities are supported by separate association fees charged to the residents of these neighborhoods.

The Summerlin Trail, a network of bicycle and pedestrian pathways, weaves throughout the community in wide, landscaped setbacks along neighborhood streets, connecting schools, parks, playgrounds, and villages. Summerlin Trail is expected to be nearly 160 miles long upon completion.

The Hughes Corporation entered into an exclusive agreement with the PGA Tour to bring a Tournament Players Club to Summerlin. This private 18-hole championship golf course, the TPC at Summerlin, opened in 1991 and is located in Hills South Village near Summerlin Parkway and Town Center Drive. Operated as a private country club, its rolling desert fairways and magnificent clubhouse make it southern Nevada's premier golf facility. Individuals may purchase a membership in the Tournament Players Club, allowing privileges at all TPCs nationwide.

The TPC stadium golf course is an innovative concept that uses earthen mounds and natural amphitheaters to provide spectator views at unobstructed vantage points during tournament play. The TPC at Summerlin became the home course for the PGA Tour's Las Vegas Invitational in 1992 and the Las Vegas Senior Classic in 1993. Beginning in April 1997, the Senior Classic will be moved to the TPC at The Canyons, a daily-fee resort course that opened in Summerlin in November 1996. The course is located in Canyons Village, less than one mile south of the TPC at Summerlin.

TPC at The Canyons is designed to incorporate its dramatic desert surroundings. The natural terrain of washes, canyons, and arroyos has been worked into the layout, while desert vegetation has been left intact, replanted, or enhanced. Because of its elevation and proximity to the nearby Spring Mountain Range, the course provides striking views of the city and of Red Rock Canyon national conservation area.

TPC at The Canyons will be affiliated with The Resort at Summerlin, a world-class hotel and casino being built adjacent to the course at Summerlin Parkway and Rampart Boulevard. In addition to serving resort guests, TPC at The Canyons is open for public play.

Summerlin is also home to three other courses, all located in Sun City Summerlin—Highland Falls, Palm Valley, and Eagle Crest. Although Sun City residents enjoy preferential tee times, the courses are open to the public as available.

Community Operations And Governance

The Summerlin Community Association (SCA) is intended to promote the sense of community. The SCA maintains the community's landscaped common areas and enforces the Summerlin covenants, conditions, and restrictions (CC&Rs). These guidelines clearly state what kinds of modifications homeowners may make to their property. The CC&Rs set procedures, standards, and a review process that balances individual rights and responsibilities with those of the community. Separate associations maintain the standards for custom-home neighborhoods and other neighborhoods where common areas require additional fees. Sun City Summerlin also has a separate community association.

While many master-planned communities have expanded their visions during the latter part of the 1990s, Summerlin's community governance structure has not kept pace. Many community associations, which were initially concerned with regulating and maintaining common areas and amenities, are unprepared to deal with their changing roles. Summerlin is presently grappling with this very issue. With Summerlin growing at a rate of 150 households every month, the company is evaluating how to govern a completed community of 160,000 residents in 30 villages.

With assistance from the Hughes Corporation, the SCA is seeking approval from its members to amend the current master declaration. This amendment would establish two additional community associations and the Summerlin Council, an entity that will oversee all three community associations and serve a community-building function by linking all residents together through common amenities, activities, and events. In addition, the amendment creates a more flexible framework for the community associations, allowing them to better adapt to future changes and trends. The purpose of the amendment is to create a system with a governance mechanism that balances multiple interests, preserves the functions of the community association, protects flexibility, and provides the powers necessary to permit an association to remain dynamic during periods of change—all while reasonably protecting property owners' interests and their expectations for an appropriate degree of certainty.

Summerlin illustrates a special cooperative effort between public and private enterprise. As part of the initial development plan, the city of Las Vegas issued bonds to fund and repay the Hughes Corporation for many improvements in infrastructure. This technique of financing infrastructure allowed the company to invest millions of additional dollars in a wide range of vastly enhanced community amenities, including improvements to the communitywide system of parks and trails, landscaping, and rights-of-way.

Two special improvement districts were created to finance the common improvements. The city issued nearly $74 million in bonds in 1989 for the first district and $40 million in bonds in 1996 for the second district. Repayment of these bonds is through a semiannual assessment to homeowners. The bonds are secured by the unpaid assessments on property within the district. The assessments, constituting a lien on the property similar to a mortgage, are paid by property owners. The assessments are apportioned per acre by the city's Public Works Department for each acre or partial acre owned.

Safety and Security

Although perceptions of safety and security are significant factors for homebuyers, the Hughes Corporation does not explicitly promote security in its marketing. Compared with other parts of the Las Vegas area, Summerlin is perceived as safe because it is new, relatively insulated, and buffered on the west by a conservation area. Nearly all neighborhoods in Summerlin are walled, and many are also gated.

Walls in the community are designed for both security and privacy. The community's design guidelines ensure added visual interest for walls, diminishing the repetitive appearance of continuous walls along major roads by varying heights, setbacks, materials, details, and openings, and by providing breaks for such uses as schools, community facilities, parks, and retail space. Gates and openings are also provided in the walls for access by pedestrians and bicyclists to selected trails and sidewalks.

The Summerlin Community Association contracts with a patrol service to complement local police service. The association currently operates three vehicles from 3 p.m. to 7 a.m. seven days a week, as well as one patrol 24 hours a day. The security patrols are instructed to protect the common area of the association and maintain a visible presence in the community. Each vehicle costs $115,000 per year to operate.

The association also employs three "compliance control officers," each with a geographic area of responsibility. Within that area, they review sites for compliance with guidelines, such as unapproved landscaping, and issue courtesy notices for violations. If the violation is not corrected, a letter is sent detailing the violation. If no response is received, a hearing with the Compliance Committee is scheduled. This committee comprises eight residents, who review each case and make recommendations to the board of directors for appropriate action, such as imposition of daily fines until the violation is corrected. Officers are expected to make every effort to maintain a high profile and serve as a deterrent to potential vandalism or mischief on the association's property.

Soft Infrastructure and Social Programming

The Hughes Corporation believes that Summerlin's success depends on the sense of community created through the services and social programming available to residents. The company recognizes that this intangible fabric of the community helps to attract potential home-buyers and influences their decision to purchase a home. According to Nancy Cook, Summerlin's vice president of finance, "Today's busy lifestyles create greater needs for residents. They want much more than just a home; they're looking for ways to feel connected with their neighborhood and their community through schools and social events and activities, and they're looking to their community to provide desired amenities and social programming."

Through the Summerlin Community Association, the company from the beginning emphasized starting the events and activities that initially shaped Summerlin's image as a vital and dynamic community. Recent market research confirms that Summerlin's events and activities have become inseparable with the community's image. The company's long-term goal is to develop a network of volunteers and fundraisers to make the community's social events self-supporting.

The SCA maintains a full-time program manager, who is responsible for developing programs and activities of interest to residents. After conducting an extensive survey of residents, the SCA established nearly a dozen clubs and organizations through the Summerlin Club Connection, a network of social, recreational, cultural, and civic groups made up of Summerlin residents sharing common interests. SCA publishes a bimonthly newsletter to highlight the community's programs, activities, clubs, and events, as well as to foster a sense of community.

The Summerlin Division of the Hughes Corporation established the Summerlin Children's Forum in September 1995 to improve the quality of life for children in the community. According to the forum's founder, Summerlin president Dan Van Epp, the organization is a natural extension of the community's philosophy: "a community built on traditional values, where families come first and bettering the lives of residents is a top priority." Born out of the desire to continue the living environment for which Summerlin is known, the forum is a nonprofit, tax-exempt corporation comprising educational, religious, and business leaders from the community, parents, and residents. The forum seeks to identify issues affecting the youth of Summerlin and to improve their well-being through educational and recreational programs.

Education

In the Las Vegas Valley, education is a major concern for most parents because of the challenges the Clark County School District faces in keeping up with the city's explosive growth. Summerlin's response has been a commitment in the form of financial support for public education. An early example was a $250,000 donation to fund a break-the-mold design for the first public school in the community. William R. Lamas Elementary School has since been recognized as the state's first "new generation" school. More recently, the Summerlin Division led the "Coins for Computers" fundraiser for Summerlin's public elementary schools. The company regularly underwrites PTA fundraisers.

Summerlin's master plan designates public school sites in almost every village, and the property is either donated or significantly reduced in price to the school district. The company actively works with the school district and the state legislature to augment local public school programs and facilities. As a result, Summerlin's schools consistently receive top rankings in the state.

Summerlin is home to five public schools— three elementary, one middle, and one secondary. Summerlin's 2,400-student high school, Palo Verde, is located in Arbors Village. Completed in early 1998, the high school is adjacent to a proposed 20-acre sports park owned and managed by the city's parks department. This arrangement, which allows the sharing of recreational facilities by students and residents, was facilitated by the Summerlin Division of the Hughes Corporation. A satellite campus of the Community College of Southern Nevada will also be located on the site.

Summerlin has expanded educational choices by bringing several private schools into the community, among them Meadows School, a college preparatory school for grades kindergarten through 12; Hebrew Academy, also for grades kindergarten through 12; two preschools, one of which also offers kindergarten; and Hillpointe Country Day School, for kindergarten through grade 6.

Recognizing the advantages to the community of having private schools, the Hughes Corporation was proactive in bringing both Meadows School and Hebrew Academy to Summerlin. Both schools helped Summerlin establish credibility and presence, and helped home sales, as parents of students attending these schools typically want to live nearby.

Health Care

The Hughes Corporation believes that state-of-the-art medical facilities are an important amenity for Summerlin. To address this need, the company built a 60,800-square-foot medical center in Pueblo Village in 1994. The Pueblo

Medical Center houses a family and urgent care facility, a medical diagnostics and imaging center, and more than 70 physicians in private practice.

The company also targeted a full-service hospital as a desirable amenity, affiliating with Universal Health Services, which had already established a network of medical centers in the eastern Las Vegas area. Universal Health Services purchased a 40-acre site in Crossing Village. The Summerlin Medical Center, developed and owned by Universal Health Services, is being built on the site in phases.

A 186-room full-service hospital opened in late 1997. The hospital provides acute, subacute, and rehabilitation services, and is the first of its kind in southern Nevada to feature all private patient rooms at no additional charge. Inpatient care includes surgical services, obstetrics, cardiology, pulmonary medicine, rehabilitation therapy, oncology, and other specialized care.

Universal Health Services also owns and operates the Senior Advantage Resource Center

Two of Summerlin's residential neighborhoods.

The Pueblo
Shopping
Center fea-
tures distinc-
tive architec-
ture of the
Southwest and
native land-
scaping.

in Sun City Summerlin. This center provides
a variety of services and benefits for members
who are 50 years and older, including free blood
pressure checks, routine health screenings,
scheduled seminars and events, and access to a
variety of health-related information and videos.

The Environment

As Summerlin's master developer, the Hughes
Corporation recognizes its obligation to be a good
steward of the environment, having carefully
preserved and protected the land for more than
50 years. To preserve this natural legacy for the
future, the company has set aside a significant
portion of the land as open space, and it incorporates environmentally sensitive land management strategies into its plans.

Water conservation is an important issue in
the Las Vegas Valley, among the most arid of the
nation's urban areas, with rainfall of less than
ten inches a year. To minimize water consumption for irrigation of landscaped areas, Summerlin adopted a landscape plan with four zones,
ranging from natural desert to oasis. These zones,
related to various land uses, are intermixed to
create an attractive and cost-effective development. In the desert zone, the land remains untouched or is restored to its natural condition. In
transitional areas, indigenous plants are grouped
abundantly to create an enhanced desert look.
A "desert garden" along major roads and open-
space areas is planted with drought-tolerant trees,
shrubs, and ground cover. A green oasis environment featuring trees, shrubs, ground cover,

and grass has been created in specific residential areas and areas with high visibility or specialized uses. Increasingly, landscaping at Summerlin creates drought-tolerant, low-water-use
environments that still are appealing for use
in marketing.

Landscaping plays a significant role in shaping
the community's image and defining the style
of each village. Entry monuments are located
at all key arterial or highway entries. A coordinated signage system creates a "Summerlin look."
The company has adopted special street light
colors and nonglare fixtures. Median areas in the
streets, landscaped by the company, are owned
and maintained by the community associations.

Employment

With more than 3,500 jobs currently located
in the community, Summerlin has a ratio of
approximately 0.35 job per housing unit. Most
jobs are located in the Crossing Business Center.
The majority of Summerlin's residents work
outside the community to the east.

The company has set a goal of creating
about 45,000 jobs in the community at buildout,
although the exact number of jobs will be a function of the market. Land use allocations in the
master plan were based on this objective. The
company sees on-site jobs as important for a
multifunctional, multifaceted community.

In the community's early years, one of the
major focuses was attracting employers to Summerlin to accelerate development of the residential neighborhoods. The company identified the

major credit card processing center for Household Credit Services, which was then based in northern California and seeking to expand or relocate, as a candidate. In a competitive recruitment process, Summerlin agreed to donate land, construct a new facility, and sell the facility to Household. Today, Household Credit is Summerlin's major employer, with more than 1,000 employees.

The second major employer to locate in Summerlin was Bank of America's western region dealer lending center. Attracting Bank of America was a very competitive process; to secure the deal, Summerlin provided many incentives, including options for Bank of America to buy additional land to expand its facility. Today, Bank of America employs between 500 and 600 people in Summerlin.

Crossing Business Center will accommodate approximately 1.2 million square feet of business facilities on 115 acres when completed. More than 700,000 square feet of office and industrial space has already been developed. The business park incorporates 11 major commercial facilities, including Bank of America, Household Credit Services, Kloehn Company, Humana Health Insurance of Nevada, and Williams-Sonoma.

Las Vegas is part of a major relocation circuit that includes Phoenix and Albuquerque, and business in Las Vegas is booming. The Las Vegas area is increasingly viewed as an attractive site for relocation of businesses because of its low cost of living, low taxes, and high employment rate. Given the current business climate, the company does not expect to offer incentives to companies to locate in Summerlin in the future.

Housing Products

Approximately 150 new houses are purchased in Summerlin each month, with the bulk of the market move-up residences, typically from $120,000 to $160,000. Housing products include single-family houses, townhouses, and condominiums ranging in price from $80,000 to more than $500,000. Custom lots are priced from $100,000 to $750,000, and custom homes sell for $1 million and up. More than two dozen production homebuilders are currently active in the community, with more than 150 model homes typically available for inspection. Housing products in Sun City Summerlin, the age-restricted community, include detached and attached houses,

with prices from the low $100s to the high $200s. The company estimates that housing in Summerlin commands an average premium of 10 percent when compared to similar products selling in other areas of Las Vegas. Special improvement district costs average approximately $5,000 per unit.

Homebuilders are responsible for land planning and product design of individual neighborhoods, including the street pattern, lot sizes, unit sizes, prices, and features, within strict guidelines established by the Hughes Corporation. The company has created guidelines for neighborhood design in each village, including the streetscape and landscaping, and reviews all builders' projects for conformance of design, grading, and perimeter walls with those guidelines.

Sales of custom homesites are very successful, accounting for approximately 22 percent of the revenue of the Summerlin Division. Custom homesites are available in a variety of sizes, with a wide range of views and choices of neighborhoods. Prices start from around $100,000 for a quarter-acre site in a custom-home neighborhood with no major recreational amenities where residents need a card to open the gate, to more than $750,000 for a premium lot with frontage on the golf course in the most exclusive gated enclave.

For buyers of custom sites, Summerlin offers a program featuring eight custom homebuilders. The builders are familiar with Summerlin's design guidelines and have established a strong track record in design of custom homes. These builders have the exclusive right to build speculative houses in Summerlin's custom-home communities. The company sells sites to these builders at a discount and requires them to always have two houses under construction and available for sale in one of Summerlin's custom-home neighborhoods, ensuring a mix of readily available custom homes for prospective buyers.

Marketing and Sales Strategy

Summerlin's marketing strategy is to provide something for everyone. It takes almost three years to complete a village in Summerlin, from design through construction. To achieve a complete range of products in each village, a color-coded plan identifies market segments and product types. The Summerlin Division constantly evaluates the number of builders in each market segment and seeks new product types and builders.

Summerlin's area is large enough that the Hughes Corporation can develop a new village in a new geographic market area. The newest villages will tap Las Vegas's southwest market, which is different from the northwest market. The geographic segmentation of the market is a result of access to employment provided by major east/west arterials. By tapping into this new geographic market, the company plans to increase total absorption in Summerlin by as much as 40 to 45 percent without significantly affecting the absorption of housing in Summerlin's northern area. Similar housing types will be offered in both markets.

Summerlin's marketing program has evolved as a result of the growth and development of the community. Initially, as a result of Sun City Summerlin's early success, Summerlin was perceived as a retirement community. To counter this perception, an advertising campaign that focused on families started in 1991. Subsequent advertising has focused more on Summerlin's natural amenities. Following a drift back to family-oriented advertising in 1995, a fully integrated campaign marketing to a full range of potential homebuyers was started in 1996 with the catchphrase "Life is choices...this one's easy."

Cooperative advertising programs are funded through a builders co-op, which is based on a contribution of 0.75 percent of sale prices. Summerlin contributes to the co-op through sales of custom homesites plus a separate contribution.

The company markets directly to brokers. About 60 percent of all sales transactions in Summerlin occur through brokers, and the company is increasing its efforts in this area. The company has a full-time sales coordinator, who works with on-site agents. Recognizing that sales are made and lost at the point of sale and that the more informed salespeople are, the better chance that traffic can be converted to purchases, the company has created a training program for sales agents to increase their knowledge of and ability to sell "the Summerlin difference."

A separate facility for Summerlin's custom homesites is part of the Summerlin Home Finding Center. More than half the buyers of custom lots ask for recommendations for builders and architects, and nearly 25 percent want to see "model" custom homes. The program of naming eight custom homebuilders, introduced in 1996, is designed to provide buyers of custom homesites with a wide range of choices and builders, and to ease the stress of designing and building a custom home. The program is designed particularly to appeal to out-of-state buyers and those who may not have the time or inclination to hire an architect, search for a builder, and supervise construction.

General Business Strategy

The Hughes Corporation, one of the most successful regional real estate investment and development companies in the United States, is involved exclusively in real estate. The company is currently developing approximately 20,000 acres of land acquired by Howard Hughes in southern Nevada and southern California. The company has earned a reputation for its innovative plans, quality developments, and capable management. Its strategy is one of long-term ownership, and Summerlin is the company's main landholding.

The company is headquartered at Hughes Center in Las Vegas and operates development of the master-planned community as an independent division. The Summerlin Division currently has a staff of about 60 people, including sales staff and the community association staff. The company's recent acquisition by the Rouse Company has not resulted in any major staff or organizational changes or affected the company's general business strategy. According to John Goolsby, president and CEO of the Hughes Corporation, "We have consistent philosophies. . . . We operate in a very conservative manner, as Rouse does." Both companies are known for their very structured, corporate-style management organizations.

One change resulting from the company's acquisition has to do with expectations for financial returns. According to Goolsby, "When Hughes was owned by the heirs, there was a great deal of pressure on short-term cash flow. Rouse has a more patient approach and is more interested in getting a consistent cash flow over the long term."

The company credits a large part of Summerlin's early success to having a full complement of amenities and community facilities in place when the community opened. The project's timing and location in Las Vegas were also key. The company recognizes that a successful master-planned community must be located in a strong market; it also recognizes that Summerlin's future success depends on, among other factors, the continued economic strength of Las Vegas.

The Hughes Corporation intends to stay in front of housing demand for the Las Vegas Valley, which will involve monitoring the marketplace and providing as many housing products as the market can absorb. Since the opening of Sun City in 1990, Summerlin has consistently captured 11 to 12 percent of the area's growth. The company will seek to increase Summerlin's market share in the future by continuing to broaden product types and prices in Summerlin. The company recently started to construct some rental housing and plans to integrate rental projects of 200 units into all future villages. Bulk land sales may also be part of its future development strategy.

A recent focus of the company was to obtain all the entitlements necessary for buildout, including obtaining a commitment from Clark County to build the Western Beltway, probably the most important factor in Summerlin's continued growth. The beltway will allow Summerlin to become an edge city, with quick and easy access to the airport. The county will fund road construction (the road may eventually become a state or federal highway); the Hughes Corporation donated eight miles of right-of-way and will excavate the right-of-way so that the road is depressed rather than at grade.

Of the current issues facing the community, Summerlin Division president Dan Van Epp identifies education and sense of community as the most crucial. Because education frequently drives housing choices, Hughes will continue to guarantee quality public and private education for Summerlin residents. The company also recognizes that what a community "lives like" is as important as what it "looks like" and will continue to stimulate a sense of community

The recreational demands of niche markets are served by various facilities throughout Summerlin. In the Willows neighborhood, a waterpark provides active recreation for children.

by staying active in community affairs and to embrace its role as community builder.

As Summerlin matures, the company will also focus on filling in the missing pieces of the land use plan: employment, by seeking a better balance between jobs and housing and the relief of the impact on regional transportation associated with long-distance commuting; retailing, by attracting retailers that complement the vision of the community, with the town center a major part of that vision; and amenities, by broadening the range of amenities provided and including amenities that appeal to specific interests. The company is eager to make sure that Summerlin avoids becoming a plain vanilla environment and remains a vibrant place for people to live, work, and play.

Celebration

Celebration, Florida
The Walt Disney Company

Celebration, a new town on approximately 9,600 acres near Orlando in northwest Osceola County, is being developed by the Celebration Company, a subsidiary of the Walt Disney Company. The company is striving to make Celebration a family-friendly, education-minded, health-conscious place to live, work, and play. The community includes a wide spectrum of housing types, a downtown district, a public school offering kindergarten through grade 12, a health care campus, an office park, an 18-hole public golf course, and parks and open space, including a surrounding 4,700-acre protected greenbelt.

Ground was broken in March 1994. The residential sales and rental program began in November 1995, residents began to move into their dwellings in June 1996, and the downtown district opened for business in November 1996. Although the unincorporated community continues to be built in phases at a pace dependent on market demand, it is expected to be completed by 2010. The site is divided by I-4; the population of the community east of the interstate will reach up to an estimated 10,000 at completion, while the type of development west of the interstate is still to be determined.

The first phase, Celebration Village, includes the 18-acre downtown district, the core of which contains a preview center, town hall, post office, bank, cinema, 68,000 square feet of retail space for shops and restaurants, 67,000 square feet of office space, and 123 rental apartments, some of which are located over retail space. Plans for a three-story, 115-room, four-star hotel to be completed in fall 1999 in the downtown district were announced in July 1998. Residential neighborhoods surrounding the downtown district include sites for a total of 360 single-family houses and are nearly sold out. The average lots range from 2,900 square feet for townhouses to 11,700 square feet for estate houses. Three-story apartment buildings, near the downtown area along Celebration Avenue and Water Street, are currently under construction; they offer one-, two-, and three-bedroom units. Additional land in the village is designated for future residential use.

Since the opening of Celebration Village, three new phases of housing have been started. Opened in January 1997, the second phase—West Village—has 95 homesites and was nearly sold out a year later. The third phase—Lake Evalyn, with 56 garden homes—sold out in six weeks. Phase IV—North Village, with over 300 homesites—began sales in October 1997 and was 36 percent sold four months later.

Adjacent to Celebration Village and the other residential phases are the 60-acre health care campus and 109-acre office park. Celebration Health's initial 284,000-square-foot facility opened in November 1997; it includes a primary care–based multispecialty center and a health activities and fitness center. The office park, Celebration Place, opened in 1995 with two buildings containing a total of 240,000 square feet.

Disney is taking the best ideas and practices from the most successful towns of yesterday and today and adapting them for a community of tomorrow. During more than eight years of planning, Disney obtained input and assistance from many people, including prospective residents, public officials, architects, community planners, market researchers, leading community developers, educators, health care visionaries, and other professionals. To guide planning and development, Disney focused on five areas, referred to as Celebration's cornerstones: health, education, technology, place, and community. Disney assembled partners for a strategic alliance to collaborate in creating the community and help distinguish Celebration as a special place to live. The partners include several local public agencies and utilities as well as major corporations, institutions, and organizations involved in education, health care, communications, building products, and financial services.

Description of the Site

Walt Disney believed that there is no "challenge anywhere in the world that's more important to people everywhere than finding solutions to the problems of our communities"; he envisioned building a new community at Disney World that could be a model for others.

In the late 1980s, the company decided that it would not need the property south of U.S. 192 for expansion of the theme park for many years. Designating the property for mixed-use development, the company commissioned a sequence of land planning and market research studies evaluating various land use scenarios. As the studies progressed, Disney executives recognized the opportunity to rekindle Walt Disney's dream of building a real town and, with the encourage-

ment and active involvement of Disney Chair Michael Eisner, set new goals for developing the community.

Celebration is located approximately 30 minutes southwest of downtown Orlando via I-4 and 20 minutes southwest of the Orlando International Airport via Florida Route 417, a newly opened toll road also known as the GreeneWay or the Orlando Beltway Extension.

Celebration sits within the nearly 30,000 acres of land southwest of Orlando purchased by the Walt Disney Company in the early 1960s. The Disney property is divided into three main areas by north/south I-4 and east/west U.S. 192. The Walt Disney World Resort, including the Magic Kingdom, Epcot, and Disney–MGM Studios, is located in the 20,000-acre northwest area. The town of Celebration, a regional mall, and other land uses are planned for the 3,500-acre southwest area. The main entrance faces U.S. 192, which continues east from the Disney

The 18-acre downtown district features apartments, shops, offices, restaurants, a movie theater, small parks, public plazas, and a lakefront promenade. Designed on the assumption that streets belong to people, not cars, most parking is placed in lots behind buildings.

Veranda Park, a neighborhood green with informal groupings of native trees, is guided by standards set by the company. The residential association maintains common property such as parks, sidewalks, and signage in residential areas.

property to connect to Florida's Turnpike; this stretch of U.S. 192 is lined by a variety of strip commercial uses.

A large portion of the site was formerly cattle pasture. Like much of central Florida, the land is characterized by a generally flat topography, a high water table, and heavily wooded areas dominated by pines and live oaks. In planning the community, the company scrupulously avoided harming wetland areas on the site; although a few major roads will cross wetland areas (because there is no alternative), all other wetland areas on the site will be preserved in their natural state. These preserved wetland areas form the framework for the open-space system that delineates neighborhoods and villages within the community.

History of the Project

Beginning in 1986, Peter Rummell, then president of Disney Development, articulated a vision for a new town in a series of memos to Eisner:

I want to describe a wonderful residential town that has human scale with sidewalks and bicycles and parks and the kind of architecture that is sophisticated and timeless. It will have fiber optics

and Smart Houses, but the feel will be closer to Main Street than to Future World. Nothing here will be different just for the sake of being different, but [it will be] designed to be enduring and comfortable. The community's special qualities will be the accent, the spice, used artfully and deliberately.... There will be a Town Center with retail and some office, but it will be residential in scale and designed for the pedestrian to co-exist with the car. There will be people living here, so it can support the level of services that go together to make a real hometown/downtown. The secret will be that at the same time it is a laboratory and experimental, exploring new ideas, new processes, it will also be practical and functioning and livable for a permanent and workable population on a day-to-day basis. It will not be full of wild architecture that is expensive and doesn't work, and it will not experiment with irresponsible financing and taxing systems or levels of community control that jeopardize the discipline needed for orderly development. Every building built will not be experimental or even necessarily award-winning. But each will have its own appropriate reflection of quality, and the overall fabric and texture of The American Town [the name of the 1989 concept] will be reaching, innovative, new without being contrived. The whole will be much greater than the sum of its parts, and it will meet both existing market demands and create new ones because it is special.

In late 1987, using the technique of parallel design exploration, Disney asked three firms to generate ideas for a planned residential community with limited commercial space. Robert A.M. Stern and Gwathemy-Siegel, both based in New York, and Andres Duany and Elizabeth Plater-Zyberk (DPZ), based in Miami, were hired. Disney liked many of the ideas from each and put the firms into collaboration. In early 1988, the firms produced a consensus plan that combined the best ideas from the individual proposals. In late 1988, Disney commissioned two firms, Cooper, Robertson and Partners, based in New York, and SOM, based in Chicago, to develop the next master plan that includes some 5 million square feet of commercial space, Disney land on both sides of I-4, and a proposed alignment for the GreeneWay toll road. That version of the plan was completed in December 1989. In 1990, Robert A.M. Stern and Cooper, Robertson developed a final master plan for the community that would be used to obtain entitlement approvals, including a more detailed analysis of the first phase and the location for the town center. They also designed most of the retail, office, and apartment buildings in the downtown district and worked with other prominent architects to design several key buildings in downtown.

During this time, Disney's in-house Celebration team collected images and plans for houses in the various neighborhoods, researched desirable apartment layouts, and decided the mixture of shops and restaurants in the town center. Market research studies and focus groups identified consumer hot buttons and revealed which were most important. These investigations verified that prospective residents were sufficiently interested in a higher-density, pedestrian-friendly new community.

As part of its research in 1992, approximately 15 members of the Disney team took a week-long tour of older towns and newly built communities, visiting Columbia, Kentlands, and Avenel in Maryland; Charleston, Kiawah, Hilton Head, and Sea Pines in South Carolina; Savannah, Georgia; and Boca Raton's Mizner Park, Coral Gables, and Seaside in Florida. Charles Fraser, developer of Sea Pines and a special consultant to Disney throughout the planning for Celebration, coordinated the tour and is credited with

coalescing the team's perspective. Jim Rouse, developer of Columbia, inspired the team to think of the community as "a garden to grow people in" and to understand that a successful community needs to have a strong and compelling vision.

The trip helped articulate Celebration's five cornerstones. The cornerstones emerged from an effort to reduce the community's vision to a succinct statement that would be used to check and validate future design and business decisions. This summary statement focused the team and educated new team members. The cornerstones were the community's founding principles, emphasizing shared responsibility, lifelong learning, good health, a high degree of voluntarism, open communication and information sharing, wholeness, a balance between work and worship, civic pride, and opportunities for renewal and innovation. According to Charles Adams, Celebration's former vice president of community development, "We had decided from the beginning that our 'software' would be more important than our 'hardware.' We were committed to quality architecture and planning, but put an even greater emphasis on the other cornerstones."

Using the cornerstones as a platform, the team worked to identify and establish mutually beneficial relationships with leading practitioners and businesses to help bring the latest products, services, and technologies to Celebration. These partners fall into two categories: corporate and strategic. Strategic partners include government agencies and educational institutions. While the anticipated benefits of exposure are certainly attractive to all alliance partners, their reasons for coming to Celebration also include the chance to use the town as a base to research new products, services, and technologies, and to introduce them into a defined market.

During Walt Disney World's initial development stages, Disney worked with the state and local governments to establish a quasi-public entity, the Reedy Creek Improvement District (RCID), to fund and provide all the infrastructure and most municipal services. Even though Disney had paid millions of dollars in local property taxes, local governments were obligated to provide only a few services. As Disney began to pursue other land uses to complement the resort and theme parks, however, adjacent local governments argued that these developments should be subject to local jurisdiction and not part of the RCID. As a result, Disney agreed to de-annex the Celebration property from RCID into Osceola County upon approval of project entitlements. A fiscal impact study estimates that the project will contribute net benefits to local government of $15 million more per year than Disney would have expended operating within RCID.

Celebration was a key element in Disney's efforts to assemble a public/private partnership that developed major transportation improvements totaling over $400 million in land and funding. Three new interchanges on I-4, improvements to U.S. 192, and extension of the GreeneWay from the airport to I-4 were built through the partnership. Disney received necessary regulatory approvals by 1994, when construction began. Because of the community's size and scope, the project was subject to review under Florida's Development of Regional Impact (DRI) process. This process took several years of effort and involved considerable expense for Disney. Osceola County eventually determined plans for Celebration were consistent with the county's comprehensive land use plan. Disney has entitlements to build up to 8,000 residential units and has flexibility in determining the product mix and locations. Final plans for each phase are subject to review and approval by Osceola County, but Disney does not anticipate any problems, as the company and the county agree on the project.

Master Planning and Design

Celebration's Phase I plan generally fit within traditional principles of town planning. Houses in the villages and neighborhoods are sited close to each other on relatively small lots with private backyards. Buildings are oriented toward the street; most feature welcoming front porches, and garages are placed in rear alleys. Strict but flexible design guidelines govern the appearance of all houses and buildings. Architectural styles and building types combine to make harmonious streets, blocks, and neighborhoods that possess a real sense of place.

Other aspects of Celebration's Phase I plan reflect the site's special character and the spirit of the community. The community is not gated. Celebration's houses are intended to have a timeless quality and seek to blend traditional southeastern exteriors designed in one of six styles: Classical, Victorian, Colonial Revival, Coastal, Mediterranean, or French. Most streets follow a grid system, modified as necessary to conform to the natural landscape and to define public open spaces. The neighborhoods are often centered around a significant public space and are linked to an address, such as Golfpark Drive and Veranda Place, referring to the central community space.

Design guidelines were prepared after much research into the architectural styles and building types of historic towns in this country. Celebration revived the use of the pattern book to guide the design of houses and neighborhoods. Throughout much of U.S. history, builders based the design of houses and neighborhoods on prototypes presented in pattern books prepared by architects. Builders largely abandoned the use of pattern books after World War II, as homebuilding became more of an industry than a craft. Celebration's pattern book seeks to restore the consensus among builders, designers, and homebuyers that in the past enabled them to create the nation's most admired and beautiful historic neighborhoods. Celebration's pattern book, published in May 1995, was prepared by Urban Design Associates, based in Pittsburgh, in conjunction with Robert A.M. Stern and Cooper, Robertson's Jaquelin Robertson. Builders found that using the pattern book lowered their in-house design requirements; they also found that residents will pay a premium for a higher-quality product.

Phase I has four basic house types: estate, village, cottage, and townhouse. All lots have approximately the same depth, but widths vary according to type of house. Estate lots are generally 90 feet wide by 130 feet deep, and most are located across from some form of public area, such as a park or the golf course. Village lots are generally 70 feet wide by 130 feet deep. Found on smaller streets, cottage lots are generally 45 feet wide by 130 feet deep. Townhouse lots are generally 30 feet wide by 100 feet deep or 22 feet wide by 130 feet deep, and are located across from community facilities. All houses are built using similar standards for landscaping and architecture to maintain the beauty and harmony of the neighborhoods. The plan allows second-story apartments over garages on all lots, and approximately half are expected to have them.

The downtown is modeled after traditional small-town retail and business districts. The Celebration Company, as developer, owner, and manager of the downtown area, chose retail tenants carefully to help position the district as a major new retail center that would support residents and attract customers from around central Florida. Internationally prominent architects were hired to design the signature buildings downtown to create a sense of familiarity and to capture the ambience of traditional town centers. The 9,275-square-foot, two-screen AMC cinema was designed by Cesar Pelli & Associates. The Celebration Preview Center, designed by the late Charles Moore, features a tower to show prospective buyers the town layout. The tower was inspired by one built by George Merrick, the original developer of Coral Gables, for the same purpose. Philip Johnson created the town hall, Michael Graves designed the post office, and Venturi, Scott Brown and Associates designed the bank.

The one- and two-bedroom apartments in the downtown range from 685 to 1,210 square feet. Ground-floor apartments on Celebration Avenue are designed so they can be converted to retail space to meet market demand. Parking is provided both on the street and in the centers of blocks behind buildings. Amenities include a lakefront promenade, a dock, fountains, courtyards, and gardens. Lakeside Park, at one end of the promenade, has tennis courts, a swimming pool, volleyball and basketball courts, a playground, picnic pavilions, and a great lawn for community events like plays and concerts.

Recreational and Cultural Amenities

Celebration's parks and open-space system include neighborhood parks, village parks, a trail network, and a golf course. Neighborhood parks range from formal to informal in character. They are typically bounded by neighborhood streets and surrounded by housing. Village parks contain pools, tennis courts, and other facilities for active recreation. The trail network consists of miles of sidewalks, trails, and pathways, both hard surface and soft mulch, for biking, walking, and jogging. The trail network includes nature trails created in cooperation with the Florida Audubon Society and designed to offer an environmental, educational experience.

The community's golf course and clubhouse opened in October 1996. Rather than being lined with homesites, the Celebration course was used to create a park setting that forms part of the

Two signature buildings in the downtown district were designed by internationally renowned architects Philip Johnson (the columned town hall) and Michael Graves (the towered post office building).

147

town's open-space system. Trees and benches line perimeter walkways, allowing all residents to appreciate the park setting.

The Celebration Golf Club is a daily-fee public golf course that is owned and operated by the company. The course, designed by the father-son team Robert Trent Jones, Sr., and Robert Trent Jones, Jr., was their first collaboration in more than 30 years. The 18-hole, par-72 course is oriented toward families and average golfers but is also challenging for avid golfers. Features of the course include forward tees for youths, minimal rough, open-entry greens, rangers to keep play moving and to provide assistance, and an unusual three-hole youth practice course.

Community Operations And Governance

Disney collaborated with state and local governments to establish two community development districts (CDDs) to reduce the burden on local government to provide basic infrastructure, to increase its control over the quality and timing of that infrastructure, and to organize a financing mechanism. The Enterprise CDD is charged with the commercial portions, the Celebration

CDD with the residential areas. The CDDs construct roads, and plan, build, and maintain Celebration's infrastructure, including recreational amenities, landscaping, streetlights, and water and sewer service. Together, the two CDDs will provide a total of approximately $100 million in tax-exempt financing.

The CDDs maintain standards in community services and assure residents of continuity in maintenance after the town's completion when residents assume control. The CDDs are public entities overseen by a board of supervisors elected by the landowners through a one-acre/one-vote system. The CDDs deliver water, sewer, and other services by purchasing capacity from the city of Kissimmee. Florida Power Corporation provides electricity. Osceola County will oversee portions of the development process and provide fire protection, police protection, and road maintenance.

Two community associations, a residential property owners association and a nonresidential association, regulate property use, and maintain and operate certain common facilities and areas. The nonresidential association regulates property use and provides maintenance and operation services, such as security for common facilities and areas in the commercial areas. The residen-

Single-family houses in Celebration are sited close to each other and oriented toward the street. Most feature front porches and large windows facing the street.

tial property owners association regulates property use in residential areas. Each association's board of directors governs, establishes a budget, levies assessments, makes and amends rules, and enforces laws and rules. The Celebration Joint Committee unifies the two associations and is authorized to levy assessments for both.

The residential association maintains and operates common property and improvements, such as sidewalks, signage, and playgrounds, guided by standards set by the company. Each homeowner is a member of the residential association and pays an amount to cover an equal share of the assessments levied by the Joint Committee and residential association.

Through the residential association, each homeowner will ultimately be entitled to have a voice in important decisions affecting the community. The association's seven-member board of directors will make many of the day-to-day decisions. As the number of homeowners increases, residents gradually gain the right to serve as voting members on the board. Residents within each village, which consists of one or more neighborhoods, will elect the voting members and are entitled to elect an equal number of directors.

The company handles architectural review and approval for all residential property, including initial design guidelines and review procedures. In the future, the company may elect to assign its right of review and approval to the residential association. Any property owner wishing to construct or modify any property will be required to submit an application for approval before construction begins.

Residences are subject to various restrictions to protect the quality of life. Customary restrictions address such items as parking, pets, and business uses. Restrictions may apply to a particular area, depending upon the type of house and neighborhood; some areas may permit the leasing of houses or home offices, while others may not. The Declaration of Covenants, Conditions, and Restrictions for Celebration Residential Properties was prepared by the Atlanta-based law firm of Hyatt & Stubblefield.

Safety and Security

Safety and security were paramount concerns during planning. Standards include requirements for large, well-proportioned windows on the front of all residences, making a gesture to the street

that indicates people live behind them. Residentially scaled streets with sidewalks that invite pedestrian traffic help keep neighborhoods safe and secure.

Although the community is not gated, it is physically isolated from adjacent areas by an open-space buffer and long entry roads. Osceola County sheriff's deputies maintain security, supplemented from time to time by security hired by the community associations. All homebuilders provide the option of installing wiring for security systems.

Soft Infrastructure and Social Programming

Disney was as interested in creating a strong soft, or civic, infrastructure as it was in creating a strong physical infrastructure with a sense of place. The company hopes Celebration's real magic will not be in buildings, physical structures, or even technology, but in the human element that will make the community great, enabling it to deal with change and to evolve over time.

In its research, the company concluded that the civic infrastructure that creates a community is often missing in modern development. Conversations with Jim Rouse and familiarity with the writings of John W. Gardner, former Secretary of Health, Education, and Welfare and cofounder of Independent Sector, a nonprofit organization dedicated to encouraging voluntarism, reinforced this point. Traditionally, kinship, place, experience, economic relationships, interests, values, age, and time have defined community. The challenge was to provide soft infrastructure that was not about reconstructing the past but about creating the future.

Disney's long-range market research was an important part of the decision to focus on community. As Todd Mansfield, former executive vice president of Disney Development, explains:

Our feeling is that as the information era matures, the days in which people establish their residency by default, based on where their employer lives, will be gone. More and more, people will be able to work anywhere they want. With this kind of flexibility, people will choose to make their homes and raise their families in places that provide a higher quality of life. As people look to determine quality of life, they will consider factors like the health of the population, the availability of programs to allow for lifelong learning, the amount of participation in and the prevalence of volunteer activities, the specifications of the telecommunications network, indications of civic pride, and evidence of firm relationships and the sense of purpose that only a strong community can provide. Specifically, people will be looking for strong civic infrastructure. It will become our responsibility as community developers to establish it. To build this civic infrastructure, we'll have to form alliances with school districts, health care providers, environmental organizations, communications companies, public agencies, and civic clubs as well. In 2010, relationships and alliances like these will be as important to the building of new communities as hammers and nails. We will no longer be able to do it alone.

The Celebration team developed an entire process to facilitate this integration and, in a way, program the software of the community. In fact, this software—or the types of events, activities, and programs that people will participate in—actually drove the development of the hardware, that is, the physical plan and development.

To nurture the civic infrastructure, the company created a nonprofit organization, the Celebration Foundation, that functions as a clearinghouse for clubs and organizations, and coordinates volunteers in the community. The foundation acts as a local chamber of commerce, with leadership eventually provided by local community members, assisted by a full-time executive director. The foundation is expected to promote ideas generated by lessons learned by the community and to channel volunteers' efforts to serve both the local and the broader community. The local bank, SunTrust, supports the foundation and provides space for an information center in the bank's lobby.

In addition to the local public school and the health center, the community's social infrastructure will also include daycare facilities, worship centers, and a public library. Children's World, an independent operator, manages the daycare facility in Celebration Place, which serves 200 children and has ties to the Celebration School. A local congregation is to build the Community Presbyterian Church, currently in the design stage, on a site designated for that use adjacent to the downtown district. A recently signed contract transfers the two-acre site to the congregation for the cost of infrastructure. The public library, located at Celebration School, opened August 1998.

Education

Disney recognized education as a very important feature for marketing the community, and it has proved to be a motivating factor for potential homebuyers. During the process of planning the community, the company chose to focus its efforts on creating a high-quality public school rather than a high-quality private one, because the company wanted to create a model with the widest possible applicability. The company worked closely with many of the nation's leading educators and with local teachers and administrators from the Osceola County public school district. The partnership with the local school district proved to be challenging and difficult at times, but the product of these efforts has become a source of pride for everyone involved. The Celebration School, a public school for kindergarten through grade 12, is located on a 36-acre campus in Celebration Village near the downtown district. The Celebration Teaching Academy, an educational facility for teachers, is also located on the school's campus.

Owned and operated by the Osceola County School District, the school will serve more than 1,000 Osceola County students each year, including those who live in Celebration. A three-member board of trustees comprising representatives from the Osceola County School Board, the Celebration Company, and Stetson University will advise the school district. The Osceola County School District spent $15.5 million to construct the school and will fund its operations, consistent with other Osceola County public schools. The company donated land, design services, funds, and other support valued at $11 million for the school's physical development. Disney provided another $9 million to fund operating enhancements for the school, training for Osceola County educators, and the development and operation of the Celebration Teaching Academy.

The Celebration School's curriculum was developed by the Osceola County School District with assistance from the company, Stetson University, leading advisers, and a consortium of Florida universities. The curriculum includes customized learning plans created with parental involvement; team teaching, with approximately

Pattern books were used to create a timeless quality in Celebration's housing. Traditional exteriors, like this Victorian-style house, blend with other styles to create harmonious neighborhoods evoking small southern towns of the region.

four teachers per group of 100 students; and access to resources and the town's Disney education programs.

The school, designed by William Rawn Associates, Architects, contains a series of academic neighborhoods comprising students of various ages that allow individual and group learning. A team of teachers can arrange flexible, collaborative learning in neighborhood classrooms according to the curriculum's and students' needs. A room has been set aside to encourage parents' involvement in their children's education. A computer network handles voice and video images, and data to permit local and worldwide access to data and distance learning. Interior wet areas for science, art, and other projects are integrated into the classroom space. Additional dedicated science labs are adjacent to each neighborhood for middle and high school students. The campus includes ten acres of wetlands, containing covered walkways and platforms so that students can study the environment. Other facilities include a gym, a media center, and playing fields.

The Celebration Teaching Academy, developed and owned by the company and designed like a teaching hospital, provides opportunities for teachers and administrators from around the nation to learn, observe, critique, and apply the best theories and techniques in education. Education experts from various universities provide guidance in curriculum, research, and evaluation. Several significant grants from the MacArthur Foundation, the BellSouth Foundation, the Knight Foundation, and the Florida Department of Education will help fund the academy's vision of educational excellence.

Under the current plan, over 4,500 educators will take part in academy programs annually. During the next ten years, the academy will donate 1,500 teacher-training days annually to the Osceola County School District as a benefit to the greater community.

Health Care

Health, another cornerstone, was considered early during the project's planning. Disney saw the office park's land sale to a health care provider as a catalyst for future commercial demand and a marketing coup for the new community. To explore the possibilities for a new health care

Townhouses, ranging from two to four bedrooms, have been built adjacent to the downtown district and add to the mix of housing available in Celebration.

system, the company teamed up with Florida Hospital, the state's largest private, nonprofit hospital.

Todd Mansfield, who had served on Florida Hospital's board, saw an opportunity for collaboration based on the hospital's 90-year commitment to health care and betterment of the community. The company and Florida Hospital devoted three years to exploring the possibilities for the new health care provider. In addition to health care experts from Germany, Japan, Canada, and the United States, the Celebration Health development team consulted with leading U.S. advisers, such as former U.S. Surgeon General Dr. C. Everett Koop and renowned futurist Leland Kaiser. Manufacturers of health care technology products and experts from Har-

vard's Mind and Body Institute, the Stanford University Center for Disease Prevention, the International Health Futures Network, and the National Institutes of Health were also brought into the loop. The consensus of the builders of this prototype health care delivery system was that health care in the future should promote good health and a healthy lifestyle.

Celebration Health's philosophy embraces wellness and proactive health management through a community-integrated system that focuses on generating good health through state-of-the-art prevention and diagnostic techniques. The Celebration Health Campus's services will be available to all Florida residents and visitors.

Celebration Health will help residents adopt healthy lifestyles by taking the health message out into the community through wellness programs and seminars. The advice of a nutritionist, physical therapist, or doctor will be available to help individuals develop a program for total personal health.

The Celebration Health Campus, designed by Robert A.M. Stern Architects, will be owned and operated by Florida Hospital and located on a 60-acre site in Celebration Place. Ground was broken in November 1995. The campus reflects Disney's approach to high-quality guest services. Visiting Celebration Health is like checking into a hotel, with amenities that offer comfort, service, and convenience. Conveniences include preregistration by telephone, valet parking, a hotel-style facility with a lobby, beepers for patients, a children's play area, shops, living room–style areas, and interactive educational computer stations.

Phase I opened in November 1997 as Comprehensive Healthcare Services, a primary care–based multispecialty center. Services offered in the 284,000-square-foot facility include intervention and inpatient surgery, diagnostic imaging and radiology, rehabilitation and sports medicine, a pharmacy, primary care services, specialty physicians, a dental clinic, and a health activities and fitness center. The 60,000-square-foot health activities and fitness center, designed to provide entertaining and enriching health experiences for the entire family, features gymnasiums, two aerobic dance studios, a lap pool, a cardiovascular fitness area, a weight- and strength-training area, health educational services, and a nursery and children's gyms.

Phase II opened July 1998 and includes more elaborate medical facilities to cover almost all of an individual's health needs, including a 24-hour emergency department.

Communications Technology

Part of Walt Disney's vision for Epcot was that new technology has the potential to solve the ills of community life. For example, monorail systems would be an antidote for traffic problems, tubes for trash disposal would be a remedy for waste management problems, and a modern factory core would be a cure for poverty and crime. Despite the sketchy concept, Disney's legacy challenged the Celebration team to reconsider the role of technology in creating a model community.

Although technology is one of the cornerstones, the expectation is only that technology will help to facilitate human interaction. The team's research indicated that although communications technology was evolving rapidly, the most advanced approaches were still too unproved and too expensive for general application. As a result, the team enlisted corporate alliance partners to subsidize the cost and provide expertise.

Eventually, a broadband, fiber-based optic network offering advanced telecommunications and information systems will link the town's residences, school, health care facilities, office park, and civic and retail spaces. The network will carry voice and video images, and data, providing high-speed communication to everyone in town. Vista–United Telecommunications (VUT) owns the physical network and provides local dial-tone and interexchange access as the local telephone exchange company certified by the Florida Public Service Commission. VUT provides transport for cable television and other video services offered by Jones Communications, which holds a franchise granted by Osceola County.

AT&T and the Celebration Company developed a Celebration community intranet that provides online E-mail, chat rooms, a bulletin board service, and Internet access via AT&T WorldNet for the entire community. The network facilitates the sense of community and helps shape it by allowing residents to electronically communicate with one another, the school, health campus, downtown businesses, and the world. The network began serving Celebration Place, the community's office park, in April 1995. Residential telephone and video services were operational in June 1996. The Celebration Community Network was introduced in summer 1996.

The company facilitates the creation of clubs through the community server. Residents can send E-mail, read and post messages to electronic community bulletin boards, tap into the Internet, read the latest headlines, search databases, and shop from home. The network serves as a valuable medical information source and a new interactive system between physicians and their patients. Long-range plans for the interactive network could bring important medical benefits to residents. In the future, health care professionals can track patients' routine indicators, such as blood pressure and pulse rate, via special devices connected to the network, making frequent monitoring possible without expensive on-site nursing. Students will be able to access homework assignments from home and ultimately an online electronic school library. Network access is designed to facilitate more communication among parents, teachers, students, and the school.

AT&T also plans to develop an advanced technology panel made up of 300 homes and apartments. Residents will be able to take advantage of a wide range of products and services to suit their advanced technological needs. AT&T will also open a customer care office in downtown Celebration. AT&T expects the forward-looking environment of Celebration to yield opportunities to create a living laboratory in which to explore how people learn about and adapt to new technologies.

The Environment

Disney is involved in a wide range of environmental programs, including food donation, recycling, water conservation, composting, energy conservation, horticulture, and research. Environmental programs planned specifically for Celebration include recycling programs; programs to teach residents, commercial property owners, and employees how to live responsibly with the wildlife in the adjacent wetland areas; and programs to promote environmentally oriented recreation activities available in the community, such as wildlife observation, fishing, and walking on the nature trail system.

Recycled water irrigates the landscaping throughout Celebration. A tree-saving program preserves many native mature trees that would be destroyed by road construction. Using the world's largest tree spade, the Celebration Company is able to move mature trees to a holding area for storage until they are needed for landscaping.

Environmentally friendly building materials are being used in all types of construction at Celebration. For example, Celebration Place uses hydrofluorocarbons for air-conditioning refrigerant rather than ozone-depleting chlorofluorocarbons, and energy-efficient materials and techniques, including fully computerized air-conditioning controls, high-efficiency insulated glass, electronic ballasts for light fixtures, low-wattage lamps, and high-efficiency motors for mechanical equipment.

Disney worked with the Florida Department of Environmental Protection, the Army Corps of Engineers, the Southwest Florida Water Management District, and the U.S. Environmental Protection Agency to minimize damage to wetlands. Disney's long-term plan for the entire property of more than 30,000 acres calls for development on approximately 18,000 acres, including Celebration. The remaining 12,000 acres will be left as wetlands, bodies of water, conservation areas, wetland creation areas, and environmentally sensitive or isolated upland areas and upland buffers. The company incorporates information about its environmental programs and initiatives in all types of marketing and public relations materials.

Employment

Marketing materials for Celebration describe the opportunities the town offers for working close to home, stressing that working and living in the same town will give Celebration residents more free time to spend with family and friends, and to take advantage of Celebration's many offerings. Many of the community's first residents plan to run businesses from their homes, taking advantage of the community's enhanced communications technology service and support. Phase I designates ten village lots specifically as a home business district intended for use by lawyers, doctors, artists, architects, or other professionals whose offices and studios have regular visitors. One of these houses is complete, and more are under construction.

The community's office park, Celebration Place, is marketed as a location for businesses that are at the forefront of health care, education, and technology. Located on the community's perimeter, the office park has high visibility and good access to I-4, U.S. 192, and the GreeneWay toll road. Celebration Place is positioned to be the premier office location for companies in the southwest Orlando area.

Plans for Celebration Place call for up to ten buildings with approximately 1 million square feet of office space. Planned amenities include an on-site cafe offering sundries and catering, an express mail station, and banking facilities. Walt Disney Imagineering and other tenants now lease the first two buildings. Designed by Italian architect Aldo Rossi, the buildings' exterior materials include red sandstone, buff-colored architectural precast concrete, and tinted glass.

Housing Products

To build the houses in the first phase, Disney selected eight of central Florida's premier homebuilders and two high-quality national homebuilding companies. The two national companies, David Weekly Homes, based in Houston, and Town & Country Homes, of Oak Brook, Illinois, are building the townhouses, cottage homes, and village homes. The local homebuilders are building the estate homes. Builders are free to set their own prices and margins. Only the estate homes are custom built.

Disney undertook extensive research to determine the desirable mix of product types. The company analyzed market growth, absorption by price point, and house and lot sizes. The research resulted in a master plan for a community that would appeal to a variety of buyers and create a vibrant town. Disney looked at what was selling in other parts of Orlando but allowed the land plan itself to influence the mix. Selling prices in all categories seem to carry a premium of at least 10 to 15 percent above comparably sized houses selling in other master-planned communities in the Orlando area. The estate homes are currently lowest in demand, perhaps because some local builders decided to set sale prices well above the recommended $500,000 price. The lowest-priced detached single-family product, the cottage, was the most popular product in Phase I, selling for around $190,000. In additional phases, an even less expensive detached single-family product, the garden home starting at $167,000, has been offered.

The Celebration Preview Center functions as an information center and headquarters for all home sales. Designed by the late Charles Moore, the center features a tower to show prospective buyers the layout of the town.

Marketing and Sales Strategy

Robert Charles Lesser & Co., based in Los Angeles, undertook initial market studies for the new community in the late 1980s. Lesser's research indicated a strong market for primary housing for young families and empty nesters, second homes, and retirement homes. The primary-home market was particularly strong because of an imbalance between the availability of jobs and housing in southwest Orlando. Rather than deal with all these markets in Phase I, Disney decided to focus on the primary-home market, as it provided the greatest support for the school and health campus. The company used covenants during Phase I to prohibit use of the houses for second homes. The first phase where houses can be used seasonally is Phase IV—North Village—which includes housing products targeted for the second-home and retirement markets and allows houses to be rented out.

Phase I required little marketing to generate high interest from consumers. Because demand was so strong, the company held a drawing to establish priority for purchasing the 351 lots and leasing the 123 apartments. Five thousand people attended the Founders Day drawing on November 18, 1995, and 1,200 prospective residents put down deposits. All advertising, kept within a budget of a few hundred thousand dollars, was local. Although there was no national advertising, the national press has been very interested in the project, requiring more public relations activity than a conventional master-planned community of the same size.

The lottery permitted entrants to participate in drawings for up to two product types. Sales appointments with the 1,200 drawing winners began in early January 1996 and were completed by mid-May 1996. Although additional drawings were not needed for openings of subsequent phases, sales appointments continue to be strong.

The Celebration Preview Center functions as an information center and headquarters for Celebration Realty, which handles all home sales. The preview center opened in August 1996; in its first 18 months, over 160,000 people visited. Its ground floor houses exhibits, sample home designs and floor plans, a video presentation, a model of the community, and an interactive computer display. Those with strong interest are escorted to the realty and design center on the second floor. Visitors may also tour homes at the model center located in North Village, the latest phase of development.

General Business Strategy

Over the years, Disney's goal has been to maintain the special values, integrity, distinctiveness, and high quality that have been the company's hallmarks, while always embracing new ideas. The company tries to look at the familiar in new ways, seeing change as the essence of creativity. According to Don Killoren, former vice president of community development and now general manager of the Celebration Company, Celebration "is a natural progression for Disney, which has a proven track record of planning and building resort hotels, commercial, retail, [and] office space, and apartments."

The company is structured like most development companies, with a general manager, a marketing division, a sales division, a residential development division that works with builders, and a financial and operations division that is responsible for financial planning, asset management, apartment leasing, and building maintenance. What distinguishes the company's structure from most other development companies is its new business development division, whose role is to establish strategic alliances and to work with partners. The company is currently staffed for full operation; it has no plans to undertake another community development project and plans to winnow down as development is completed.

Don Killoren speaks of a special "charge" that Charles Fraser gave to the Celebration team. Says Killoren, "Charles Fraser shared with us some things he would have done differently as well as those that worked." Fraser spent an average of two days per month with the Celebration team throughout planning and is generally credited with helping the team to stretch its thinking.

The Celebration Company tried to create something that would serve as a model for others. The company believes that others can replicate almost everything about the community, including the town center, the use of a pattern book, and the creation of public/private partnerships for information technology, education, and health. Disney does not see its role as educating other developers, however, and will leave to others the challenge of drawing conclusions from its experience.

The strategic alliances with corporate partners proved to be win/win situations. Celebration's alliances bring industry leaders together to help create and mold the special components that form the town's cornerstones. Since they were initiated in 1992, alliances typically have evolved through several steps: research and identification of potential partners, sharing information, letters of understanding, an operations plan, formal agreements, operations, vision, and expansion of the alliance. The last step often results in the identification of new products and opportunities for Disney, creating value that the company did not have in the past.

The alliances often created synergistic relationships. Because the partners were brought together with the common purpose of creating community, they were asked to focus not only on their own areas but on the entire town. For example, Florida Hospital is not just building a health center for the entire community; it is also on the team that is developing the school's curriculum. SunTrust is not only building a bank, but is also working to combine its ATM card with the school library card and an individual's personal health record.

The company acknowledges that it would be considerably more difficult for most developers than it was for Disney to undertake so much advance research and development. The special circumstances that made it possible were that Disney owned the land, had access to substantial financial resources, and was able to tap into strong market demand. Nevertheless, the company points out that it has a pro forma for each element of the project and that every element is programmed to generate an appropriate return over time. Moreover, building the infrastructure using CDDs helped the economic equation greatly. At the front end, the project required the company to stretch its corporate culture, its financial resources, its human resources, and its development resources.